100 THINGS GUARDIANS FANS SHOULD KNOW & DO BEFORE THEY DIE

Zack Meisel

TRIUMPH
B O O K S

The Library of Congress has catalogued the previous edition as follows:

Meisel, Zack, 1989–
  100 things Indians fans should know & do before they die / Zack Meisel.
    pages cm
  ISBN 978-1-62937-032-3
    1. Cleveland Indians (Baseball team)—History. 2. Cleveland Indians (Baseball team)—Miscellanea. I. Title. II. Title: One hundred things Indians fans should know and do before they die.
  GV875.C7M45 2015
  796.357'640977132—dc23
          2014041807

This book is available in quantity at special discounts for your group or organization. For further information, contact:
  Triumph Books LLC
  814 North Franklin Street
  Chicago, Illinois 60610
  (312) 337-0747
  www.triumphbooks.com

Printed in U.S.A.
ISBN: 978-1-63727-329-6
Design by Patricia Frey
Photos courtesy of Getty Images unless otherwise indicated

For my son, Charlie, who on his first day of life in 2022 watched Owen Miller hit a game-tying homer in the bottom of the ninth for the Guardians...before they lost in extra innings.

Welcome to Cleveland sports, kid.

Contents

Foreword

I wish I would have been good enough as a player to have played at this level, but I wasn't. So for me, becoming the radio announcer in Cleveland was the next-best thing to being a major league player. There are only 30 of these jobs and I was one of the lucky ones who got one of the 30. The odds of that aren't very good for a guy who grew up on a dairy farm in Wisconsin.

Listening to Milwaukee Braves games and then the Brewers when I was growing up, this job seemed like the impossible dream, but it became a reality. I can't quite get over the fact that it really happened. From a professional standpoint, the Cleveland Guardians mean everything to me. I can't think of a better organization to have worked for. We can't think of a better city to have raised our four children. We came here with a two-month-old and now have four children and we never had any thoughts of going anywhere else. We had other opportunities, but never seriously considered them because we thought that much of the organization and the city.

I know how blessed we have been to get this opportunity and to have witnessed a ballpark that helped revitalize a city, a ballclub that ended all of the national jokes about Cleveland. You think of this ballpark and those teams in the '90s—that was the end of late-night talk shows taking shots at Cleveland. It ended it. To have seen all of those great moments and the great Hall of Fame players who have played here, I've been really blessed.

You never know how fans are going to take you. I think I was really fortunate that I worked with Herb Score for eight years, since Herb was such an icon. Because Herb accepted me, that opened the door for fans to accept me. It was very fortuitous to be able to work with Herb.

You want to work in a city where the fans care. The worst thing is apathy. Florida has great weather. So do California and Arizona. But in a lot of those places, those people didn't grow up with those teams. They moved to those cities, so they may be fans, but they don't live and die with it like they do here in Cleveland and some of the other Midwest cities.

I always wanted to live in the Midwest, as did my wife. We wanted to raise a family in the Midwest because we believe in those values. But also, the fans care so much. If fans care, it can't help but make you be a better broadcaster. You may have a bad season, but you know how much they care for that night's game.

This job has given us a great life. We owe everything to baseball. The home we live in, the ability to send our kids to college—we owe all of that to baseball. Outside of my family, nothing means more to me than what the Guardians have meant.

—Tom Hamilton

Introduction

There's no cheering in a press box. When a player hits a walk-off homer, your fingers are too busy stroking the proper keys on your laptop to engage in applause. To keep your coverage fair and respectable, you have to keep your biases out of it. As a conduit between fans and the players and teams they love, you have to remain objective so they're as informed as possible and can draw honest conclusions about who blew a game, who was responsible for a winning streak or who should be traded. You can't sit in a press box with your face painted orange and brown ready to write analysis about Cleveland's quarterback if you expect anyone to take it seriously.

Perhaps contrary to popular belief, it's not too difficult to divest yourself from that fandom, and that's coming from someone who grew up a Cleveland fan, who first started paying attention to sports when the Indians were scripting memorable Octobers. As a kid, I watched every minute of some pitiful Cleveland teams, devoting far too much of my time to Chris Magruder, Chris Gatling, and Chris Gardocki. I first had aspirations of a job in sportswriting when, as an awestruck third grader in attendance at Jacobs Field, I watched Randy Johnson zip a fastball near Kenny Lofton's head in 1998, sparking a benches-clearing brawl, and wrote about it the next day at school—not for any particular assignment, but just because I felt compelled to scribble down my thoughts about what I had witnessed.

That upbringing, though, armed me with knowledge of what makes a Cleveland fan tick, what keeps a Cleveland fan hopeful, and what makes a Cleveland fan so loyal, year after year, gut punch after gut punch. So even though I'm not sitting at Progressive Field rooting for the Guardians to make a magical run through the postseason, I can certainly understand the plight of so many of my readers who have waited years, decades—three-quarters of a damn century—to witness a World Series triumph. Sportswriters don't root for teams, per se, but we can root for our readers, we can root for stories, we can root to have a front-row seat for the greatest spectacles in sports. And along those lines, there's nothing I'd cherish the chance to chronicle more than a World Series parade down E. 9th Street in early November.

The Indians were a charter member of the American League in 1901. The franchise carries enough history to fill thousands of pages. To an eight-year-old in April 1998, the Johnson–Lofton feud felt like the most noteworthy event in team history, but over time, I learned it's barely a blip on the radar. Here are 100 of those more pressing and distinguished moments, personalities, events, and activities. And maybe one day, we'll be able to update this book again to include a chapter or two about a Guardians World Series triumph.

1 The Rebirth of the Franchise

During the construction of Jacobs Field in the early '90s, players and team employees would occasionally ride a bus to the site to view the progress. They listened to a tour guide wax poetic about the 17,000–square foot batting cages, the SwimEx pool, the sauna and steam room and other amenities they couldn't even imagine while spending 81 days a year at Municipal Stadium, a cavernous dungeon on the shores of Lake Erie.

One day, Kenny Lofton tossed on a hard hat and followed the group out to center field to see where he would eventually chase down fly balls. Only, Lofton couldn't find it.

"There's no damn center field," he said. "What is this?"

"You're *standing* in center field," the guide replied.

Once they built the stands, the vision became clearer. At the time, it was just a vast plot of dirt. They installed home plate on June 25, 1992, a spectacle that lured TV stations and suite holders and employees. Charles Nagy and Mel Harder, who delivered the first pitch at the old stadium 60 years earlier, completed ceremonial tosses to Sandy Alomar Jr. With home plate in place, they could map out the mound, the bases, the foul lines, the distances to various walls and, of course, center field.

The countdown to Opening Day 1994 was under way.

The Indians were set to host an open house at newly minted Jacobs Field on April 3, 1994, a Sunday afternoon. It snowed. The event was canceled. It wasn't the most promising omen for the grand opening of a new ballpark set to happen the next day.

The Friday before Opening Day, the Indians dedicated a statue to Hall of Fame pitcher Bob Feller outside of Gate C, out beyond center field. A day later, the Indians and Pirates squared off in an exhibition game intended to serve as a test for ballpark operations. Fans poured into the stadium until it was packed to near capacity.

The open house was supposed to give fans who didn't have tickets to Saturday's affair a chance to explore the new building. Mother Nature, however, refused to cooperate. Fortunately for the team, Opening Day brought sunny skies, albeit with chilly temperatures. It was 48 degrees at first pitch.

"You're walking in there," said shortstop Omar Vizquel, "like, 'Wow. This is like Disneyland. This is beautiful.'"

Just how much better was Cleveland's new venue compared to old Municipal Stadium?

"It was night and day," said first baseman Paul Sorrento. "It was the past and the future."

"Every single day showing up there was like Christmas Day," said longtime executive Dan O'Dowd. "For us, it was that beautiful. It was that much of an upgrade."

"Everything tasted better. Everything looked better," Lofton said. "You go into the bathroom and even the toilet looked better. You felt like you could sit in there. You used to go into the bathroom before and get in and get out. Now, you're like, 'Let me get the stats and read the stats while I'm in here for a while now.' You felt like, 'Damn, this is cool to sit in here for a long time.' The other one was like, 'I gotta get up out of here real quick.'"

And its debut received a dramatic amount of attention.

President Bill Clinton tossed out the ceremonial first pitch for the inaugural game at the new building. Draped in a blue Indians windbreaker and blue Cleveland hat with a red brim, Clinton wore a light brown mitt on his right hand as he heaved a baseball down the middle to catcher Sandy Alomar Jr. Ohio Governor George

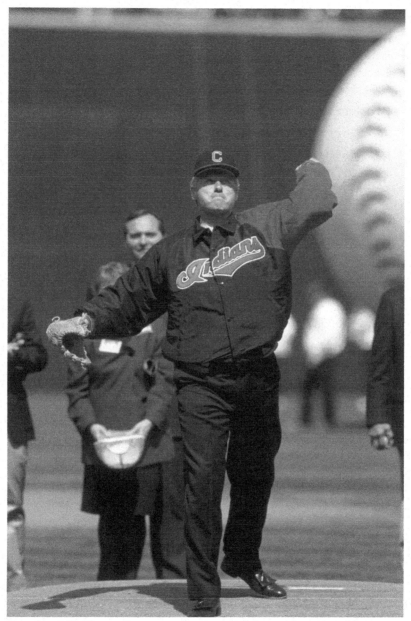

President Bill Clinton throws out the ceremonial first pitch on Opening Day 1994 before the Indians and Mariners squared off. It was the first-ever game at Jacobs Field.

Ballpark Firsts

Plenty of history has been made at the corner of Carnegie and Ontario, where Progressive Field, then named Jacobs Field, opened in 1994. The ballpark's firsts include the following:

First pitch: President Bill Clinton on April 4, 1994

Actual pitch: Dennis Martinez on April 4, 1994

Hit: Seattle Mariners outfielder Eric Anthony, a home run, on April 4, 1994

Home run: Anthony on April 4, 1994

Hit by a Cleveland player: Sandy Alomar on April 4, 1994

Home run by a Cleveland player: Eddie Murray on April 7, 1994

Grand slam: Paul Sorrento on May 9, 1995

Inside-the-park home run: David Bell off of Seattle's Randy Johnson on April 15, 1998

No-hitter: Angels right-hander Ervin Santana on July 27, 2011

Triple play: Casey Blake to Asdrubal Cabrera to Victor Martinez on August 27, 2007

Unassisted triple play: Asdrubal Cabrera on May 12, 2008

Voinovich and Feller followed with ceremonial first pitches of their own.

The Indians had planned for this day. They rebuilt their roster, devoting long, trying years to developing young players. When that green talent started to blossom, they cashed in on the free-agent market and pieced together a group that they felt could contend, all right as the organization opened the doors on a brand-new ballpark. The endeavor culminated in that Monday afternoon. All the hard work and pain suffered through decades of losing, the long, miserable nights at a massive, mostly empty stadium—it was all set to dissipate in favor of a new era, one Cleveland hoped would be rife with triumph and glory.

And then Seattle Mariners pitcher Randy Johnson held Cleveland hitless through the first seven innings of the first game.

Alomar finally ended Johnson's bid at an Opening Day no-hitter with a single to right field with no outs in the eighth. The base knock came after Feller, the only pitcher in major league history to toss a no-no on Opening Day, broke into the broadcast booth and attempted to jinx Johnson on air. Alomar's hit moved Candy Maldonado, who had walked, to second. Both runners advanced a base on a wild pitch and Manny Ramirez brought them home with a double off the wall in left field to tie the game.

The matinee extended to extra innings and both teams plated a run in the 10th. In the 11th, the Indians christened their new home with a fitting finale to its first affair. Reserve outfielder Wayne Kirby slapped a two-out single to left field off of Seattle reliever Kevin King. Eddie Murray scored from third and the Indians celebrated.

"How that all unfolded," Jim Thome said, "I think the magic kind of started from that."

The Indians would take an immediate liking to their new residence. They won a franchise-record 18 consecutive home games from May 13 to June 19 in their inaugural year at Jacobs Field. The club had the best home record in the league in 1994, at 35–16. Of course, it all began with that Monday afternoon. What a fortuitous finish and a proper culmination to everything the organization had worked toward.

"I would contend that that was the singular most important day in franchise history," said Guardians vice president of public affairs Bob DiBiasio. "It provided us the ability to carry forward, where if this thing is not built, we're gone. There is no baseball in Cleveland."

"We were waiting for that," said second baseman Carlos Baerga. "Now we had a place we could call our house. When everything is new, you see the ballgame in a different way. And everything changed. We had 455 nights in a row with that ballpark packed. It was amazing."

"What a great time to be in Cleveland," Thome said. "When we moved in from the old ballpark, it was a feeling like no other. And once we started to win, you could really see the city come alive."

2 A Long Time Coming

For four decades, Cleveland had waited for September 8, 1995. And it felt like Jeff Huson's pop-up took four decades to fall toward the Earth and settle in Jim Thome's glove.

By early July, the Indians knew a division title was inevitable in '95, but that didn't dampen the celebration after the club captured its first playoff berth since 1954.

The Indians won 100 games in 1995, a strike-shortened season that limited teams to 144 contests. They outscored their opponents by nearly two runs per game, finishing 14 games ahead of any other American League team and 30 games ahead of the second-best finisher in their division, the Kansas City Royals. Cleveland led the American League in runs, hits, home runs, stolen bases, batting average, on-base percentage, slugging percentage and total bases. Indians hitters struck out less frequently than any other offense, while the pitching staff's ERA was nearly a half-run better than that of any other AL staff. They issued the fewest number of free passes and recorded the third-most strikeouts.

"The season was just a magical season," said manager Mike Hargrove. "It was like the perfect storm. We just beat people to death with our bats. We scored a lot of runs. The thing that struck me with that team, that made it so magical, other than the 27 come-from-behind victories, was the fact that there never was a bump in the road with that ball club all year long."

Jason Giambi was a rookie infielder for the Oakland Athletics in 1995. They went 0–7 against the Indians that season.

"If you could go into Cleveland and play well, you knew what kind of ballclub you had," Giambi said, "because they were so good and so stacked that if you could play with them, you had a good team."

The Indians finished at least nine games over the .500 mark in each full month of the regular season. Their worst showing came in July, when they posted an 18–9 mark. They didn't slow down in August or September, when the division title was all but a guarantee. The players wanted to out-do one another. They sought bragging rights within the clubhouse. They didn't want to stop. The hunger to exceed their own standards and those of their peers drove them to new heights.

"'Who's pitching for them? Let's go kick their butt,'" said center fielder Kenny Lofton. "That's the idea and the mindset we had. Who was on the mound? What was their ERA? We didn't give a damn. Bring it."

The Indians sat at 85–37 on September 8. They gripped a commanding 22½-game lead in the division. That Friday evening, they hosted the Baltimore Orioles in a series-opening affair. An eager group of 41,656—a sellout crowd, of course—filled Jacobs Field, knowing what was likely to come after nine triumphant innings. In the third inning, Omar Vizquel opened the scoring with a sacrifice fly. Eddie Murray followed three batters later with a two-run single. Cleveland coasted from there. Orel Hershiser didn't need any more backing. The back end of the bullpen—Paul Assenmacher, Julian Tavarez and Jose Mesa, who earned his 40th save—cruised through the final frames.

As Thome straddled third base, waiting—for eons, seemingly— for Huson's two-out pop-up to descend from the stratosphere, fans shrieked with excitement. Thome squeezed the division-clinching out in his glove, kept his left arm raised and dashed to the mob scene at the center of the diamond. Indians coaches embraced in the home dugout as fireworks exploded high above the outfield. The players dumped a cooler of Gatorade onto Hargrove.

Radio announcer Tom Hamilton shouted, "The season of dreams has become a reality. Cleveland: You will have an October to remember!"

It marked the earliest any team in the divisional play era had clinched a postseason berth. It marked the Indians' first ticket to October in 41 years. It marked a new beginning for a franchise that had suffered through decades of ineptitude.

The team raised a flag after the game to signify its accomplishment. Lofton was granted the honor of pulling it, as Garth Brooks' "The Dance" played on the ballpark sound system, a request called in by Hargrove. It was the favorite song of Steve Olin, the Indians relief pitcher who died—along with teammate Tim Crews—in a tragic boating accident just two years earlier. As the Indians paid tribute on this momentous evening, tears streamed down the players' faces.

Looking back on the memory of
The dance we shared 'neath the stars above
For a moment all the world was right
How could I have known that you'd ever say goodbye
And now I'm glad I didn't know
The way it all would end, the way it all would go
Our lives are better left to chance, I could have missed the pain
But I'd have had to miss the dance

Upon clinching a playoff spot, the front office received congratulatory phone calls from former players, including Gary Bell, Max Alvis, Duane Kuiper, and Pat Tabler. Former Cleveland

Browns head coach Sam Rutigliano wrote the team a note commending the group for captivating the city.

"Once the years go by," Lofton said, "and you start to compare, they say, 'That '95 Cleveland team was something else.' That's what really makes it sink in."

3 A Year to Remember

In February 1948, Cleveland's baseball writers hosted a party for Lou Boudreau, the team's shortstop and manager. Boudreau had been at the center of trade discussions over the winter, before he signed a new two-year contract.

Boudreau gave a speech to the group, saying: "We now have a team with pennant possibilities. This is the first time that I've been able to say that since I've been manager."

The Indians had everything in 1948. They had three starting pitchers with at least 19 wins: Bob Lemon (20), Gene Bearden (20), and Bob Feller (19). They had hitters who produced sparkling offensive numbers: Joe Gordon (32 home runs, 124 RBIs), Lou Boudreau (.355 average, 18 home runs, 106 RBIs), Ken Keltner (.297 average, 31 home runs, 119 RBIs), Larry Doby (.301 average, 14 home runs), and Dale Mitchell (.336 average, 204 hits).

Hank Greenberg, the Hall of Fame first baseman who had shifted into a vice president role with the club, said after a doubleheader sweep of the Red Sox in early May, "You know, I think the boys learned today that they can win the pennant."

Cleveland had three players (Boudreau, Gordon, Keltner) in the All-Star Game starting lineup and two more (Lemon, Feller) on the pitching staff. They had a player/manager (Boudreau) who also captured the American League MVP award and had plenty of motivation. Owner Bill Veeck had planned to trade Boudreau during the previous offseason before rumors swirled and overwhelming backlash convinced the boss to keep him. They also had a landmark midseason addition in Satchel Paige, a legend in the Negro Leagues who contributed to Cleveland's stout pitching staff down the stretch.

The Indians topped their opponents by five or more runs on 43 occasions. Their hurlers tossed 26 shutouts. It was a complete team, one that jockeyed with the New York Yankees and Boston Red Sox for American League supremacy throughout the summer. The Indians spent about half the season in first place. They never held a lead larger than 3½ games and never trailed by more than 4½ games. Facing their most daunting deficit with only three weeks remaining in the regular season, they rattled off a pair of seven-game winning streaks in September to erase the gap.

A key to Cleveland's summer surge?

"If we win the pennant this year, a lot of the credit will be due to the great improvement of Doby," said team owner Bill Veeck. "Ever hear of Stan Musial? Doby will be better than him."

The Funeral

When the Indians were mathematically eliminated from the pennant race in 1949, owner Bill Veeck captained a funeral for their status as world champions, acquired when they won the World Series the previous year.

They folded up the pennant flag and buried it in a coffin. Player/manager Lou Boudreau, his coaching staff and several front-office executives served as pallbearers. They placed the coffin into a hearse, which Veeck drove around the field at Cleveland Municipal Stadium. The players joined in on the ceremony as the team nestled the coffin into a grave in center field.

The Indians finished the 1949 campaign with an 89–65 record, good for third place in the American League.

Cleveland held a two-game lead entering the final series against the Detroit Tigers at Municipal Stadium. The Indians sent their three-headed monster of Lemon, Bearden, and Feller to the mound, but the Tigers took two of three to force Cleveland into a one-game playoff with the Red Sox. The winner would advance to the World Series to face the Boston Braves.

Bearden started the playoff game, despite twirling a complete-game shutout just two days earlier. He logged another nine innings against the Sox, as Boudreau socked a pair of home runs and the Indians proceeded to their first Fall Classic in nearly three decades with an 8–3 triumph.

Harry Jones' article in the Cleveland Plain Dealer read:

Cleveland's beloved Indians, after all the anxious months of stress and strain and sweat in the closest race in American League history, have finally won the pennant.

They were proclaimed the champions—and deservedly so—at 3:54 this afternoon as Gene Bearden, a rookie southpaw who indelibly inscribed his name in the book of baseball immortals, pitched the final out for an 8-to-3 victory over the Boston Red Sox at Fenway Park in the winner-take-all, one-game play-off for the league's crown and world series money.

Bearden was carried off the field on the shoulders of his deliriously happy teammates, who had gained the privilege of meeting the National League's Boston Braves for the world championship by soundly thrashing the Red Sox, with whom they were tied at the close of the regular season.

Roelif Loveland wrote about the clinch as if the club had endured centuries without reaching the World Series:

Shortly before 4 yesterday afternoon the sun trembled in his orbit and the stars shivered violently in the heavens.

The earth gave itself a couple of extra spins, and a great voice cried: "Behold, the Cleveland Indians, winners of the 1948 American League pennant."

As if in answer, the city of Cleveland, which had waited long, went completely and noisily wacky.

The Indians captured the championship in six games, clinching the series at Braves Field. It was a series dominated by pitching; in only one game (Game 5) did either team score more than four runs. Bearden relieved Lemon in the eighth inning of Game 6 to close out the decisive victory, as the Indians recorded the second championship in franchise history.

Bearden, Paige and Keltner arrived at the Cleveland airport after taking a flight home the night of Game 6. As Alvin Silverman detailed in a *Plain Dealer* article: *If things to come were indicated in the spontaneous reception the three baseball stars received at Cleveland Airport from a group of persons who had little advance notice of their arrival, the planned celebration for their teammates this morning could be a welcome comparable to that which Cleveland gave Franklin D. Roosevelt and Charles A. Lindbergh. The sensational rookie pitcher, Bearden, and the gallant veteran, Keltner, scarcely had time to embrace their wives after stepping off a United Air Lines DC-6 before almost everyone at the airport surrounded them.*

The following day, they held a parade in downtown Cleveland, with three lanes of cars carrying players down Euclid Avenue. As a local broadcaster described: "Hundreds of thousands of cheering fans lined the street from Union Terminal, all the way out to Western Reserve University." The team's announcers captured the celebration, as they interviewed everyone from the players to the bat boy to the head of the stadium ushers. During their broadcast, Mel Harder, who had retired after the 1947 season following two decades with the club, said, "I don't know if the 1920 World Series was this big or not. Was it, Tris Speaker?"

"Well," said Speaker, the Hall of Famer who had taken a role as a team advisor, "we won it at home, and we didn't have to have this parade downtown. This is the biggest thing I've ever seen."

4 Breaking Barriers

Larry Doby's son would ask him to share stories from his playing days, to wax poetic about breaking the American League color barrier. Doby, though, leaned on two replies.

"Go look it up in the history books."

"That was yesterday. I deal with today."

His son never knew if the memories were too painful to recount or if there was some other reason for his reticence. Doby powered plenty of pitches into the outfield seats during his Hall of Fame career, but he preferred to instead marvel at teammate Luke Easter's majestic blasts. Larry Doby Jr. would eavesdrop when reporters called the home telephone or when his father dialed Don Newcombe, his best friend in the league. Doby twice led the AL in home runs, he once finished second in the MVP voting and he helped guide the Indians to a pair of World Series appearances, but only when his son met Doby's old teammate, Bob Lemon, did he receive confirmation that his father compiled an impressive career.

Lemon was the manager of the White Sox. Doby was his hitting coach. When Doby Jr. asked if his father was any good, Lemon laughed and assured him "he was one of the best."

"That was all I needed to hear," Doby Jr. said. "That was that. He just wasn't the kind of guy who talked about himself or about what he did or about the bad stuff that happened."

Jackie Robinson broke the Major League Baseball color barrier for the Brooklyn Dodgers at the start of the 1947 season. It was a calculated operation and both Robinson and the Dodgers had time to prepare. Doby's addition to the Indians later that year was done hastily and without public knowledge. Like Robinson, Doby dealt with cold shoulders from teammates and backlash from opposing players and fans.

Doby Jr. remembers his father regularly reminding him: "You treat people the way that you want them to treat you."

"What he said was, when you're off the ballfield," Doby Jr. said, "that's when you generally felt the prejudice, because you couldn't stay with your teammates. You couldn't socialize with your teammates. But when they were on the field, they had a common goal, and it was like they didn't care what color he was. 'Can you help us win?' Those were his happy times. Obviously, there were jeers from the stands and people and certain players who said stuff, but they were united in the cause of a common goal when they were on the field. So, that was his sanctuary, to a degree."

Doby suited up for the Indians for the first time on July 5, 1947, at Comiskey Park in Chicago. Bill Robinson, who joined the Indians when he was still a teenager in 1950 as the assistant traveling secretary, was tasked with coordinating Doby's travel and accommodations. They developed a close bond. Robinson would sometimes have to tip cab drivers extra to convince them to allow Doby in their vehicle. Doby parked his car at Robinson's parents' house in Cleveland Heights when the team left for a road trip. Robinson's mother would occasionally invite Doby in for a drink. Neighbors would call the police. At hotels in certain cities, Robinson had to sneak in Doby through a back door and up a secret elevator to accompany him to his room. Robinson recalled a couple of locker room confrontations, including one in which third baseman Al Rosen fought a player acquired in a trade who used a racial slur to describe Doby. He never spent much time on those details, though. Doby Jr. only ever heard about the respectful teammates. Doby spoke highly of Lemon, Joe Gordon, Jim Hogan and Steve Gromek.

"He accentuated the positive," Doby Jr. said.

Doby had played mostly middle infield in the Negro Leagues, but Gordon and Lou Boudreau were entrenched at shortstop and second base, respectively. So in his first big league season, Doby played sparingly, occasionally serving as a pinch-hitter. He blossomed during his first full season in 1948, as he posted a .301 batting average and .384 on-base percentage, with 14 home runs and 66 RBIs. He played center and right field and helped Cleveland to the American League pennant. The club defeated the Boston Braves in six games to capture its first World Series title in 28 years, and Doby became the first African American player to homer in a World Series game.

Doby developed into a middle-of-the-order threat and a perennial All-Star. He was selected to seven consecutive All-Star teams from 1949 to 1955 and he slugged 20 or more home runs for eight straight seasons. Doby finished second in balloting for American League Most Valuable Player in 1954, when he tied a career high with 32 home runs and established a personal best with 126 RBIs. That year, Cleveland tallied 111 wins in the regular season to put a temporary end to the New York Yankees' dominance.

About seven years after he played his final big-league game, Doby was elected into the team Hall of Fame in 1966. The franchise retired his No. 14 on July 3, 1994, and the Veteran's Committee inducted him into the Baseball Hall of Fame in 1998. On July 5, 2012, 65 years to the day he debuted with the Indians, the team renamed a portion of Eagle Avenue—the street that runs adjacent to the ballpark beyond left field—Larry Doby Way. In July 2015, the club unveiled a bronze statue of Doby outside the center field gates at Progressive Field.

Doby debuted with Cleveland 81 days after Jackie Robinson did so with the Dodgers. Doby Jr. believes "somewhere in the deep, deep reaches of his heart," his dad wished that his courage would have resonated as profoundly as Robinson's deed.

"What he always said to me," Doby Jr. said, "was that America didn't change from April 15 to July 5, when he started. It was the same thing."

5 Filling the Seats

On display in the upper deck at Progressive Field are the names and retired numbers of Bob Feller, Larry Doby, Bob Lemon, Earl Averill, Lou Boudreau, Mel Harder, Jackie Robinson, Frank Robinson and Jim Thome. On an adjacent wall rests one other retired number, perhaps the most cherished in team lore. It reads, "455: The Fans."

From June 12, 1995, to April 4, 2001, Cleveland fans filled Jacobs Field to capacity. The club established a Major League Baseball record with 455 consecutive sellouts. It became the first team in the league to sell every ticket to every game for an entire season. It did that for five straight years.

The Red Sox eventually topped the Indians' sellout streak in 2008, but Cleveland's stretch will never be forgotten near Lake Erie. The Colorado Rockies had owned the league's longest streak, at 203 games, before the Indians bested that mark.

"The convergence of things that resulted in 455 consecutive sellouts is a miracle," said Bob DiBiasio, Guardians senior vice president of public affairs. "People just don't truly understand. It never happened in the history of baseball. Not once."

On June 7, 1995, 36,363 watched the Indians top the Tigers in 10 innings on a Jim Thome walk-off home run. For nearly six years thereafter, every green seat and silver metal bench in the ballpark was occupied. Jacobs Field was a new entity, a shiny new toy in the forefront of the downtown landscape. Fans were going to flock to the building for a while anyway. Then, the realization of the team's potential began to spread.

"As that talent on the field started to be more and more evident to our fans, they started to feed off of it," said former team president Mark Shapiro. "The packed houses were no longer here just to see a new ballpark. They were here to see one of the best teams in baseball in one of the nicest ballparks in baseball. It just became an incredible amount of civic pride bubbling over in a combination of what was a crown jewel building with a team that they were proud of."

The lineup included a litany of All-Star caliber players: Kenny Lofton, Carlos Baerga, Albert Belle, Manny Ramirez, Sandy Alomar Jr., and Thome. Those talents boasted flamboyance, flair, and swagger, and they backed it up on the diamond. Fans lined up to partake in that powerful aura.

"Their offense was unreal, with Thome, Manny, Alomar, Kenny, all of them," said former Cleveland center fielder Michael Bourn. "Everybody knew about them in the '90s."

The attraction was evident to even the visitors. Shapiro can recall the honking horns from cars mired in traffic on the streets of downtown Cleveland after each game, the dominance of the Indians' potent lineup, and the intimidation and fear the group instilled in opposing pitchers.

"It was the place to go," said Jason Giambi, a rookie infielder for the Oakland Athletics in 1995. "It was unbelievable. They were selling out every game. Some of the best players in the game were playing there. The fans were coming out in droves, The Flats, that city was bumping. It was fun to play there."

People wanted to watch them on the road, too. Former Indians closer Chris Perez was raised near Tampa Bay, Florida. He can remember venturing to Tropicana Field to watch Thome and Ramirez and David Justice launch home runs against the hometown Devil Rays.

"People would come in here knowing, 'All right, we're going to get our ass kicked,'" DiBiasio said. "It was that simple. And then when the Tribe came to their city, it was, 'Oh shit. Let's see if we can get one out of these guys this weekend, because they're going to beat the devil out of our pitching.'"

The star power was signed or drafted and then developed in the Indians' system at the start of the run. As time elapsed, however, the Indians employed one of the league's highest payrolls—a benefit of the new ballpark, the height of the fan interest, and the newfound success. Shapiro compared the organization to the Los Angeles Dodgers and Boston Red Sox. He said the club's ability to impact the free-agent market and operate differently from most of the league was "incredible."

"They had the perfect pieces of the puzzle," Giambi said. "They had homegrown guys, free agents, Thome and these guys. Albert Belle left, and they brought in David Justice. They would just replace one piece of the puzzle with another. It was just unbelievable to watch. One free agent would leave, and they would bring somebody else in or a kid would take over. It was pretty special."

To amass a record number of sellouts required a perfect storm of sorts, an unforeseen confluence of variables that garnered the team such an unheralded, dedicated following. The economy was thriving; people had disposable income available to spend on the various costs incurred when attending a game. The city's NFL franchise had relocated: owner Art Modell moved the Browns to Baltimore after the 1995 season.

At the time the Indians opened the doors to their new establishment in April 1994, they had a talented crop of young players that was prepared to contend for the postseason. The timing worked wonders. The fans caught on quickly.

"It was the coolest thing," DiBiasio said. "Our guys knew. That energy building up, from about 3 o'clock on. Three hours before games, people just started lining up. Kids played catch on the grass.

Jacobs Field, pictured at full capacity. Between June 12, 1995, and April 4, 2001, the Indians established a Major League Baseball record with 455 consecutive sellouts.

"A remarkable set of circumstances came together with a team with such sparkle. This team was dynamic."

From the time Jacobs Field opened in 1994 until the end of the streak, the club sold out 95 percent of its regular season games. The Indians eclipsed the Rockies' sellout record on September 9, 1997. They attracted more than 19 million fans to the ballpark during the streak. When it began, the Indians had played the first two months of what would be their first playoff season in more than four decades. The club qualified for the postseason for five consecutive years, but when it fell one game short in 2000, ticket sales suffered. Fans packed the stadium for Opening Day in 2001, but the second game of the season featured a crowd of only 32,763, about three-fourths full. The sight of empty green seats had not existed for 2,122 days.

On April 22, 2001, less than three weeks after the sellout streak was snapped, the Indians unveiled the red letters and numbers on a pillar in the right-field mezzanine. No one will ever again don the numbers worn by Feller, Lemon, Harder, Doby, Boudreau, Averill, the Robinsons or Thome. And, in all likelihood, no era of Cleveland baseball will spark the long-term, widespread fanaticism that the teams from 1994–2001 did.

"The most difficult barometer for us is being measured by the '90s," DiBiasio said. "It's so difficult for the franchise to have to live up to that and be measured by it, but that's our goal.

"Our goal is to turn the town upside down like we did then."

6 A Historic Winning Streak

The collection of memorabilia tells the story of a team that couldn't lose. The Baseball Hall of Fame is in possession of three items: one of the baseballs Corey Kluber tossed during his complete-game shutout that notched the 2017 Indians their 20th consecutive win, the red uniform top Mike Clevinger donned during their 21st win in a row, and second base from win No. 22.

The team saved the last-out ball from wins 15 through 22, the lineup cards from wins 20 through 22, a Roberto Pérez bat and Jay Bruce's navy uniform top from the final win in a record-setting streak. That Bruce jersey survived a Gatorade shower, splashes of water and a cyclone of baby powder. Teammates tugged at the threads from every direction to celebrate the hero who lifted them to yet another win before another raucous crowd on September 14, 2017.

It's the longest winning streak in major league history...depending on who you ask. In 1916, the New York Giants pieced together a 26-game unbeaten streak, but that included one tie, which sparked a ton of debate as Cleveland marched to 22 straight victories.

"[We have] the record," pitcher Adam Plutko said. "I don't care what anybody says about the tie or whatever. In my mind, it's the record."

There wasn't much drama along the way. Throughout the streak, players and coaches downplayed the evolving achievement, leaning on clichés about taking things one day at a time and focusing on the task at hand. They were quite ho-hum about making history.

The Indians, coming off a World Series trip and boasting both a formidable lineup and the stoutest pitching staff in the league—their staff actually logged a higher WAR total than any other pitching staff in the history of the sport—had been sort of uninspiring for the first four months of the season. And then, they went unbeaten for 527 hours and 43 minutes. Here are some astounding statistics from their streak, which included a series-finale win against the Red Sox, a sweep of the Royals, a sweep of the Yankees in the Bronx, a sweep of the Tigers at Comerica Park, a four-game sweep of the White Sox on the south side of Chicago, a sweep of the Orioles, another sweep of the Tigers and another win against the Royals:

- They outscored the opposition, 142–37, and they scored 30 runs in the first innings alone
- They trailed after only eight of 199 innings
- They hit more home runs (41) than the opposition scored runs (37)
- They posted a 1.58 ERA as a team and recorded seven shutouts
- Their starting pitchers limited the opposition to two runs or fewer in 19 of 22 games
- They registered three consecutive shutouts for the first time in 61 years

- They increased their lead in the AL Central from 4.5 games to 13.5 games

"There weren't many nail biters," said closer Cody Allen.

By the end of the streak, the media contingent covering the team on a daily basis had ballooned in size. Attendance at Progressive Field had spiked. Oddsmakers vaulted the club to the top of the list of World Series favorites.

"CNBC wanted to interview me in the middle of it and talk about it," said general manager Mike Chernoff. "I'm like, 'What the hell? CNBC?'"

A year earlier, the club rattled off 14 consecutive wins at the start of summer to emerge as a contender. This streak topped that one by more than a week, and it benefited a bunch of homeowners. A local company, Universal Windows Direct, offered reimbursements to customers who purchased windows after July 1 if the Indians compiled a 15-game winning streak. Sure enough, they paid out $1.7 million in rebates—well, their insurance provider did—after they held a watch party at Progressive Field during win No. 15.

No triumph, however, proved as dramatic as the final one. Francisco Lindor delivered a two-out, two-strike RBI double in the ninth to push the game to extra innings. Bruce then socked a walk-off double in the bottom of the 10th to spark pandemonium in downtown Cleveland.

Outfielder Greg Allen: "Down to our last strike with Frankie. It gives you goosebumps."

Assistant hitting coach Matt Quatraro: "You just felt like it was going to happen."

Infielder Erik Gonzalez: "It was like we won the World Series. Everybody screamed."

Reliever Dan Otero: "You hate to say it's never going to be broken, but hopefully not."

The next night, the club fell short against Kansas City. It felt foreign. Even the postgame notes sheet the team distributes after the final pitch mistakenly displayed the Indians as 4–3 winners in the box score. It had become such a habit to mark them as victors.

"What we did was kind of crazy," Otero said. "Three weeks without losing a freaking game. Looking back on it, it almost seems unattainable and history kind of proves that—it's never been done before.

"Maybe they'll make a movie out of us."

Win 1: Thursday, August 24—Indians 13, Red Sox 6
Quatraro: "We knocked [Chris Sale] around pretty good. That made us feel good, beating those guys."

Win 2: Friday, August 25—Indians 4, Royals 0
Yan Gomes, catcher: "To win 22 games, it doesn't happen by luck. You might get a five-game win streak or something like that with things going your way. Twenty-two games—every day, you have to be clicking. Everything was: hitting, pitching, bullpen, baserunning, defense. Everything was clicking."

Win 3: Saturday, August 26—Indians 4, Royals 0
Otero: "Any time we took the lead, it was like, 'OK, they're not going to score any more runs. We're going to win the game.' It was crazy."

Win 4: Sunday, August 27—Indians 12, Royals 0
Cody Allen: "I maybe had, like, four save opportunities. In 22 wins. We were playing really, really well. That was one thing we did the year before in the 14–game win streak. I remember we joked about it. [Bryan] Shaw and I, we hardly pitched the year before, in 14 games. Our starting pitching was so good, and we scored early and we scored late."

Win 5: Monday, August 28—Indians 6, Yankees 2

Otero: "We know how hard it is to win baseball games. Winning four or five in a row is a feat in itself."

Win 6: Wednesday, August 30—Indians 2, Yankees 1

Josh Tomlin, starting pitcher: "You hear, six in a row, seven in a row, [and it's], 'They're hot.' And you look back and, golly, we had two more weeks of winning after that."

Win 7: Wednesday, August 30—Indians 9, Yankees 4

Otero: "I wasn't there for [the Yankees series]. We had our third kid, Sable, and she hadn't lost a game.... Sable didn't lose a game her first 22 days of life. I was like, 'You're a good-luck charm.'"

Win 8: Friday, September 1—Indians 3, Tigers 2

Greg Allen: "I came up and joined the team about a week in. So those first few weeks up, I didn't know what it was like to lose at the big-league level."

Win 9: Friday, September 1—Indians 10, Tigers 0

Otero: "You don't sweep doubleheaders in Major League Baseball very often. You try to, but those are hard to do. It doesn't matter who it's against. You use your best arms maybe one game and then you can't use them in the next game. Everything has to fall in place. To me, that was another remarkable part of the streak."

Win 10: Saturday, September 2—Indians 5, Tigers 2

Plutko: "When you look in the 'Last 10' column and see 10–0, the team's pretty hot. For me, it's two times through the rotation and then it's like, 'The team's feeling pretty good about itself right now.'"

Win 11: Sunday, September 3—Indians 11, Tigers 1

Tomlin: "We were pitching really well at that time and our offense, in the first two or three innings, they'd put together four or five runs. You'd go out there and you're already built on this momentum of pitching well and you'd get this run support early on and you're like, 'Even if my stuff isn't that good that day, let them put the ball in play and see what happens.'"

Win 12: Monday, September 4—Indians 5, White Sox 3

Gomes: "We didn't even quite understand it when we were doing it. We just knew we were extending our lead the whole time. You definitely look back on it now and realize how hard that was to do."

Win 13: Tuesday, September 5—Indians 9, White Sox 4

Kluber: "Right around when we were getting close to what we did the year before, I kind of started paying attention to it, or was aware of it. It's not like we came in every day looking to extend the winning streak. You're aware of it, just because people are talking about it."

Win 14: Wednesday, September 6—Indians 5, White Sox 1

Quatraro: "Once we got past the 14, then people were like, "Really? This is happening again?" We had been so mediocre and then after the All-Star break, when we opened up out west, we were terrible. It was like, 'What are we doing? We can't rely on 14 straight to pop up.' And then all of a sudden, it's 22. Obviously, you can't rely on that, but once we got past the 14, I think sometimes we'd look around, like, 'Really? Another one?'"

Win 15: Thursday, September 7—Indians 11, White Sox 2

Otero: "I didn't think much of [the windows deal]. 'We're not going to get to 15 in a row.' They only gave you two months to do it. It wasn't even the whole year, just August and September. And, sure enough, it happened."

Win 16: Friday, September 8—Indians 5, Orioles 0
Chernoff: "Jay Bruce was here for a few losses at the start and then, essentially, the guy came here and hadn't lost. You bump into him after a road trip and you're like, 'How are things going?' And he's like, 'Well, pretty good. We don't ever lose around here.'

Win 17: Saturday, September 9—Indians 4, Orioles 2
Lindor: "I remember a couple times where—the last game of the series, we'll get together and we all hug each other and we'll be like, 'Good series. On to another one.' Then, the next time, same thing. 'On to another one.' All of a sudden, it's like, 'We've been winning all these series?' I couldn't remember if we really had won that many games in a row until everybody started saying, 'Oh, they're at 16 games, 17 games.' By then, it was like, 'I don't care who you put out there. You're not winning.'

Win 18: Sunday, September 10—Indians 3, Orioles 2
Chernoff: "For the first 15 or 16 games, we're just going down to Tito's office the same way we always do, talking about the game, not really thinking about it. As we got closer to 20 games, you start getting in your own head. 'I don't want to say the wrong thing to Tito. I don't want to put pressure on the guys.' So you start playing that game a little bit."

Win 19: Monday, September 11—Indians 11, Tigers 0
Cody Allen: "I think once it started getting national attention, when we were getting close to 20, that's when it became a little more of a challenge to tune it out. But up until then, it was just, 'All right, who's pitching for us? Who's pitching for them? Who are we playing? Who's hot in their lineup?'"

Win 20: Tuesday, September 12—Indians 2, Tigers 0

Chernoff: "I remember going into Tito's office after 20 wins and Chris [Antonetti] went to shake his hand. We all thought that was so weird. We don't ever shake hands after a win. He shook his hand, and we took a moment and looked at each other, like, 'This is pretty cool,' with some congratulations. That's a moment that really stands out to me.... [A's GM] David Forst texted us right after that win, 'Congratulations, I remember being in Oakland when this happened. It's hard to think of it now, but when you step back and look at the cool things in baseball, this is one of those moments. I hope you guys always remember it.'"

Win 21: Wednesday, September 13—Indians 5, Tigers 3

Clevinger: "We were still pushing for the division title, but at the same time, there was a game right there that was bigger than all of us and we couldn't avoid it. We can say that's probably once in a lifetime. I'm not saying it can't be done, but it would be really, really rare to see something like that."

Win 22: Thursday, September 14—Indians 3, Royals 2

Lindor: "I was watching the last couple innings of [a] Houston-Oakland [game] and they said something about the team that won 20 straight games coming back for a reunion or something. And I was like, 'Shit, we won 22!' I was thinking, 'Yeah, that's pretty cool. It's special. Maybe they'll be calling me to come back for a reunion for winning 22 games.'"

7 Ten-Cent Beer Night

There were crude chants and obscene shouts. There were streakers and flashers, and the trespassing led to arrests. Add it all up and you get a disruption of a major league game, a forfeit and one of the most infamous nights in franchise history.

So much went wrong at Cleveland Stadium on June 4, 1974, that the night lives on in sports infamy. Certainly, had the Indians—and, more specifically, Jackie York and Carl Fazio, the organization's promotions team—had any inkling that the night may have gone awry, they would have scrapped the idea. But in 1971, they held Nickel Beer Night. It went on without a hitch.

"It went smoothly," said Bob DiBiasio, Guardians senior vice president for public affairs. "They thought they'd do it again and raise it to a dime. But there were issues."

A week earlier, the Indians played at Arlington Stadium in Texas, where the Rangers hosted their own Ten Cent Beer Night. After a bench-clearing brawl, fans became unruly and heaved beer and food at Cleveland's players in the visitors' dugout. Rangers manager Billy Martin did not endear himself to the Cleveland community when he claimed the city lacked the number of fans necessary to repeat those actions when the teams met again a week later.

"They won't have enough fans to worry about," Martin quipped.

Martin taunted the fans at Cleveland Stadium by blowing them a kiss prior to first pitch on June 4. That did not help measures, either.

Cleveland radio host Pete Franklin doused the fire with gasoline when he spent the days leading up to the Rangers' arrival by building up the rivalry, Martin's antics, and the need for retaliation. He urged fans to venture to the ballpark.

"A lot of people think Pete Franklin had something to do with it," DiBiasio said. "When we were in fisticuffs with the Rangers on the previous road trip and the radio was playing up that fireworks were going to be happening at the game—you add the beer to it…"

The cheap beer—a drink that typically cost about 65 cents at the time—provided the final spark for the crowd of 25,134. Throughout the game, fans were removing clothes, running onto the field, throwing hot dogs, and yelling obscenities. One woman bolted onto the field in an attempt to kiss umpire Nestor Chylak. Fans tried to slide into bases. They pulled down their pants and mooned the crowd. A man wearing nothing but one black sock streaked across the field.

In the ninth inning, everything took a turn for the worse. The Indians had tied the game, 5–5, with a pair of runs in the final frame.

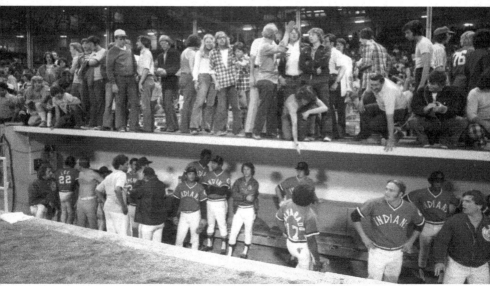

Fans became increasingly rowdy on Ten Cent Beer Night at Cleveland Stadium on June 4, 1974. Their belligerence intensified from standing atop the dugouts to finally storming the field in the ninth inning.

Then, one fan entered the field of play in an attempt to retrieve the hat off of the head of Rangers right fielder Jeff Burroughs. He ran up behind Burroughs, snatched the ball cap, dropped it, looked up and locked eyes with the player. Burroughs attempted to kick the fan and fell down and fans spilled out onto the field and swarmed Burroughs. A melee broke out. Rangers players poured out of the dugout, wielding bats, in support of Burroughs. The Indians followed suit, joining forces with their American League adversaries to fend off the feisty fans. Reliever Tom Hilgendorf was struck in the head with a steel folding chair. It was pure belligerence and hops-infused chaos. Fans stole all three bases on the infield.

The umpires called the game. The Indians were forced to forfeit. Some left the field bearing wounds. Some were taken to the hospital. Some were arrested. The Indians never held Ten Cent Beer Night again…until July 18, a mere 45 days later. That night, they limited fans to two beers per transaction.

Now that infamous night is celebrated in the form of commemorative T-shirts and parodied ballpark promotions. At the time, though, no one was condoning the behavior. Martin declared it "the worst sportsmanship in the history of baseball." Chylak dubbed the fans "uncontrolled beasts." Cleveland sports chronicler Hal Lebovitz pinned much of the blame on the promotion: "They weren't baseball fans," he wrote. "They wanted the beer."

There were bruises, threats, and plenty of blood. There was debate about whether to deliver a warning over the loudspeaker or call the game early. In the end, it was a night no one will forget.

"I don't know who's to blame," Aspromonte said after the game, "but I'm scared."

"I guess these fans just can't handle good beer," Martin said.

Tito

After he was dismissed from his managerial role with the Phillies, Terry Francona assisted with the Indians' scouting efforts in 2001. Whenever then-general manager Mark Shapiro asked Francona—who served as a special assistant that season—for his thoughts on a particular player, Francona steered him away. Ultimately, Shapiro asked Francona why he had not approved of any prospect.

"He said, 'You haven't said yes [to anyone],'" Francona said. "I figured the odds were in my favor if I said no. How do you know?"

Francona—whose father, Tito, played 15 years in the major leagues—was once a highly touted prospect himself. With the Tigers in 1959, Tito asked Detroit general manager John McHale for a $500 raise, extra income that would help support the son he and his wife, Roberta, were expecting. McHale scoffed at the notion, saying it wasn't his problem. The Tigers dealt Tito to the Indians that March. Terry was born a month later.

In 1980, the Expos selected Francona with the 22nd overall pick in the first-year player draft. Naturally, McHale happened to be Montreal's GM.

Tito said to McHale: "Do you remember that son that I wanted the $500 for?"

McHale remembered.

"Well, it's going to cost you a lot more now," Tito said, as both parties laughed.

A few days after he was drafted, Francona's University of Arizona team captured the college national championship. After the title game, Wildcats coach Jerry Kindall approached Francona, who had been named the Most Outstanding Player of the tournament and told him it was time for him to move on to the next level.

"The only thing I was really stressed about," Francona said, "was I had done so horrible at class that semester that I was thinking, 'If I don't sign, I'm going to have to take summer school.'"

The Expos offered Francona a $100,000 signing bonus, which he accepted. Jim Fanning, Montreal's director of scouting, flew into town; Francona grew up in the small community of New Brighton, Pennsylvania. Tito and Roberta had Francona pick up Fanning from the airport and bring him back to the house. Roberta cooked a meal for everyone, and they all chatted for a few hours. A week later, Francona officially joined the Expos organization.

He was almost a Chicago Cub. Before he ever attended college, Francona was drafted by the Cubs in the second round. They offered him an $18,000 signing bonus, but he was adamant about earning a $40,000 stipend.

Francona was well regarded. He panicked during his senior year of high school when his batting average "slipped" to .700. His stress level increased even more when he then separated his shoulder, which sidelined him for six weeks. He always dreamed of following in his father's footsteps. His seventh-period Spanish teacher often dismissed him from class early. He would drive his Mustang down to the baseball field and drag the dirt. When his effort did not finish the job, he would douse the field with four or five gallons of gasoline and light it on fire.

"I remember teachers saying, 'Damn, I thought the fucking building was burning,'" Francona said. "Nowadays, you'd probably go to jail. My Spanish teacher, she knew I didn't [care] about Spanish. I just wanted to play."

A handful of scouts flocked to New Brighton to watch him take batting practice off of his coach during his senior year. Longtime Cincinnati Reds scout Elmer Gray organized a showcase for Francona in which he performed a series of drills, including a pair of 60-yard dashes, two at-bats against a live pitcher, and a set of outfield throws.

Tito's Tales

Did you hear the one about the bad dream the night before Game 7 of the 2016 World Series?

Throughout his Cleveland tenure, Terry Francona offered a daily dose of humor, self-deprecation and stories that only he could tell. He once ate 17 popsicles in one sitting, but insisted it was OK because they were low-calorie popsicles. He ordered $44 worth of room service ice cream in the middle of the night ahead of Game 5 of the 2016 World Series. His tooth popped out during the National Anthem before Game 3 of the 2016 ALCS, forcing him to meet with a dentist at 1:00 AM. He swallowed a chunk of his tooth after it broke off as he ate pasta he failed to thoroughly cook one night during spring training in 2023. He has woken up in the morning covered in M&Ms or melted ice cream. His seat on the team plane resembled that of a messy toddler.

Anyway, Game 7 of the 2016 World Series: Francona woke up thinking he had experienced a nightmare. He felt a sharp pain in his side. He had fallen asleep on his remote control, which was lodged in his ribs. He also had peanut butter on his glasses, the result of dozing off while dunking pretzels in the jar.

When the Cubs refused to up their offer, however, Francona enrolled at Arizona. Then, as the clock wound down toward his first class, he became homesick and developed feelings of regret about turning down Chicago's proposal. Negotiations could continue until a player attended his first college class, so Tito checked back with the Cubs one final time to see if they would budge.

They did.

They offered Francona $19,000.

He went to class.

Those experiences provided Francona with plenty of insight that came in handy when he joined the Indians staff in 2001. Francona lasted parts of 10 seasons in the big leagues, as he compiled a .274 batting average with 16 home runs in 708 games. He hit .346 in 58 games for the Expos in 1984 before a knee injury marred his season. He never lived up to his billing as a first-round draft choice, and he said when he went out with Shapiro to scout in 2001, he "was humbled."

"You just never quite know," Francona said. "You see guys hit .350 in Triple-A and they get to the big leagues and if they have a hole—it may take the league [a while] to find it, but [they will]. There aren't a lot of guarantees."

Francona had more skill in communicating with players and practicing in-game strategy. He started managing the Phillies at the age of 37 in 1997. He led the Phillies for four years—all losing seasons, which included a pair of last-place finishes in the National League East—before he received a pink slip.

The Indians swooped in and hired him as a special assistant. He traveled with Shapiro to New Orleans to scout Tulane infielder Jake Gautreau and Louisiana State infielder Mike Fontenot. The Indians did not select either player. Francona sat in the team's draft room and observed. He spent time with the organization's minor league staff at each stop in the farm system. The Indians had an impending hole to fill in center field, as Kenny Lofton, then 35 years old, was bound to hit free agency. Francona evaluated seven or eight center fielders. Eventually, the club settled on a trade for 23-year-old Milton Bradley. Francona spent the year building a tight bond with Shapiro and his assistant, Chris Antonetti. Those relationships became the foundation for a reconnection later down the road.

The Indians sputtered to an abysmal 68–94 finish in 2012. A 5–24 showing in August derailed their faint postseason hopes. With six games remaining in the regular season, the club cut ties with manager Manny Acta. Bench coach Sandy Alomar Jr. served as interim skipper for the final week, and he instantly became a finalist for the job. So, too, did Francona. It took one phone call from Shapiro and Antonetti and the man who directed the Red Sox to two World Series titles was interested in the opening. Francona said Cleveland was the only destination in which he desired to coach again, more than a year removed from an undesirable conclusion to his tenure in Boston. To prove his commitment, Francona crafted a 17-page manifesto outlining his firmest baseball beliefs, from his stance on smart baserunning to how he handles difficult roster decisions. He wrote the document in all caps.

A 94-loss team hauled in a two-time world champion to infuse a winning attitude into its clubhouse.

"I don't think that we felt like it was definitively going to be some miracle cure," Shapiro said. "We felt like Terry was going to bring credibility and a change in culture and bring a huge injection of positive energy and he was going to bring experience."

Francona flourished in Boston, with a team stacked with quality veterans every year, thanks to the loaded pockets of the club's ownership. In Cleveland, he arrived into the opposite situation. That did not deter him from signing on.

"I remember being so amazed at his open-mindedness at bringing in people and getting their opinions," Shapiro said. "That set an immediate tone for the organization, like, 'OK, everybody's important. Whatever helps us be successful, whatever helps us win, that's what we're going to do.'"

His credibility helped the club lure free agents Nick Swisher and Michael Bourn to town. Immediately, the players in the clubhouse took a liking to their new commander. In Francona's first year, the Indians capped a 92-win regular season with a 10-game winning streak that catapulted the club into the playoffs. Cleveland hosted the American League Wild Card game, which it lost, 4–0. Still, it represented a 24-game turnaround. That year spent scouting prospects and networking in the organization, those experiences gained through the draft process—all of it paid off for both Francona and the organization. He became the winningest manager and the longest-tenured manager in franchise history.

Under Francona, Cleveland captured four division titles. He won three Manager of the Year awards. After 11 seasons with the franchise—the last few spent dealing with a variety of health maladies—Francona retired at the end of the 2023 campaign.

"I came here for the right reasons," Francona said. "I think I'm leaving for the right reasons. And in between, it's been really good."

Francona was a master of communication, finding ways to connect with everyone in the organization, from the star players to the rookies young enough to be his grandkids to the ballpark ushers and security guards to the clubhouse attendants who combed through his lawn looking for his car keys. Despite his credentials, he dodged credit at every turn, preferring to poke fun at himself for his food-spilling episodes or on-field shortcomings rather than focus on his game-changing bullpen machinations or shelf full of awards. His players wouldn't let him slip out of Progressive Field without soaking up the spotlight, though. After his final home game as Cleveland's manager on September 27, 2023, José Ramírez blocked the dugout steps, forcing Francona back onto the field for a well-deserved curtain call.

9 Visit Ray Chapman's Gravesite

The gray headstone displays only his name, Ray Chapman, the year he was born, 1891, and the year of his tragic death, 1920. An imposing maple tree stands guard in a shady section of Lake View Cemetery, a hilly, 285-acre peek into Cleveland's past that includes the resting spots for President James A. Garfield, law enforcement ace Eliot Ness and business magnate John D. Rockefeller.

No one at the Polo Grounds on that dreary afternoon more than 100 years ago imagined Chapman's life was in danger, even after Cleveland's shortstop crumpled to the ground. Tris Speaker,

Chapman's teammate and manager, had absorbed a fastball to the noggin a few years earlier, but returned to the lineup after a little more than a week. But hours after Yankees hurler Carl Mays nailed Chapman's left temple with a dirtied baseball, Chapman died at St. Lawrence Hospital in New York City, the only player in major league history to sustain a fatal, on-field injury.

Chapman was a .300 hitter in three of his last four seasons. He had earned acclaim for his speed, which fueled a bevy of infield singles and stolen bases. He led the league in walks and runs in 1918. A year earlier, he swiped 52 bases, which stood as the franchise record until Miguel Diloné came along in 1980. Ross Tenney of the Cleveland Press anointed Chapman "the greatest shortstop in the game."

He was a hit off the field, too. Tenney once described him as a "peppery shortstop whose ever-bubbling-over spirits were a big factor in the life of the ball club." Chapman was known to gather teammates for a morale-boosting concert after a loss, often to sing "Dear Old Girl." He delivered jokes, provided pep talks and captivated audiences with his storytelling. He befriended famous performers such as Al Jolson and Will Rogers. American League umpire Billy Evans once said, "If there were more men like Chapman in baseball, umpiring would not be a half-bad job." When Chapman was stuck in a hospital bed for the first six weeks of the 1914 season because of a broken ankle, Henry P. Edwards, former sports editor of *The Plain Dealer*, wrote that it "was like traveling with the mourners. Never a song, never a funny story, never a thing to bring a smile. It was the most discouraged aggregation of ballplayers I ever saw, and it remained such until Chapman rejoined the team." Manager Joe Birmingham characterized the absence of "Chappie" by saying he was essentially missing "more than half of my team."

When Mays' pitch struck Chapman on that day in 1920, the shortstop dropped to his knees, blood flowing from his left ear.

The umpire called for a doctor from the stands and Chapman was rushed to St. Lawrence. Speaker called Chapman's wife, Kathleen, who was pregnant with their first child, a daughter she would name Rae. Kathleen was traveling by train to New York when her husband passed. Her younger sister, Margaret, once said Kathleen never attended another baseball game.

The gravesite still attracts visitors, more than a century later. Baseballs line the top of the headstone, many weathered and discolored, some reduced to eroding clumps of yarn. One note, scribbled in Sharpie on one of the baseballs, reads, "You were such a good player. RIP you will be missed."

In Chapman's funeral pamphlet, Speaker was quoted as saying, "I can't say the things Ray Chapman deserves. He was an inspiration to the whole team, both with his playing and his personality. With Ray in there, things went with a snap and ginger. Without him—well, I don't know. I've lost one of the finest players in the game, but more than that, I've lost the kind of a man the game cannot afford to do without."

In the ensuing weeks, a committee was formed to create what the members described as a "monumental bronze on a slab of antique marble" that would be "secured in a manner to make its removal impossible." The ultimate composition combined two of the 50 designs submitted by an array of artists and bronze manufacturers. Chapman's father-in-law, M.B. Daly, the president of the East Ohio Gas Company, granted final approval for the tablet, which initially hung inside the Lexington Avenue entrance of League Park in 1921. It was removable, however, as it was ultimately relocated to Municipal Stadium and then disappeared for a while before it was tacked onto the brick facade in Heritage Park in 2007. It reads, "This tablet is erected by lovers of clean sport as an affectionate tribute to his inspiring enthusiasm, cheerfulness and unfailing loyalty to his club."

Rev. Dr. William Cullen presented the eulogy at Chapman's funeral and depicted him as "a glorious example of that great American spirit," with "smiling cheerfulness," "unswerving devotion" and "gentle courtesy." Mays, meanwhile, griped in a *Sporting News* essay four decades later that no one ever considered his 207 career wins, his .622 winning percentage or his 2.92 ERA. "What happened to me in August of 1920 is the only thing anybody remembers," he asserted. He suggested he and Chapman shouldered "equal responsibility" since hitters took "a foothold, digging in, right on top of the plate and almost defying the pitcher to throw to the inside corner of the plate." "I love baseball," penned Mays, who eventually served as a scout for the Indians and several other clubs. "It has been good to me. It has been my life. The only thing that hurts is that I am remembered for only one thing—an accident."

The Indians dropped eight of 11 following the tragedy before putting together a 24–8 run to close out the regular season and fend off the Yankees and White Sox in a three-team pennant chase. They downed the Brooklyn Robins in the World Series to secure the franchise's first championship, only eight weeks after Chapman's death. The team awarded Kathleen a full World Series share.

"Down through the years," began a *Cleveland Press* contribution to Chapman's funeral pamphlet, "Chapman sacrificed and teamworked his team to victory, never sulking, always cheerful, always optimistic, always praising the other fellow.

"How does your record stack up with Ray Chapman's?"

10 What's In A Name?

There might not have been a more polarizing topic in Cleveland sports than the baseball team's name change. The charter member of the American League went by the Bluebirds (often shortened to Blues), the Bronchos, the Naps and then, for 106 years, the Indians. But in 2018, the franchise ditched its longtime Chief Wahoo logo, and in 2020 the club initiated the process of identifying a new name. The consideration came about, according to the organization's leaders, in response to social unrest and the decision by the NFL's Washington franchise to move on from its old name. Team owner Paul Dolan said the decision came after months of "discussions with fans, business leaders, players, social activists and researchers focused on Native American culture and issues."

They cycled through nearly 1,200 options for the new name, from Spiders to Walleye to Buckeyes. (For what it's worth, Naps won out in a public vote before the 1903 season over other nominations such as Cyclops, Emperors, Gladiators, Giants and Metropolitans.) Spiders received a lot of attention early in the process, but those in the organization preferred to avoid a connection to the Cleveland Spiders, who sputtered to a 20–134 record in their final year of existence in 1899. They finished 84 games out of first place. The name Buckeyes presented some hurdles because of obvious ties to Ohio State University. Throughout the process, Guardians always made the most sense to those charged with deciding on the ultimate choice. The only hiccup: a local roller derby team also named the Cleveland Guardians sued the club in an effort to halt it from unauthorized use of the name. The sides eventually reached a settlement.

In the early 1930s, the city of Cleveland built a pair of art deco–style stone sculptures, known as the Guardians of Traffic, along a newly constructed bridge in the heart of downtown. The monuments withstood harsh Cleveland winters and drastic modifications to the city's downtown landscape. Now they stand tall on the Hope Memorial Bridge, as bicycles, cars and buses hum along below them, a brief five-minute walk down the street from the ballpark that hosts the team named after them.

The team hired Academy Award winner Tom Hanks to narrate a video announcing the name change. Hanks studied theater in Cleveland in the late '70s and developed a fandom for the franchise.

"Together we stand with all who understand what it means to be born and built from The Land," Hanks said in the video, which was revealed to the public on July 23, 2021. "This is a city and a game we believe in. And together we are all Cleveland Guardians."

They retained the red, white and navy color scheme. They added a bit more character to their Block C logo, gave it a white border and rebranded it the Diamond C logo. They also crafted a logo that featured a pair of winged "G" symbols adorning a baseball. The club continued to wear "Cleveland" on its road tops, with a script "Guardians" on its home uniforms. That November, the team removed the script, 80-foot-wide "Indians" display atop the Progressive Field scoreboard. They later replaced it with a script "Guardians."

There's debate over whether "Indians" was chosen ahead of the 1915 season as a tribute to Louis Sockalexis, a Native American outfielder who played in Cleveland from 1897–99. Sockalexis died in December 1913. A January 17, 1915, *Cleveland Plain Dealer* article carried the headline, "Baseball writers select Indians as best name to apply to the former Naps."

"We're not asking anybody to give up their memories or the history of the franchise," Dolan said. "That will always be there."

11 Near-November Reign

A little after midnight on July 31, 2016, the Indians and Yankees completed a trade sending Andrew Miller to Cleveland, but the two front offices agreed they didn't want to wake the players and their families, so they opted to wait to inform them until the morning. Meanwhile, in Cleveland, everyone was waiting to learn whether Brewers catcher Jonathan Lucroy would waive his no-trade clause and solidify the most glaring weakness on the Indians' roster.

Morning came, and the trade was complete: Miller, the league's most imposing reliever, a 6-foot-7 slider-slinging, strikeout-stacking cyborg, was headed to Cleveland. A couple hours later, Lucroy officially vetoed his trade. His loss.

Miller was the prized acquisition, and he proved to make a substantial difference when it mattered most. That October, with Danny Salazar and Carlos Carrasco sidelined and after Trevor Bauer's pinkie lost a late-night fight with a drone—yep, the fall of 2016 was something else—Terry Francona's club leaned on its bullpen more than ever. And that meant Miller would lead the charge, with multi-inning appearances at any critical juncture of the game.

The Indians' run to the 2016 World Series—and to within one win, one run, one Mother Nature interference of their first title since 1948—was as improbable as any.

The roster had plenty of talent, but it was nowhere near full strength. In addition to the pitcher injuries, Michael Brantley was on the shelf with a shoulder injury that pestered him throughout the season. They unearthed the winning formula, though: an elite bullpen, just enough starting pitching and key hits at precisely the right time.

The team rattled off 14 consecutive wins in late June, which convinced both the clubhouse and the front office that the roster was ready for reinforcements that could pay dividends in October. The final victory in that streak, by the way, was a 19-inning thriller in Toronto, in which Carlos Santana produced the decisive home run. Mike Napoli provided power and leadership. José Ramírez emerged as a steady force in the middle of the lineup. Corey Kluber anchored a dominant rotation. And Miller cemented Cleveland's bullpen as the best in the league.

They soaked the visitors' clubhouse in Detroit with champagne in late September to celebrate their first AL Central crown in nine years. And then they swept the Red Sox in the opening round of the playoffs, following that familiar recipe for success. In Game 1, Francona deployed Miller in the fifth inning and he and closer Cody Allen combined for eight strikeouts (and 80 pitches) across 3⅔ scoreless innings. Roberto Pérez, Jason Kipnis and Francisco Lindor all homered in a span of four batters in the third inning. In Game 2, Kluber logged seven shutout frames. And in Game 3, with Boston fans chanting his name in a futile method of intimidation, Josh Tomlin pitched Cleveland to a series sweep.

Kluber, Miller and Allen were the catalysts for the club. They combined on a shutout in Game 1 of the ALCS against the Blue Jays, a series that had everything. Bauer was pushed back to Game 3 because he sliced his pinkie on a drone, and then exited that start in the first inning as blood dripped from his finger like a leaky faucet. Cleveland's bullpen patched together 8⅓ innings to secure the victory. During the national anthem that night, the veneer on one of Francona's teeth popped off. Francona met with a dentist in downtown Toronto at 1 AM to repair the tooth. The Indians turned to Ryan Merritt, who had one start and 11 career innings to his name, to take the hill for Game 5. Toronto slugger Jose Bautista said the rookie would be "shaking in his boots." Instead, Merritt delivered 4⅓ scoreless innings, and Cleveland advanced to the World Series. After the game, in the middle of a smoke-filled, beer-scented clubhouse, rested a bottle of champagne inside a cowboy boot.

The Indians clashed with the Cubs in the World Series, a meeting of the two teams saddled with the league's longest championship droughts. Cleveland's hex dates back to 1948. The Cubs hadn't celebrated a title since 1908. Francona's club raced out to a 3–1 series lead, as Jason Kipnis, a kid from the north side of Chicago, punctuated the Indians' Game 4 victory with a three-run

A Plea to the Baseball Gods

Jason Kipnis, Lonnie Chisenhall, Mike Napoli and Chris Gimenez snuck away to Target in downtown Minneapolis the morning of July 16, 2016. They bought a rotisserie chicken, candy, a piñata, capes, costumes, maracas, kazoos and tambourines. You know, the essentials in the middle of a baseball season. They spent about $500, all in hopes of reversing the course of Yan Gomes' miserable season.

The team gathered in the visitors' clubhouse that afternoon, closed the doors and dimmed the lights. Napoli read a monologue. Gomes, wearing a white sheet and holding flowers, sacrificed the chicken with a dramatic slice as "Circle Of Life" and "Hakuna Matata," classic tracks from *The Lion King*, blared on the clubhouse speakers.

Napoli, sporting a rainbow cape and his patented "Party At Napoli's" T-shirt, placed his left hand on Gomes' head and read, "We have prepared this exorcism to honor thy holiness and to absolve Yan Gomes of any wrongdoing that he may have committed towards thee. We urge you to forgive his obsession with the octagon and bestow him with your guidance and grace on the diamond. Please accept these offerings as atonement for him straying from the righteous path. Be kind and just in your willingness to accept him and not condemn him any further. In the name of Jobu, amen."

Gomes struck the piñata to spray candy across the room. The catcher, a Silver Slugger Award winner two seasons earlier, was batting .163 with a .198 on-base percentage at the time. A day after the ritual, Gomes took a spill at first base and dislocated his shoulder.

blast at Wrigley Field. The Cubs won the next two contests to force a decisive Game 7 on an unseasonably warm early November night in Cleveland.

Kluber was on fumes after pitching on short rest for most of the postseason, and he endured his worst start of the Indians' run. Cleveland carved into Chicago's lead when a pair of runs scored on a wild pitch, with Kipnis dashing to the plate from second base, reminiscent of Kenny Lofton's scamper against Seattle in the 1995 ALCS. Then, trailing 6–4 and representing the tying run, Rajai Davis supplied perhaps the most memorable moment in franchise history, with a home run that narrowly cleared the 19-foot-high wall in left field on a 100-mph fastball from Aroldis Chapman.

Dan Otero: "I threw our bullpen bag in the air so everything that was in the bag flew out. I jumped on the fence like a spider monkey. I was all over the place. I lost my voice."

Lonnie Chisenhall: "I remember almost fainting. The legs went jelly on me."

Jason Kipnis: "It was literally a euphoria feeling. We were all celebrating like little kids."

Josh Tomlin: "I felt like a four- or five-year-old kid."

Yan Gomes: "I remember jumping the highest I've ever jumped and acting like a fool."

Andrew Miller: "I kind of blacked out."

Mike Chernoff: "I almost fell out of the suite."

Tyler Naquin: "It gives me goosebumps every time I think about it."

Danny Salazar: "You know sometimes when you're screaming [or] you're laughing and all of the air you have inside comes out, but you can't stop and you see [nothing but] black? That was me for, like, five seconds."

Brandon Guyer: "I was like, 'You gotta be kidding me, man. It's meant to be. We're going to win this.' I've never felt those emotions when I've been on a baseball field."

Cleveland's momentum, however, stalled during a 17-minute rain delay after the ninth inning. The Cubs scored a pair of runs in the top of the 10th off Bryan Shaw. The Indians mounted a mini rally, as Davis delivered an RBI single, but Michael Martinez grounded out as Chicago secured its first title since 1908.

12 Rapid Robert

Mark Shapiro had settled into his new office at the Indians' spring training complex in Tucson, Arizona, when he heard a noise.

Thump. Thump. Thump.

Shapiro's office shared a wall with the outfield at Hi Corbett Field and it sounded as though someone was throwing a ball against the cinder block. Shapiro, then an assistant in the baseball operations department, walked outside to check. Sure enough, there was 73-year-old Bob Feller chucking a baseball over and over.

Feller spent his entire 18-year career with the Indians. He hung around the club long after his playing days, wore a Cleveland cap into the Baseball Hall of Fame upon his induction in 1962, and has a permanent seat in the Progressive Field press box.

"I think he's one of the great players in the history of the game," Shapiro said, "and for him to play his career here and do what he did off the field, too, was pretty remarkable."

Feller amassed 266 wins, the most of any pitcher in franchise history. He won 20 or more games six times. He led the league in strikeouts on seven occasions and tallied a career-high 348 in 1946, the seventh-most in any season in the modern era. He led the league in innings pitched five times. He made eight All-Star teams, logged 279 complete games, and tossed three no-hitters (including the only one ever on Opening Day) and 12 one-hitters. He fanned 15 in his first career start as a 17-year-old and 2,581 in all. Feller blew away batters with his blazing fastball, an asset that earned him national recognition and buzz, including magazine covers, radio coverage, and a competition in which he threw the pitch while a motorcycle whizzed by at full speed. He finished in the top five in balloting for Most Valuable Player four times.

"I go over all of his records and think, 'Holy, moly,'" said Feller's oldest son, Steve. "I just think, 'How did he do that?'"

Yet perhaps what Feller is most respected for is his military service and his unabashed willingness to serve his country. Feller enlisted in the Navy in 1941; he was crossing a bridge into Illinois, where he was headed to negotiate his contract for the upcoming season, when he heard a report on the radio about the Pearl Harbor bombing. The next day, Feller placed his budding baseball career on hold and joined the Navy. He was sworn in at a recruiting office in Chicago.

"I don't know how many guys today, including myself, would ever do that," Steve said. "Geez, Louise."

Feller spent four years as an anti-aircraft gunner aboard the U.S.S. *Alabama*. He was the first major leaguer to enlist, a leader, a trendsetter, a trailblazer. He earned six campaign ribbons and eight battle stars, but he also refused commendation for his efforts.

He is known for his quote: "I'm no hero. Heroes don't come back. Survivors return home."

"Over time, having a lot of conversations with him," Shapiro said, "he was also a guy that the more you talk to him, the more you were impressed by what a strong man he was. He was an impressive person."

To honor Feller's service and selflessness and those who follow in his footsteps in their own way, the Indians created the Bob Feller Act of Valor Award in 2013. The distinction recognizes three individuals who reflect the values, integrity, and dedication to serving the country that Feller also possessed. The award is presented annually to one U.S. Navy Chief Petty Officer, one member of the Baseball Hall of Fame, and one active major leaguer.

"His service in the Navy meant more to him than all of his records," Steve said. "I heard him say that probably hundreds and hundreds of times. He was adamant about that. He really was."

Former Indians designated hitter Travis Hafner, who spoke to Feller on occasion during the Hall of Famer's annual spring training visits, spoke highly of Feller's choice to serve instead of pitch.

"He didn't do anything half-hearted," Hafner said. "He put everything he had into what he did and he had his beliefs that he believed in. He was a very strong man."

When clearing out the Bob Feller Museum in Feller's hometown of Van Meter, Iowa, Cleveland executive Bob DiBiasio discovered a Western Union telegraph sent to Feller from Jackie Robinson, who congratulated the hurler on being inducted into the Hall of Fame and expressed how honored he was to share that ceremony with him in 1962. Robinson and Feller, along with Bill McKechnie, elected by the Veterans' Committee, were the only inductees that year.

The Indians honored Feller in 1994 with a statue erected outside of the brand-new Jacobs Field. In his later years, he spent every game in the third row in the press box, in the section closest to the door and the seat closest to home plate. After his death in 2010, the Indians placed a memorial of sorts on the desk at that seat, which will never again be occupied.

"His whole life," DiBiasio said, "he probably was one of the greatest ambassadors of the game of baseball there ever was around the world and he did so as a Cleveland Indian."

When considering the lengthy history of the Cleveland franchise, which dates back to 1901, perhaps no name better represents the organization than Feller.

"Without question," DiBiasio said. "He was a man who committed his life to the city of Cleveland and to the one team. He performed at a Hall of Fame level. I don't see how you could say there's anyone else. He is the singular name. He is the true face of our franchise."

13 The Pinnacle of Heartbreak

The champagne was prepped to be popped. The Most Valuable Player trophy was etched and ready to be awarded. The walls of the visitor's clubhouse were draped with plastic to control the unshakeable tradition of spraying bubbly.

It all unfolded so quickly, so shockingly, so painfully for the Indians.

Every so often, Sandy Alomar Jr. receives a phone call. His friends will inform him when a replay of Game 7 of the 1997 World Series between the Indians and the Florida Marlins is on TV. He will not watch it.

"Let me know when it's on when the ending changes," he tells them.

After the Indians forced the decisive affair with a win in Game 6, radio announcer Tom Hamilton joined vice president of public relations Bob DiBiasio and his wife, Penny, in South Beach to celebrate. Hamilton said they were the only people in Miami who even knew the World Series was taking place.

"That's when you knew how different it was," Hamilton said. "You knew back in Cleveland the town was going wild."

The state of emotions would reverse course pretty quickly.

Anyone involved in the game can remember the date: October 26. They can remember how skipper Mike Hargrove—who was celebrating his 48th birthday—opted to start the kid, Jaret Wright, instead of the grizzled veteran workhorse, Charles Nagy. They can still envision the raucous crowd of 67,204 at Pro Player Stadium. Years later, Wright remembers everything about the entire series.

"What I ate, what I was thinking, the whole deal," he said.

Mark Shapiro, then the Indians' director of minor league operations, had moved out of his seat to the portal behind home plate, where he watched the events unfold with special assistant Bud Black. Shapiro said he felt constant jitters, even after Tony Fernandez supplied Cleveland with a 2–0 lead on a two-run single in the third inning. He felt unrelenting knots in his stomach as Bobby Bonilla sliced into the Indians' advantage with a solo home run on Wright's first offering of the seventh.

"It just exponentially increased to the point that you were just sick to your stomach," Shapiro said. "Especially with how it ended. It was just incredibly deflating to go through that range of emotions in such a short period of time."

The Indians carried a 2–1 edge into the ninth. League officials had initiated the proper postgame preparations. Indians players, coaches, and executives were on the top dugout step, ready to spill out onto the field and commence a celebration not experienced by a professional Cleveland franchise since 1964.

"The feeling that we had in Game 7 of the '97 World Series, sitting at the edge of the dugout, waiting for the explosion of the players to go out and celebrate on the field and just thinking what that would have meant to generations of Indians fans, we think about it all the time," DiBiasio said. "We got so damn close to bringing that to reality.

"You really have a sense of how difficult it really is to win."

Singles by Moises Alou and Charles Johnson gave the Marlins runners at the corners with one out against closer Jose Mesa. Craig Counsell followed with a sacrifice fly that lured right fielder Manny Ramirez toward the warning track. Florida had tied the game. Mesa had blown the save.

"You could feel the momentum start to shift a little bit," Hargrove said.

League bigwigs had to remove Chad Ogea's name from the MVP trophy. The Indians had to resist the temptation to permit the deflating feeling from swallowing them whole. There was still baseball to play. The game proceeded into extra innings.

"It's a scar that never goes away," Alomar said. "You play in two World Series and have a chance to win them, but Game 7—anything could have won that game. It does bother me."

In the bottom of the 11th, with Nagy on the hill, Bonilla opened the frame with a single. The right-hander retired Gregg Zaun, but Counsell hit a grounder that scooted under Fernandez's glove. The miscue by the typically sure-handed fielder placed runners on the corners with one out. Nagy intentionally walked Jim Eisenreich and got Devon White to tap into a force out at the plate. It all came together in the Marlins having the bases loaded with two outs. Edgar Renteria then lined a series-winning base hit that skimmed off the tip of Nagy's glove and shot into center field. Counsell scored and Cleveland suffered. Pitching coach Mark Wiley lived in the Miami area at the time and said he took a lot of grief from his neighbors.

"It was bad," Alomar said. "We're scarred for life. It still, to this day, bothers me. I was sad that we couldn't pull it out. I got over it when we had more games, but that was one of the biggest missions we had here, to win a World Series, and we didn't."

The Indians boasted a championship contender each year from 1994–2001. They never came closer to the ultimate triumph than they did in 1997. Hell, no team can come closer than that without actually capturing the crown.

"I told them to be proud of themselves," Hargrove said, "they're a good ball club, that they played a good series and they had a very good postseason and there's no reason for them to feel ashamed or sad or anything. Feel the loss, but don't feel bad about who they are and where they've come from and where they've gone. They should feel proud of themselves. I told them to keep their heads high because they were champions. They were winners."

14 Little Lake Nellie

Steve Olin always scribbled his No. 31 beneath the brim of his cap, with the one extending into an arrow that pointed toward home plate to remind him of his most elementary instruction.

Throw the ball straight.

Olin didn't throw hard—junk, mostly. Everything moved. Late break, dramatic sweep. Nothing stayed straight, so if he could just release it the way he wanted, batters would flail at the baseball as it spun their direction. And, well, that could be easier said than done, considering Olin's unorthodox motion. He would whip his body around, scrape the dirt with his right knee and fling the baseball from his hip to conceal it as long as possible to confuse the hitter.

The Indians selected Olin in the 16th round in 1987, a Portland State product with mid-80s velocity and a funky delivery. Scouts were skeptical he would amount to much, but he survived with pinpoint command and a knack for converting a hitter's eagerness into his downfall. His grandfather, who signed with the Dodgers just before joining the Navy ahead of World War II, implored him to aim every sinker no higher than the knees; the pitch would fade at the final instant, leaving hitters unable to lift the pitch, which explains how Olin allowed only 14 home runs in four major league seasons.

Olin's knees wobbled and knocked together during his big-league debut in July 1989. His first opponent: Jim Rice, an eventual Hall of Famer. Rice tapped a weak grounder back to the mound for a harmless groundout. Two weeks later, Olin's parents watched him from the stands for the first time in Oakland. He struck out Rickey Henderson and Jose Canseco on three pitches apiece.

By the summer of 1991, Cleveland manager Mike Hargrove handed over ninth-inning duties to Olin. In the spring of 1993, Olin was penciled in as the team's closer on the heels of a season in which he recorded a career-best 2.34 ERA with 29 saves, a performance that landed him a two-year contract.

The Indians, training in Winter Haven, Florida, after nearly a half-century in Tucson, Arizona—and only because Hurricane Andrew had wrecked the club's original spring complex in Homestead—opted not to make up a rainout against the Dodgers on March 22, 1993. Hargrove feared a player mutiny on the club's only scheduled off-day of the spring. For the rest of his tenure, Hargrove ensured the team never again had a blank space on the spring slate. Tim Crews, a new addition to Cleveland's bullpen, had wanted to throw a party at his ranch on Little Lake Nellie in Clermont, Florida, about 40 miles north of the team's facility. Crews, Olin and fellow pitcher Bobby Ojeda boarded Crews' 18-foot bass boat. To Olin, Crews and Ojeda were a step above strangers, but a baseball season has a way of bonding even the most transient players and gathering on Crews' Skeeter for a bass hunt was a first stride toward fraternization, a nightcap of fishing after a day of cooking out and riding horses.

In 1993, a long-pitiful team was ready for a renaissance. A submarining closer was ready for the prime of his career. Olin was ready for the prime of his life, with a wife and three young children, a new contract, a new house.

And in an instant, in the time it took for Crews' boat to slam into a dock, Olin was gone.

Olin and Crews didn't survive the crash. Ojeda suffered severe injuries. Crews' blood alcohol content was ultimately measured at .14, exceeding Florida's legal limit of .10. The tragedy rattled the organization to its core and spawned a slew of what-ifs. Team officials met at 4:30 AM to map out a plan. They held one press conference after another. Players arrived at the facility the following morning and, when they spotted an endless line of news trucks, they assumed the club had swung a seismic trade. Then they noticed everyone in the building crying and consoling each other.

Two weeks later, Cleveland hosted its final Opening Day at Municipal Stadium. The widows of Crews and Olin accepted their late husbands' jerseys during a somber pregame ceremony. Yankees players in the visitors' dugout, who had never met either reliever, shed tears.

Olin's children cling to their father's keepsakes, to his baseballs, framed jerseys, bomber jackets, Cleveland caps and cowboy hats. Olin's mother decorated his father's office with his memorabilia, a team pennant and his 1989 minor league Reliever of the Year award. Olin's only son, Garrett, caught the baseball bug. Garrett used his dad's old glove, with his dad's nickname, Oly, written on the side. Garrett played in high school in Oregon and, to start each high school outing, he would stand behind the mound, exhale and mutter to himself, "Here we go, Dad. Let's go." He printed a 31 on his left forearm and would glance at it whenever he needed a reset. When he turned 18, he adapted it into a tattoo of his dad's old number.

15 Planning Ahead

Commissioner Fay Vincent was sitting in a golf cart behind home plate at Municipal Stadium during batting practice when he issued a stern warning: If voters didn't pass a measure for a new ballpark on the May 1990 ballot, he could not guarantee the team would remain in Cleveland long term. The referendum would tax sales of alcohol and cigarettes in Cuyahoga County, with the money financing a new venue. Issue 2 passed...barely, 51.7 percent to 48.3 percent.

"I think if there were a club that people in baseball said needs to be moved in the late '80s and early '90s, it would have been the Indians," said former general manager John Hart. "Our owner made it very clear that wasn't going to happen. The politicians and the city made a decision to keep the club in Cleveland."

At that time, Cleveland's front office executives knew they would have a brand new, state-of-the-art ballpark on the forefront of downtown in less than five years. They also knew they needed to field a team worthy of such an edifice. They could strike gold if they built a club that blossomed just as the new venue opened.

They did just that.

"It played out even more perfect than the vision," said longtime Cleveland executive Dan O'Dowd.

The wheels started turning later in 1989. The Indians acquired 23-year-old Sandy Alomar Jr. and 21-year-old Carlos Baerga from the Padres for Joe Carter. The 29-year-old Carter had emerged as a force in the center of Cleveland's lineup, but by the time the Indians would be ready to contend, he would be past his prime. Two years later, the club acquired Kenny Lofton from Houston. Two years after that, Omar Vizquel relocated to Cleveland from Seattle.

When Gabe Paul ran the franchise in the '60s, he operated on the merits of showcasing star power to attract fans. He reacquired former fan favorite Rocky Colavito, who had been traded away years earlier. It didn't work. The team struggled.

This was a different approach, one installed by Hart and his predecessor, Hank Peters. The trades flooded the farm system with burgeoning talent. The club excelled in the amateur draft, as Albert Belle (1987, second round), Charles Nagy (1988, first round), Jim

Change in Ownership

Dick Jacobs and his brother, David, purchased the Indians in 1986. Steve O'Neill had owned the franchise until his death in 1983 and his estate owned the organization thereafter until the Jacobs got involved. Under Dick Jacobs' ownership—David died in 1992—the Indians enjoyed a resurgence following four decades of malaise.

In 2000, Larry Dolan bought the team for $323 million, more than eight times what Jacobs had paid for it 14 years earlier. Jacobs paid $6.3 million to keep the name of the ballpark as Jacobs Field for another six years. It was renamed Progressive Field in 2008.

Thome (1989, 13th round), Manny Ramirez (1991, first round), and Chad Ogea (1991, third round) all eventually paid dividends.

Of course, the Indians had no idea that their tactic would actually pan out. They had accumulated a cluster of young talent, but they needed the kids to develop in time.

"We really, really thought we were onto something," O'Dowd said.

In between tantrums, Belle arrived as a feared power hitter. He led the league with 129 RBIs in 1993. Nagy became an All-Star in his second full year in 1992. That same year, Lofton's first in Cleveland, the center fielder led the league in stolen bases and finished second in balloting for American League Rookie of the Year.

"We knew we had talent," said Mark Shapiro, who joined the front office as a baseball operations assistant in January 1992. "Seeing Albert Belle start to emerge, seeing what Jim Thome was capable of, Sandy Alomar, Charlie Nagy, Carlos Baerga—there were certain guys that already started to demonstrate it. Other guys were clearly getting close."

Shapiro was immediately hooked by Hart's strategy.

"I bought into it," Shapiro said. "John was a pretty persuasive guy with a strong vision and one he was passionate about. The vision that they painted and the plan that they talked about was, 'We have a core of young players, and we are going to be developing and peaking as a team coinciding with moving into a new ballpark, and that will allow us the revenues to be able to keep the team together.' It was that simple."

The next step of the plan included the team locking up some of its rising stars, such as Alomar and Baerga, to long-term, affordable contracts.

"We tied these guys up to multi-year deals, getting control of free-agent years and arbitration years and a lot of cost-certainty for long-term deals," Shapiro said. "We did that on a mass scale, with some guys who ended up being core players and some guys who didn't."

In 1993, the Indians amassed a 76–86 record for the second straight year. They were better, though. They improved their run differential by 50 runs. Their starting rotation was a train wreck, but their core pieces had developed as hoped. The team was clearly on the ascent and was prepared to move into its new building, so it complemented its talented youth with established veterans. On December 2, 1993, the Indians introduced Dennis Martinez and Eddie Murray as free-agent acquisitions at the new ballpark. There was a shift in perception about the club. Fans finally had a reason to back their team and opposing players had justification for respecting it.

"Probably in '93, the end of '93, going into '94, you could feel it," Hargrove said. "Our guys had enough big-league experience by that time. They had the belief that they could play with anybody."

By Opening Day on April 4, 1994, there was a palpable energy and buzz about the team, its new home, and its future. The blueprint sketched out five years earlier had worked. Now it was all about converting it into a period of sustainable success.

"It's rare that a plan that's articulated like that comes to be like that one did," Shapiro said. "There were probably things involved in that that weren't part of the plan, like the Browns not being here, which was part of it extending and being as successful as it was. It was just a magical time."

16 The Drumbeat of Cleveland

On April 7, 2023, on a chilly, overcast Friday afternoon, they filed into Progressive Field and marched directly to the top of the left-field bleachers. That's where John Adams would sit, on the end of the last green bench, beneath the scoreboard, in front of a wall with weathered white paint and blotches of rust. His 26-inch bass drum sat in the aisle, in front of a step with a yellow stripe that has been painted and re-painted and re-painted again. The guy with the drum was so profound, such a fabric of Cleveland baseball, so meaningful to so many strangers that fans made a beeline for his ballpark residence before they grabbed a hot dog and a beer and settled in their seats for the Guardians' home opener. He was so profound, the team wore a jersey patch with his initials, even though he never played or coached or swung a trade.

Adams died in January 2023 after a few years of battling a series of health maladies. The illnesses had prevented him from voyaging to the ballpark since the 2019 season, halting his remarkable run as a fixture at the top of that bleacher section. When he was a kid, Adams and his dad would board the Union Ave. bus to downtown Cleveland for 15 to 20 games per season. They would hop off at the corner of E. 4th Street and Prospect and journey toward the cavernous structure on the shores of Lake Erie. Adams loved to describe the moment Municipal Stadium came into view, saying his perspective morphed from black-and-white into vibrant colors, like when Dorothy arrived in the land of Oz.

Then, on August 24, 1973, Adams toted his drum to the ballpark. Sixteen East Tech High students filled the row in front of him that night. One of the kids turned around, sized up Adams and his drum and asked, "You're not going to hit that, are you?" Adams brought the drum for a more practical manner of noisemaking than the traditional clanging on the metal benches, which could make the customary crowd of a few thousand sound like a group five times the size. But he didn't want to disturb those around him, so he obliged when a man making a beer run encouraged him to relocate to the last row of Section 55. When Bob Sudyk of the Cleveland press wrote that Adams' drumming would become a nightly ritual, Adams felt impelled to return. So, he did. Again and again. And again and again and again. He missed an average of one game per season through the 2019 campaign, totaling nearly 4,000 contests. Adams regularly referred to the ballpark as a "magical land" and an "escape from reality," somewhere he could partner with the stranger beside him to "solve half of the world's problems." Adams often said he had connected with fans from every continent but Antarctica, and the only hurdle keeping him from completing his global mission was that penguins didn't purchase bleacher seats.

Adams' steady drumbeat was the soundtrack of every Cleveland baseball season for almost a half-century, year after year, through miserable slogs during brisk evenings on the lakefront and during magical October moments. As the opposing pitcher received his catcher's signs in the ninth inning of a close game, you could hear the beat in the background, an unassuming hum that built toward the moment the hurler came set. Then, a Cleveland hitter produced a key hit and the drumbeat evolved into a rapid rattle that reflected the energy of the erupting crowd.

Fans knew him. Players knew him. Opposing players noticed him. His drumbeat, via an audio recording, was the only shred of

John Adams' 26-inch bass drum served as the soundtrack to Cleveland baseball for nearly half a century.

normalcy during the pandemic-altered 2020 season. For the 40th anniversary of his first game with the drum, former second baseman Carlos Baerga tossed a ceremonial first pitch off the instrument.

In 2022, the Guardians inducted Adams into their Distinguished Hall of Fame and honored him with a bench in Heritage Park featuring a bronze sculpture of his drum. That drum, which went on display in the Baseball Hall of Fame in November 2023, delivered the heartbeat of Cleveland summers. There was nowhere Adams would rather spend a Friday night in June or a Sunday afternoon in September than his post in the left-field bleachers. He never intended to make his trek to the ballpark a daily habit, but as he reflected on his permanence at Progressive Field four decades into his residency, he asked, "Am I not the luckiest guy in the world?"

17 Perfection

The game-time temperature was a chilly 49 degrees. Nearly 7,300 fans trickled into Cleveland Municipal Stadium. (Tens of thousands more claim to have been in attendance.) On May 15, 1981, Len Barker tossed the 10th perfect game in major league history.

He remembers how much bite his curveball had that night. He started to throw the pitch with frequency after the third inning, even though he was more known for his heater. He remembers having pinpoint control. He could throw any pitch to any desired location, and he would record a strike. He threw only 19 of his 103 pitches out of the zone. He remembers walking out to the mound for the ninth inning, how he picked up the baseball off the dirt, stepped on the rubber, dropped the ball and nearly fell off the mound because he was so nervous. Every time he is asked about that brisk, damp Friday night, he stresses that the historic feat was a team and city-wide achievement, not just an individual accolade.

Barker was in control from the start. He induced three quick groundouts in the first inning. He did not reach a three-ball count on any of the 27 batters he faced.

Second baseman Duane Kuiper would signal to first baseman Mike Hargrove if Cleveland's pitcher was about to throw an off-speed pitch to a left-handed hitter so Hargrove could hug the line. Hargrove was so focused on Barker's every pitch that Kuiper couldn't get his attention to offer a heads-up when Barker was throwing yet another curveball.

"As those games go on," Kuiper said, "your concentration level gets so high that you can't hear anything, you don't notice anything. Everything is dead air."

The ninth inning arrived with the Indians ahead 3–0. A horde of reporters and cameramen gathered next to the dugout, ready to pounce.

"Those usually start to sink in after about the fourth or fifth inning," Kuiper said, "when you realize that nobody's reached. And then the crowd starts to let you know if you don't know. And then things get weird where you stay away from the pitcher, and he sits alone in the dugout."

Rick Bosetti led off the ninth for the Toronto Blue Jays and lifted a harmless pop fly into foul territory, short of third base. Toby Harrah squeezed it for the first out. Barker then fanned Al Woods on an off-speed pitch. Ernie Whitt, a pinch-hitter, was Toronto's last chance.

"I never like guys who are hitting under .200 in that situation, because you almost figure that guy's due," Kuiper said.

"Fly ball, center field," broadcaster Herb Score shouted as Whitt lofted Barker's offering to the outfield.

Center fielder Rick Manning spread his arms as wide as they could go to call off his fellow outfielders. He took a series of excited steps toward the spot where he would make the catch.

"Manning coming on. He's there."

In one, swift motion, Manning caught the ball, raised his arms above his head, jumped up and down and then sprinted in toward the mound.

"He catches it! Len Barker has pitched a no-hitter! A perfect game for Len Barker!"

Barker was immediately mobbed by catcher Ron Hassey and Hargrove. Pitchers and media members followed. Barker had thrown the second perfect game in franchise history and the first in 73 years.

"It was exciting," Barker said, "not only for me and my teammates, but for the whole city of Cleveland."

Manning presented to Barker the baseball from the final out, but the hurler gave it right back to the center fielder.

"He came running in," Barker said, "gave me a hug and he said: 'Here's the ball,' and I said, 'No. I'm giving it to you for all the things you've done.'

"It wasn't me just pitching a perfect game. It was the whole team and the whole city. That's the way I always treated it through my whole career. People would ask me, and I'd say, 'No. It was all of us.'

"I couldn't have done it without my teammates and the city. They were always behind us."

Said Kuiper, "It was a big deal when Lenny did this for a team that nobody thought was going anywhere. We weren't getting a lot of publicity. For at least a week, it put us on the map. It made everybody feel pretty doggone good."

18 O Captain, My Captain

A year after George Burns won the American League Most Valuable Player Award, Cleveland manager Jack McCallister named him the franchise's first official captain in 1927. Tris Speaker had unofficially served the role in his 11 seasons with the club. He moved on to the Washington Senators in 1927, and Burns took command of the team. Speaker was player/manager for his final eight seasons with the Indians. Lou Boudreau and Frank Robinson later filled similar roles. None of the three was technically captain, but that status might as well have been included in their job descriptions. The team was named after Nap Lajoie during his Cleveland tenure toward the start of the century, so captain would be far down on his résumé, too.

But as for a specific captain, it's been a rare position in franchise lore, and it has gone unoccupied since the late '80s. The

Forest Citys, a professional outfit in Cleveland from 1870–72, had captains. In the 1850s, the New York Knickerbockers tasked captains with assigning players to positions which, obviously, now falls under the manager's duties.

For a long time, though, the team captain provided a sort of shield for the manager. Ossie Vitt charged Hal Trosky with the role of captain in 1940 after the players, dubbed the "Cleveland Crybabies" after the episode, held a mutiny against the manager. But as Trosky told manager Roger Peckinpaugh the following year, after Vitt was forced out, according to an article from beat writer Gordon Cobbledick, "The captaincy brought him only grief and trouble while he held it." As captain, Trosky was tasked with relaying Vitt's instructions from the dugout, which left Trosky in the line of fire, as fans fueled their frustrations toward him instead of the manager. In 1941, he said, 'I don't want to have anything on my mind but playing ball," and he resigned from his post, forfeiting a $1,000 bonus.

The club didn't have another captain until Vic Wertz in 1958. Wertz earned a $500 bonus, which general manager Frank Lane joked was for a "sword and epaulettes." Manager Bobby Bragan referred to Wertz as a "liaison man" who would pass along messages to pitchers during an inning and walk the lineup card to home plate before first pitch, obligations now carried out by a pitching coach and a bench coach, respectively.

In 1977, manager Jeff Torborg asked infielders Duane Kuiper and Buddy Bell to serve as co-captains. The big change stemming from that appointment? The team decided to exercise as a group before each game.

In 1985, manager Pat Corrales named Andre Thornton captain during spring training. When Thornton asked who elected him to that position, the manager replied, "I had a meeting with myself in my room. No one else got any votes." Thornton was initially reluctant but agreed to take on the role. Corrales said he was "a guy who can relate to everybody, from the president of the club down to a Class A ballplayer."

Thornton's career ended in 1987, and the following season, manager Doc Edwards named Joe Carter and Mell Hall co-captains. Hall was traded in the spring of 1989, but Carter remained a Cleveland captain until he was traded that December for Chris James, Sandy Alomar Jr. and Carlos Baerga.

19 Hometown Hero

Sandy Alomar Jr.'s 1997 season was nothing short of magical. Had it been a Hollywood script, it would have been deemed too cheesy and unrealistic to excel at the box office.

The veteran catcher socked a home run in five consecutive games during the season's first week. After the Indians' first seven games—he played in six of them—he was batting .538 with five home runs, 13 RBIs, and a 1.231 slugging percentage. He had multi-hit games in seven of his first eight contests and 21 hits overall. On April 13, he was batting .618. That was just a precursor of how the rest of his campaign would unfold.

Alomar had come back to Earth once the weather warmed up. He entered a game against the Orioles on May 25 with a .331 average. He went 1-for-4 in that affair. He followed that up with two hits the next day in Chicago and one base knock the day after that. This became a pattern. Alomar strung together a 30-game hitting streak before he finally went hitless in an 0-for-4 effort in Minnesota on July 10, the Indians' first game following the All-Star break.

In Cleveland's 8–2 loss to Minnesota at the Metrodome, Alomar struck out in the second and fourth innings, grounded out in the seventh, and popped out for the final out in the ninth. He fell one game short of the franchise-record hitting streak of 31 games, logged by Nap Lajoie in 1906. He fell four games short of Benito Santiago's record mark for a catcher, established in 1987, Santiago's rookie campaign.

It wasn't as though Alomar cooled off during the All-Star break. He tallied a crucial hit in the Midsummer Classic, too. In the eighth inning of the annual duel between the American and National leagues, Alomar slugged a 2–2 off-speed pitch from San Francisco's Shawn Estes into the left-field bleachers for a go-ahead two-run home run. The long ball broke a 1–1 tie with two outs in the seventh inning.

Joe Buck's call to a national TV audience declared Alomar a "hometown hero," as the catcher sent those in attendance into a frenzy. The American League held on for a 3–1 victory. Alomar became the first player to club a home run in the All-Star Game in his home ballpark since Braves slugger Hank Aaron teed off at Atlanta Stadium in 1972.

Alomar dedicated the game to his grandmother, who had passed away four days earlier. He earned the Most Valuable Player award, which he lifted high in one hand while he held his son, Marcus, in the other. Alomar attributed his performance—both during the game and overall that season—to his good health. Injuries limited Alomar to fewer than 90 games in each season from 1991–95.

Alomar finished the regular season with a .324 batting average, .545 slugging percentage, 21 home runs, 83 RBIs, and 37 doubles, all career-best marks. He racked up 15 hits that gave the Indians the lead in a game. He batted .321 with runners in scoring position and .309 with runners in scoring position and two outs. He hit .397 with a 1.043 OPS when the game was considered "late and close" and .371 with a 1.024 OPS during "high leverage" situations.

No at-bat came with more on the line than his trip to the plate in the eighth inning of Game 4 of the American League Division Series against the New York Yankees. Four outs from elimination, the Indians trailed 2–1 in the game and 2–1 in the series. With two outs and no runners on in the eighth, Alomar sent a 2-0 pitch from 27-year-old, first-time All-Star reliever Mariano Rivera into the first row of seats in right field. The game-tying home run saved the Indians' season. Alomar shouted, wound up his right arm and pumped his fist as the ball landed out of the reach of Yankees right fielder Paul O'Neill. After the game, car horns were blaring in downtown Cleveland for hours. Fans didn't want to leave the ballpark, even though there was another game the next day.

"I cherish that postseason," Alomar said, "and hitting the home run against Mariano was huge because it gave us a chance to go to the next game, in which we ended up beating the Yankees. That, to me, is what baseball is all about. It's about winning games and championships. That was the most important home run in my career."

Omar Vizquel delivered an RBI single in the ninth to force a decisive Game 5. Once Brian Giles squeezed the baseball in his glove on Bernie Williams' fly out to left field, Cleveland claimed that contest 4–3 to advance to the American League Championship Series against the Baltimore Orioles. Alomar's home run the previous night, though, is remembered for rescuing an eventual World Series team from an early postseason dismissal.

How many players can boast about a clutch home run in both the Midsummer Classic and the postseason? Alomar understandably covets the October long ball a bit more.

"That was more fun, when we were playing the Yankees in the postseason and had the chance to beat them," Alomar said. "Hitting home runs in the postseason [is] more challenging and important than a home run in the All-Star Game."

What a debate to even consider. That's a microcosm of Alomar's miraculous 1997 season.

"For the first time, I felt completely healthy," Alomar said. "I had so many problems with the microfracture [surgery] that I had, that I had to make a lot of adjustments in my mechanics and stuff like that. That year, I felt like I put it together. I felt pretty good. It was a fun year. But more importantly, I was able to help the team and we were able to go to the World Series. That was the most fun year I had."

20 Check Out Heritage Park

Beyond the center-field fence at Progressive Field, tucked behind the trees and shrubs that give the concourse a green thumb, in a space previously occupied by picnic tables, resides a shrine of Cleveland baseball lore.

It's hallowed ground, filled with beacons of history. It's a refreshing spot to visit before or during a game, a place to learn, to reminisce, to appreciate. It's dubbed Heritage Park and it was unveiled on Opening Day in 2007 as a means to preserve team history, "to honor excellence," and "to connect generations," as detailed on a plaque at the center's entrance.

Walk down a short set of steps to the area's rotunda, where all members of the franchise's Hall of Fame have a plaque with a depiction of them. There is Sandy Alomar Jr. in full catcher's gear, with his mask resting on the top of his head. There is Rocky Colavito, holding his bat high above his head with both arms. There is Bob Feller, rocking back into his patented windup, with his left leg stretched out into the air. There is Mike Hargrove,

Top Achievements

There are 37 large, dark bricks in Heritage Park that commemorate some of the franchise's most prolific individual achievements. Here is a complete list.

- Gaylord Perry won the American League Cy Young award in 1972
- Sam McDowell tossed back-to-back one-hit shutouts in 1966
- Albert Belle became the first player in franchise history to hit 50 home runs in a season in 1995
- Chris James set a club record with nine RBIs in a game on May 4, 1991 (and Lonnie Chisenhall tied it in June 2014)
- Dick Bosman threw a no-hitter against the defending champion Oakland Athletics on July 19, 1974
- Rocky Colavito slugged four home runs in one game on June 10, 1959
- Herb Score was named American League Rookie of the Year in 1955
- Len Barker threw a perfect game on May 15, 1981
- Al Rosen clubbed two home runs during the 1954 All-Star Game
- Jolbert Cabrera slapped the game-winning single in the Indians' 15–14 win against the Mariners on August 15, 2001
- Sandy Alomar Jr. was named the 1997 All-Star Game Most Valuable Player
- The Indians hit four consecutive home runs during a win against the Los Angeles Angels on July 31, 1963
- Marquis Grissom stole home for the winning run in Game 3 of the 1997 American League Championship Series against the Baltimore Orioles
- The Indians sold out 455 straight games from 1995–2001
- Tony Fernandez socked the game-winning home run in Game 6 of the 1997 American League Championship Series
- Dennis Eckersley strung together $22\frac{1}{3}$ consecutive scoreless innings in 1977
- CC Sabathia hurled his first big league shutout on August 15, 2003
- Travis Hafner hit six grand slams in 2006
- Kevin Kouzmanoff slugged a grand slam on the first pitch he saw in his major league career on September 2, 2006
- Bob Feller won the pitching triple crown in 1940
- Frank Robinson became baseball's first African American manager in 1975

- Earl Averill hit a home run in his first major league at-bat in 1929
- Johnny Burnett set a big-league record with nine hits in a game on July 10, 1932
- The Indians registered their first win in the American League on April 27, 1901
- Bob Feller recorded 17 strikeouts in a game as a rookie on September 13, 1936
- Lou Boudreau went 4-for-4 in a one-game playoff against the Boston Red Sox in 1948 to determine the American League World Series representative
- Larry Doby broke the American League color barrier with the Indians in 1947
- Bob Feller threw the sport's only Opening Day no-hitter in 1940
- Luis Tiant tossed four straight shutouts in 1968
- Addie Joss threw the franchise's first perfect game in 1908
- The Indians recorded the first postseason unassisted triple play and grand slam in Game 5 of the 1920 World Series
- Kenny Lofton won the American League stolen base crown for five consecutive years from 1992-96
- Stan Coveleski earned three victories during the 1920 World Series
- Carlos Baerga homered from both sides of the plate in the same inning on April 8, 1993
- Omar Vizquel collected six hits in a 22-0 win against the Yankees on August 21, 2004
- Tony Peña hit a walk-off homer in the club's first playoff game in 41 years on October 3, 1995
- Jim Thome set a new franchise record with 52 home runs in 2002

the "Human Rain Delay," doing what he did best—stepping out of the batter's box with one foot and regrouping in a means of stalling for time. There is Kenny Lofton, his eyes glued to the pitcher, with his hands gripping a bat as he prepares to lay down a bunt. There is Omar Vizquel, his left knee gracing the infield dirt, making a backhanded stop from his shortstop position. There are Larry Doby and Carlos Baerga, clutching their bats with their right hands after following through on a swing.

The ground is made up of bricks that bear names of—and messages from—fans. Each section of bricks is topped with a dark gray square dedicated to a specific achievement. There's a square commemorating Frank Robinson for becoming the first African American manager in major league history. There's a square honoring Addie Joss for throwing the franchise's first perfect game. There's a square noting Lofton's five consecutive American League stolen base titles.

Take another set of steps down to a vast, open area, where on a giant brick wall rest squares with the names and signatures of the top 100 all-time players in franchise history and the 100th anniversary starting lineup, chosen by fans in 2001. Fans can read about Cleveland's Negro League history (the Cleveland Buckeyes played in the league from 1943–1948 and again briefly in 1950) or about the harrowing tale of Ray Chapman, who is honored with a large plaque and a script about his story. There is a plaque to honor Doby and two smaller displays with information about Steve Olin and Tim Crews, a pair of relievers who died in a boating accident during spring training in 1993. An oversized bronze baseball that bears the club's "Distinguished Hall of Fame" for non-uniformed personnel is also on display. That includes past owners Bill Veeck and Dick Jacobs; broadcasters Mike Hegan, Jimmy Dudley, and Jack Graney; front office executives John Hart, Hank Peters, Dennis Lehman and Cy Slapnicka; athletic trainer Jimmy Warfield; traveling secretary Mike Seghi; longtime drummer John Adams; clubhouse manager Cy Buynak; and adviser Johnny Goryl.

Heritage Park serves as a mecca of Cleveland baseball history, a destination spot for anyone fascinated by the greatest feats and figures in the franchise's existence.

21 A Bug's Life

Squirrels, seagulls, and chickens have played a hand in happenings at Progressive Field. No creature, however, can compare to the impact provided by swarms of midges in October 2007.

Just ask Joba Chamberlain.

In Game 2 of the 2007 American League Division Series between the Indians and Yankees, pesky bugs pushed Cleveland to victory and a 2–0 series lead. The infestation of little flies didn't seem to fluster Fausto Carmona, who tossed nine dazzling innings for the Indians. The right-hander limited New York to one run on three hits. Unfortunately for the Indians, Andy Pettitte matched him.

The Yankees carried a 1–0 lead into the eighth inning. Then, the midges stole the show. Chamberlain, clearly bothered by their presence, walked Grady Sizemore to start the eighth. He heaved a wild pitch, sending Sizemore to second. Asdrubal Cabrera bunted Sizemore to third. Travis Hafner lined out, but with Victor Martinez at the plate, Chamberlain tossed another wild pitch. Sizemore raced home from third to tie the game.

"You can't prepare for it," Chamberlain said. "So you don't know how you're going to react."

During the inning, Yankees staff attended to Chamberlain on the mound, as they sprayed down his uniform with insect repellant. Home-plate umpire Laz Diaz doused his body in the spray as well. He then passed the green can to Yankees shortstop Derek Jeter, who applied the stuff to his gray uniform. The rest of New York's infield joined in, as Alex Rodriguez and Robinson Cano covered their jerseys with the sticky substance. There's just one problem. Unlike mosquitoes, midges don't bite, and they're actually not

What's My Age Again?

During the winter of 2012, the Indians learned that the 28-year-old Fausto Carmona was actually a 31-year-old hurler named Roberto Hernandez. The right-hander was arrested in his native Dominican Republic on charges of using a false name. He received a three-week suspension from Major League Baseball, restructured his contract with the Indians, and was required to perform community service.

Hernandez expressed remorse over his transgressions—he had assumed the identity of a distant cousin in order to convince the Indians he was 17 when they signed him in 2000. He did not, however, delve into the details of his ordeal.

His teammates didn't bother asking the tough questions. (Justin Masterson asked Hernandez if he could call him "Bob." Hernandez approved.) They took it easy on the pitcher. For the most part, at least.

Once Hernandez was granted a new visa and arrived at the Indians' clubhouse on July 22, 2012, his teammates presented him with three birthday cakes to cover the difference in his actual age. On a table sat one round cake with candles shaped in the numerals 2 and 9, as well as two rectangular-shaped cakes with plastic balloons and red, yellow, and green frosting.

attracted to humans—just other midges—so bug spray doesn't offer much of a solution.

The bugs latched onto Chamberlain's face and neck. They crawled into his mouth and under his shirt. In fact, he said, "there was not a place or an orifice where they weren't." The infielders spent the inning swatting them away, wiping them off, and trying to gain a line of sight toward the plate.

"I've never seen anything like that before," Jeter recalled seven years later, upon his final visit to Progressive Field as a player. "It was like that for both teams. It wasn't like they just came out when we decided to go on defense. Those were by far the oddest conditions I've played in. I didn't enjoy it. It wasn't fun. They were all over the place. You really couldn't shake them. That's what made it difficult."

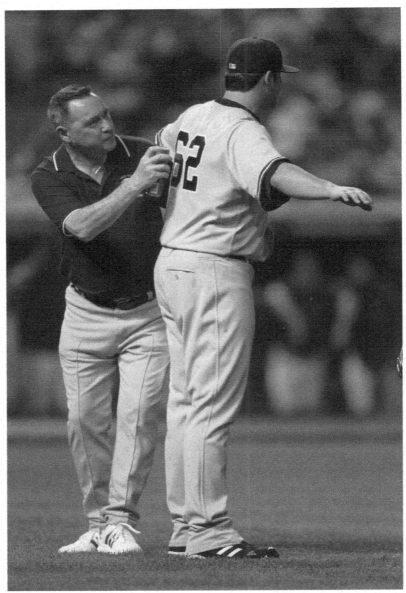

A member of the Yankees staff sprays pitcher Joba Chamberlain with insect repellant late in Game 2 of the 2007 ALDS against the Indians. The bugs caused Chamberlain to give up the Yankees' lead in the eighth inning and seemingly helped the Indians, who weren't nearly as bothered by them, win the game.

There have been other odd conditions. The Indians defeated the Kansas City Royals 4–3 in 10 innings on June 11, 2009, when Shin-Soo Choo singled home the winning run. Choo chopped the base hit up the middle. A flock of seagulls had gathered in center field. When the baseball came bouncing in their direction, they scattered, shielding center fielder Coco Crisp's view. The ball deflected off the wing of one of the birds and rolled past Crisp as he attempted to corral it and fire a throw toward home plate. Instead, Mark DeRosa scored, and the Indians won.

Maybe it's just a dose of home-field advantage. The midges didn't appear to torment Cleveland's players the way they did the Yankees. Or was it simply a showcase of the club's toughness?

"I will never make an excuse," Chamberlain said. "I didn't execute pitches and we ended up losing the game and that's on me."

"Both teams had the bugs," said Mark Shapiro, then the club's general manager. "It bothered one team. It didn't bother the other team. It wasn't like the bugs were only there for the Yankees. They were there for our guys, too.

"Fausto Carmona sat there and was so focused. There were bugs crawling all over his face and he didn't even notice it, whereas Joba Chamberlain was spraying himself and swatting himself. There was Fausto, just locked in.

"I felt like that was a triumph of our toughness and our resilience. That's what stood out to me with that group of guys."

The game lasted until the 11th inning, when Hafner supplied a walk-off single with the bases loaded and two outs. Cleveland captured the series in four games and advanced to the American League Championship Series against the Red Sox.

Just how bedeviling were the bugs?

"I'm sure they'll be back," Jeter surmised. "Next time they're out, just stand outside for a little while. You'll be able to answer that."

22 Tito's Bloop Troop

Austin Hedges approached Steven Kwan and Will Benson in the hallway outside the visitors' clubhouse at Globe Life Field.

"You're all underage," the veteran catcher quipped. "No more alcohol."

"Underage?" Kwan asked. "I'm 25."

It just *seemed* like the Guardians' 2022 roster was full of kids. But a roster that celebrated the big-league debuts of 17 different rookies throughout the season cruised to a division title and covered that Texas clubhouse in beer and champagne in late September. Who would have imagined such a scene in March or April or even early August?

The first day of spring training, Terry Francona met with José Ramírez and Amed Rosario. If the Guardians were to function properly on offense, those two needed to set the tone with their hustle and their aggressiveness on the bases. They needed the cast of young players to follow their lead.

But first, Ramírez needed to sign a contract extension. The club was leaving Arizona after weeks of negotiations during spring training led nowhere. Ramírez expressed how he wanted to remain in Cleveland for the rest of his career, even if it meant sacrificing future earnings. He and the team hammered out the parameters of an extension on the final day of spring, briefly delaying the team flight out of Phoenix. Had Ramírez not urged the two sides to unite at the last minute, he likely would have been a Padre or a Blue Jay…and the magical 2022 season never would have materialized.

The Guardians employed the youngest roster in the league, and the roster underwent quite the face lift as the season unfolded.

Kwan blossomed as the club's everyday left fielder, leadoff hitter and Gold Glove recipient. Oscar Gonzalez emerged as a late-season hero who walked into the batter's box to the SpongeBob SquarePants theme. Andrés Giménez broke onto the scene with an All-Star campaign. Shane Bieber, Triston McKenzie and Cal Quantrill formed a reliable trio atop the rotation. The bullpen was the best in the league after the All-Star break, which explains how they went 13–6 in extra innings and 28–17 in one-run games. And they employed that style of play Francona presented to Ramírez and Rosario in spring training. Tito's Bloop Troop slapped the ball around the field, making far more contact than any other team in the league. They piled up more infield hits than anyone else. They stole a ton of bases. They dashed from first to third at every opportunity, placing unrelenting pressure on opposing pitchers and defenses.

That was enough for the Guardians to hang around throughout the summer, and in September, they caught fire. They went 21–4 to close out the regular season. After White Sox infielder Elvis Andrus, the antithesis to Miss Cleo, predicted the Guardians would "crumble" down the stretch, they instead steamrolled past their AL Central competition to cruise to a division title. In a span of nine days, they increased their division lead by seven games, blooping the ball across the diamond and running from first to third, running from second to home and running away from the rest of the pack in the AL Central.

"What's wrong with being young?" Bieber said.

They first partied in Texas, a division crown in hand, as Hedges covered the plastic sheets protecting each locker with champagne, Francona buzzed the hair of replay coordinator Mike Barnett (which had become a ritual to jump-start the club) and team president Chris Antonetti embraced Ramírez to thank him for spearheading such a run with his decision to sign the extension. Otherwise, Antonetti wasn't sure he could imagine the scene unfolding in the clubhouse.

"In what fairy tale?" he said. "The fact he committed and wanted to be here for the long term gave us a great foundation to build upon."

The Guardians advanced to the first round of the playoffs against the Rays, and on Gonzalez's 15th-inning blast to the bleachers off former Cleveland hurler Corey Kluber, they proceeded to the ALDS against the Yankees. The Guardians split the first two games in the Bronx and then Gonzalez capped a ninth-inning comeback with a walk-off hit in Game 3 to inch Cleveland to within one step of MLB's final four. The Yankees, however, turned to Gerrit Cole and, thanks to a rainout, Nestor Cortes to shut down Cleveland's offense in Games 4 and 5 and take the series.

No one foresaw such a run for the Guardians. Even those in the front office admitted they were hopeful the team could compete in 2022 but deemed it unfair to expect anything like what transpired. The surprising rise earned Francona, who guided a classroom full of kids through a demanding schedule that included 11 doubleheaders, his third AL Manager of the Year award since joining the franchise in 2013. A team that started the year praying it could retain its All-Star third baseman, a team that opened the year with Bobby Bradley, Yu Chang and Franmil Reyes in its starting lineup, a team littered with rookies, a team projected by *USA Today* to finish 74–88 and in the basement of the AL Central somehow played into the third week of October.

23 Ring the Belle

The man with the muscle, the stout frame, and the surly scowl had plenty of nicknames. Some, he embraced. Others, no one said to his face.

Albert Belle, ever the explosive personality, has cultivated a tumultuous relationship with the Indians organization ever since he first donned a Cleveland uniform in 1989. He was Joey. He was Albert. He was Mr. Freeze. He was Snapper. And through it all—through the corked bats, the bulging biceps, the spats with reporters, the run-ins and chase-downs with trick-or-treaters, the fits of rage in the clubhouse—he remained the same driven individual who simply wanted to be the best. He also wanted to be paid like the best.

"They put a thoroughbred in the gates to run the Kentucky Derby and they have the blinders on [him]," said Bob DiBiasio, Guardians senior vice president of public affairs. "When he put his tunnel vision on, his blinders, to get ready to compete at a high level and you tried to penetrate those blinders on Albert, he bit your head off. You had to learn when you could connect with him."

Nearly two decades after Belle played his final game for the Indians, DiBiasio gave the former slugger a call. The two had maintained contact off and on since he departed the organization that drafted him in the second round out of LSU in 1987. DiBiasio asked Belle if he would grant his approval on the team creating a bobblehead in his likeness.

"It's about time!" Belle responded.

Before DiBiasio could utter another word, Belle requested that the ceramic model pose in the stance the once-chiseled outfielder made infamous. In Game 1 of the 1995 American League Division Series, after Belle's 11th-inning home run off of Red Sox reliever Rick Aguilera, Boston skipper Kevin Kennedy asked umpires to check the outfielder's bat for a cork filling. Though untimely, it wasn't the most far-fetched request. Belle had been caught red-handed a year earlier and slapped with a suspension. This time, though, it was all in the muscle. Belle stood on the edge of the dugout, demanded attention from the Red Sox bench and pointed to his flexed right biceps, which was bulging out from under his uniform sleeve, a patch of white cotton that appeared to be hanging on for dear life.

"Bobbleheads are no good unless they tell a real story," DiBiasio said.

Belle's story has many layers, many unforgettable incidents, and many learning experiences.

While at Triple A Colorado Springs in 1990, he destroyed a clubhouse sink during a fit of rage, which earned him a five-game suspension. Later that summer, he checked into counseling to cope with his alcohol dependency. After two months of help at the Cleveland Clinic, Belle issued a statement that declared he had received the necessary help and that he was now to be referred to by his first name, Albert. He had previously gone by the nickname Joey, short for Jojuan, his middle name.

No matter the moniker, the fiery personality remained the same. He was kicked out of the Puerto Rican winter league in 1990 for his typical temper tantrums. In May 1991, he drilled a heckling fan in the chest with a baseball. That merited him a six-game ban. A year later, he charged the mound after Kansas City hurler Neal Heaton heaved a pair of pitches that he deemed too close for comfort. Both players were ejected, as the benches cleared and players spilled out onto the field. Belle received a three-game suspension. In May 1993, Belle brawled with Royals pitcher Hipolito Pichardo after the right-hander plunked him in the shoulder. As a result, he was hit with another three-game ban.

In July 1994, White Sox manager Gene Lamont accused Belle of employing a corked bat. The lumber was confiscated and stored in the umpires' locker room to be examined. After the game, the umpires discovered the bat had been switched, so the Indians were required to hand over another one, which contained cork. Belle contended that the White Sox swiped his bat and corked it. Nonetheless, he was dealt a seven-game suspension.

Reporters learned to stay out of Belle's way. He was known to gripe or yell if a member of the media looked at him in a certain manner or even said hello to him. Prior to Game 3 of the 1995 World Series, he shouted obscenities at reporters in the Indians dugout as they prepared to conduct interviews. Belle was later fined $50,000 for his actions.

His temper warranted him the nickname "Snapper" from some of his teammates. He could erupt, without warning, at any moment. He earned the nickname "Mr. Freeze" after he grumbled about the temperature in the clubhouse, turned down the thermostat and then shattered it with a bat. He once executed the same treatment on Kenny Lofton's boom box.

On Halloween in 1995, a group of teenagers tossed eggs at his house after he refused to supply them with candy. So, Belle chased after them in his SUV. He was convicted of reckless operation of a motor vehicle and fined for the incident. In 1996, Belle struck a photographer with a baseball, and he knocked Milwaukee Brewers second baseman Fernando Vina to the ground with a sturdy forearm because Vina was standing in his path in the baseline as he tried to turn a double play. Belle served a two-game suspension for his bullying.

Once, after he made an out, Belle retreated to the dugout tunnel and launched a bat into a wall. A new teammate shouted, "What the hell was that?" But Belle's action barely registered with the rest of the players and coaches. "Ah, it's just Albert," said catcher Sandy Alomar Jr. "Don't worry about him."

For years, the team put up with his antics because of what he provided on the field. He recorded the first 50/50 season in major league history when he tallied 50 home runs and 52 doubles in only 143 games in 1995. He was named to four consecutive All-Star teams while with Cleveland. He led the American League in RBIs on three occasions. He finished in the top three in the balloting for the Most Valuable Player award each season from 1994–96. During those years, he logged a .325 batting average, .414 on-base percentage, and .671 slugging percentage, averaging 42 doubles, 45 home runs, and 125 RBIs. All six of the walk-off home runs he swatted in his career came during that stretch. Two of them were grand slams.

"Nobody could outwork Albert with hitting," Alomar said.

"He was the ultimate competitor," said manager Mike Hargrove. "He wanted to win. He wanted to be the best."

Belle's peak production coincided with the team's ascent from a bottom-feeder to a perennial World Series contender. The team reached the Fall Classic in 1995 and qualified for the postseason in '96. And yet, it wasn't enough. The ego was always there, though not in a self-absorbed, pompous fashion. Belle simply presented an unfiltered, steadfast belief in his ability. He was set in his ways, unwavering in his conviction that his on-field exploits deserved proper compensation and acknowledgement. He strived to be the highest-paid player in the league, an aim that triggered the deterioration of his relationship with the Indians organization. He hit the free-agent market and the White Sox—Cleveland's AL Central adversary and the team that uncorked the secret behind his booming bats—scooped him up with a five-year, $55 million pact.

Fans were upset by how the situation unfolded, how a player who served as part of a blossoming team could abandon everything. That Belle acted in such a manner, however, surprised no one. Perhaps the vanquishing of his baggage and his inevitable tirades and tantrums and riots would cleanse the clubhouse. The team certainly had the lineup pieces to cope with his departure, especially since general manager John Hart swung a trade for powerful third baseman Matt Williams.

Belle proceeded to bat .274 with 30 home runs in his first season on the South Side. When he made his first appearance at Jacobs Field as the enemy on June 3, 1997, fans showered him with Monopoly money in left field. He resumed his offensive onslaught in 1998, when he compiled a .328 batting average, .399 on-base percentage, and .655 slugging percentage, with 49 home runs, 152 RBIs, and 48 doubles.

After the '98 campaign, he invoked a clause in his contract that required he remain one of the three highest-paid players in the league. Chicago refused to meet his contract demands, so he became a free agent and signed a five-year, $65 million deal with the Baltimore Orioles. Belle hit 60 home runs over two years for the O's before a degenerative hip condition forced him into retirement.

"Every time he stepped to the plate," said pitcher Charles Nagy, "magic was going to happen."

24 The Catch (and the Sweep)

Between 1921–64, the New York Yankees captured the American League pennant 29 times. They won 20 of the 29 World Series in which they appeared during that span. Their most prolific stretch came in the middle of the century. The Yankees emerged victorious in seven games over the Brooklyn Dodgers in the 1947 Fall Classic. In 1948, the Indians edged the Yankees by two-and-a-half games in the standings. They tied the Red Sox and won the subsequent one-game playoff for the pennant to advance to the World Series, which they won.

After that, however, the Yankees rattled off five consecutive titles. They seemed poised for a sixth straight, as they amassed 103 victories during the regular season, more than they tallied in any of the previous five years. Cleveland, however, totaled 111, which earned the club the right to square off—as a heavy favorite—against the New York Giants in the World Series.

"The Yankees had taken over baseball," said Bob DiBiasio, Guardians senior vice president of public affairs. "People don't realize, the Yankees won every year except for '54."

That would hold true even after the '54 campaign. The Yankees reached the World Series in each of the following four seasons and nine of the ensuing 10, led by stars in Mickey Mantle, Yogi Berra, and Whitey Ford. They fell short in '54, though, and the Indians instead sought their second championship in a seven-year span.

Willie Mays had other ideas.

Vic Wertz had his way with Giants starter Sal Maglie in Game 1. Cleveland's first baseman socked a two-run triple in the first inning and singles in the fourth and sixth. So when Maglie issued Larry Doby a free pass and served up a single to Al Rosen to begin the eighth, Giants skipper Leo Durocher opted for southpaw reliever Don Liddle to face the left-handed-hitting Wertz with the score tied 2–2.

Wertz delivered again, as he punished a ball to deep center, a spacious abyss at Polo Grounds. Mays had been playing a relatively shallow center field, so he had miles and miles of ground to cover as he chased after the soaring baseball. As gravity dragged the baseball toward the earth, Mays, his back turned to home plate, used his glove like a basket and hauled it in. His cap flew off as he twisted his body and fired a throw back toward the infield while he fell to the ground. Doby had to race back to second base, tag up and advance to third. The Indians failed to take the lead in the inning.

The Hebrew Hammer

For about five years, Al Rosen was one of the most feared sluggers in the game. The Indians third baseman submitted one of the finest offensive single-season showings in franchise history in 1953. That year, one in which he took home the American League Most Valuable Player trophy, Rosen batted .336 with 43 home runs, 145 RBIs, and 115 runs scored. He came within one hit of winning the Triple Crown, as he lost the batting title by .001 to Washington's Mickey Vernon.

The next year, when the Indians captured the American League pennant, he hit .300 with 24 home runs. Rosen clubbed 156 round-trippers from 1950 to 1954. Nagging injuries ultimately limited his career to 10 seasons (seven full ones at the big-league level), but he was a four-time All-Star and twice led the American League in home runs and RBIs. Rosen was inducted into the Indians Hall of Fame in 2006. The team hasn't had an MVP winner since.

The Giants proceeded to win 5–2 in 10 innings on a pinch-hit, three-run home run by Dusty Rhodes.

As Mays modestly said years later, "Everybody said, 'Well, it was a hard catch.' I said, 'It was an easy catch.'"

Mays did admit that he may have prevented a run from scoring. Given how far Wertz's shot took Mays, Doby might have been able to tag up and score from second had Mays not swiftly returned the ball to the infield. Mays said he could not see where he was throwing, but his frenzied heave was right on target to the cutoff man.

"The key there is catching the ball," Mays said, "and I think that hurt Cleveland very dearly. If I miss that ball, it might have been an inside-the-park home run. They could have scored easily. That was a big catch as far as the World Series was concerned."

Cleveland's bats remained dormant for the rest of the series, as the Indians scored only nine runs in the four games. A change in venue did not help. The Giants finished off the sweep at Cleveland

Municipal Stadium. The Indians prevented the Yankees from winning another title, but they fell short in adding to their own collection.

25 The Clock Strikes 2:00 AM

Bob Costas and Bob Uecker had engaged in meaningless drivel. Only caffeine and a lack of a finite outcome were keeping them going.

"It was a long, cold, wet game," said manager Mike Hargrove.

Shortly after 2:00 AM on October 4, 1995, Cleveland had captured its first postseason victory in 47 years. Perhaps the most unlikely hero sent a full house of fading fans home happy.

The Indians were no strangers to dramatic victories at Jacobs Field in 1995. Among their 100 wins, 27 came in their final at-bat, including nine in the form of a home run. Albert Belle slugged three, Manny Ramirez clubbed two, and Sandy Alomar Jr., Jim Thome, Paul Sorrento and Eddie Murray each delivered one. Tony Peña wasn't an offensive threat. He batted .262 with five home runs and 28 RBIs in 91 games in 1995. His role was to form a rapport with the pitching staff; hitting was secondary.

A 39-minute rain delay pushed back the game's first pitch. A 23-minute rain delay interrupted the eighth inning, with the score tied 3–3. Boston's Tim Naehring provided the Red Sox with a one-run advantage in the top of the 11th when he deposited a pitch from Jim Poole over the fence in left field. Belle, however, evened the score in the bottom of the frame as he swatted a Rick Aguilera offering into the bleachers. A third delay ensued when Boston manager Kevin Kennedy yelled to the umpires to confiscate Belle's

A Bulging Bicep

The pose is iconic in Cleveland, and not just because its likeness now exists as a bobblehead. After Albert Belle tied the score in Game 1 of the 1995 American League Division Series with a home run, Red Sox skipper Kevin Kennedy requested that the slugger's bat be checked for cork.

At that moment, Belle pointed to his right bicep and pointed to Indians history. That stance, from the home dugout, would never be forgotten. As he flexed his muscle, veins protruded from his right forearm. His eyebrows curled as he initiated a menacing glare toward Boston's dugout. His mustache wrapped around his upper lip as he shouted at Kennedy. He squeezed his right fist as his bicep pushed his white uniform to its limit.

He seemed primed for a fistfight, ready for confrontation. His bat checked out clean. The Indians knocked out the Red Sox in three games to advance to the American League Championship Series against the Seattle Mariners.

bat, which the skipper contended was corked. Belle stared at the Red Sox from the home dugout, flexed his right bicep and pointed to the bulging muscle. The umpires checked the slugger's lumber but found nothing afoul.

When Peña stepped into the batter's box with two outs in the bottom of the 13th, the clock had ticked past 2:00 AM and Costas was taking playful jabs at Uecker's unheralded playing career. Red Sox southpaw reliever Zane Smith misfired with his first three offerings to the 38-year-old. Hargrove gave Peña the take sign. There was no need to swing at a 3–0 pitch, especially given Peña's offensive limitations. Peña didn't listen.

Uecker was mid-sentence when Costas cut him off and shrieked, "Oh man! Oh man! Tony Peña! On 3-and-0! Sends everybody home!"

Smith left a pitch over the plate. Peña took a healthy swing and immediately flipped his bat away, toward the Indians' dugout. The baseball landed in the first row of the bleachers, perched above the 19-foot-high wall in left field. A group of fans clad in orange ponchos chased after the ball as Peña raised both arms in the air and circled the bases. He slapped hands with second baseman Carlos Baerga before he was mobbed by the rest of his teammates at home plate.

"That was a key game for us," Alomar said, "to believe that, 'Hey, we can go through Boston, no problem.'"

The Indians hadn't competed in a playoff game since 1954, when they were swept in the World Series by the New York Giants. What a way to make the wait worthwhile. A wet, dreary night—turned morning—ended in thrilling fashion, a style to which Indians fans had quickly grown accustomed.

"That went right along with what we had done all year," said pitching coach Mark Wiley. "It was unbelievable."

26 "One Moment to Shine"

Rajai Davis still watches the YouTube video with his son on a regular basis. Jordan Michael Davis has viewed it so many times he could give detailed commentary about every second of the clip: how his dad choked up on the bat as the battle with Aroldis Chapman unfolded, how fans erupted once the baseball disappeared onto the home run porch, and every motion his dad made while circling the bases.

Prior to November 2, 2016, Davis' signature moment, according to the man himself, was a walk-off grand slam with the Tigers two and a half years earlier.

"But nothing in the playoffs, when more people watch," he said.

Davis can recall every shred of action from that night, too. He knows he hadn't hit a home run in a couple months—since August 30, to be exact. He knows Chapman hadn't allowed a homer since June. And he remembers thinking how he wished he would have taken his mindset from that at-bat and applied it to every plate appearance of his 14-year big-league career.

"It was a more focused approach," he said. "I was intentional. I wanted to win."

Davis was a decade into his major league career, one that almost ended before it started. He wanted to bail on baseball when he was a minor-leaguer not being afforded the opportunities he was certain he deserved. While in Double-A, he thought he was being overlooked and others were passing him by, even though he had passed every test sent his way.

"I was really discouraged," Davis said. "'Why am I playing this game?'"

Fast forward to that unseasonably warm evening in early November 2016. Earlier in his career, Davis said, he wouldn't have been prepared for such a chance at a historic contribution. But on the grandest stage imaginable, Game 7 of a World Series between a pair of franchises bearing the league's longest title droughts...

"It's really remarkable how everything lined up for that moment."

...he supplied perhaps the most unforgettable home run in team history.

Had Cleveland emerged on top, that declaration would not be debatable. Since the Cubs prevailed in 10 innings, the conversation can get a little murky. The moment itself was inarguably electric, magical and implausible. It was also fleeting, the buzz in the ballpark ultimately quelled by an untimely rain delay and then a Chicago rally.

But for a moment, Davis was on top of the world.

"What you're thinking," Davis said, "is, I have to battle and my battle is against one man. Not nine guys. One man. I know what he's throwing. I faced him two other times in the series. He's got one pitch. I know what's coming. All I had to do was be ready for it, be ready for one pitch. So, I have a focus. At that time of year, it's later on in the year, so that's heavy. You want to make sure you get the bat on the ball. I want to control that thing. That's where the choke-up comes in. In my mindset, I'm gonna win this battle. He's Goliath. I'm David. I have my bat. He had the ball. I just felt with the help of God on my side, I couldn't fail. I felt really confident."

Davis always believed that when he received daily playing time, he could offer plenty with his bat. When he played sporadically, it was more difficult for him to make adjustments to pitchers. He was filling a part-time role during the 2016 playoffs, but he had squared off against Chapman in Game 2 (a five-pitch strikeout) and Game 5 (a sixth-pitch single). In their three encounters, Chapman threw him 18 pitches, all fastballs.

There were no surprises. Davis was seeking fastball, and on Chapman's seventh offering to him in the eighth inning of the seventh game of a dramatic World Series, Davis got one he could yank over the 19-foot-high wall in left field to spark pandemonium at Progressive Field.

"It was 16 years of preparation," Davis said, "for one moment to shine."

27 Quite Frankly

The temperature hovered around freezing on Opening Day in 1975, when the Indians hosted the New York Yankees at Cleveland

Stadium. Nearly 57,000 fans braved the conditions and sat in their seats around the tundra to watch Frank Robinson, the league's first African American manager, direct the Indians in his first game. Robinson, a two-time Most Valuable Player award winner—once in each league, the first player to accomplish that feat—came over in a trade with the California Angels near the end of the 1974 campaign.

He became manager prior to the 1975 season and, despite settling into a reserve role, was still a player at the time. He inserted himself into the No. 2 spot in the Opening Day lineup on April 8. In his first at-bat, he launched a solo home run to left field off of right-hander Doc Medich. The Indians proceeded to claim a 5–3 victory.

When Cleveland general manager Phil Seghi offered Robinson the role of manager, the job came with a $200,000 salary. Robinson realized he was already in line to earn $180,000 as a player.

"I was no math genius," Robinson said. "I said, 'Phil, you mean to tell me you're going to pay me $20,000 to manage?' He said, 'That's right. Take it or leave it.' I had a decision to make, and I made it, for the better. I'm glad I did."

Not only did Robinson have to deal with daily managerial rigors and extra attention for his trailblazing achievement, but he had to balance his own playing time and keep his players' egos in check.

In his Baseball Hall of Fame induction speech in 1982, Robinson quipped, "If I had wanted to go after personal goals, I could have inserted myself into the lineup much more often in Cleveland when I was a player-manager, but as a manager I had better sense than that. I knew I had better ballplayers than Frank Robinson at that time, so I played the best that I had."

Of course, he adhered to his hunches from time to time. On June 11, 1976, Robinson called upon himself to pinch-hit in the bottom of the 13th inning. The Chicago White Sox had taken a

4–3 lead in the top half of the frame. With two outs and a runner on third, Robinson batted for Orlando Gonzalez and clubbed a walk-off home run. It was one of only three home runs he hit that season, his last as a player. He finished his career with 586 home runs, fourth-most in history at the time of his retirement.

Robinson managed the Indians from 1975–77 and finished with a 186–189 record. He would eventually manage the San Francisco Giants, Baltimore Orioles, and Montreal Expos/Washington Nationals. During his presidency, Gerald Ford once sent Robinson a telegram commending him on becoming the first African American manager in baseball history.

The Indians honored Robinson with a statue at Progressive Field in 2017. They also retired his No. 20. Hank Aaron attended the festivities that afternoon in late May and told his pal he was jealous he never won the Triple Crown like Robinson had done.

"You did it and did it with ease," Aaron told him.

"I should've done it at least three or four times," Robinson snapped back.

Robinson later stepped up to a podium to deliver a speech and said, "[Hank] thought that winning a Triple Crown was easy. I'm going to tell you one thing—it is not easy. He doesn't realize how long I had to chase him and look up at him doing something great. It started in the minor leagues. All I ever heard was, 'Hank Aaron hit one here [and there].' I get to the big leagues two years later. 'Hank Aaron. Hank Aaron.' Then I had to see it personally. 'Hank Aaron.' I said, 'Yeah, this guy is a pretty good ballplayer.' I was chasing him and trying to do what he would do, for 21 years. I couldn't do it. But I'll tell you one thing—he made me a better ballplayer."

Aaron reciprocated the kind words.

"I remember one or two players telling me, 'There's [a certain] way you have to pitch to Frank,'" he said. "I said, 'Yeah, hold the ball and pray.'"

28 A Series to Remember

Maybe.

It's a word with which Herb Score qualified his historic call, a five-letter filler that hedged the radio announcer's premature exclamation.

"The Indians are going back to the World Series!" Score shouted once Tony Fernandez's fly ball landed in the first row of seats atop the right-field wall at Oriole Park at Camden Yards on October 15, 1997.

"Maybe," he then added, realizing that Baltimore still had its last at-bat in the bottom of the 11th inning.

It was a perfectly flawed moment to cap a wacky, dramatic, mistake-filled set of six games. Fernandez wasn't even supposed to play that day. Bip Roberts was drilled on the left thumb by a line drive during batting practice. He couldn't properly grip a bat, which made him unavailable for Game 6 of the American League Championship Series. Naturally, Fernandez was the culprit at the plate who sprayed the line drive toward Roberts' digit.

Roberts was the team's spark plug, installed as the leadoff hitter after being acquired from the Royals less than two months earlier. Fernandez had a solid season at the plate and tied his career high with 11 home runs, but he was more of a defensive specialist. He had never hit a homer in 145 trips to the plate in his postseason career.

To even arrive at Game 6 requires a wayward journey through a maze of crazy contests. The Orioles knocked out the Indians in the AL Division Series the year before, and they were the better team throughout the 1997 regular season, winning 98 games to Cleveland's 86. Baltimore boasted a stout pitching staff, anchored by Mike Mussina, Scott Erickson and Jimmy Key, plus a balanced lineup centered around Brady Anderson, Roberto Alomar and Rafael Palmeiro. They cruised past the Mariners in the ALDS, while the Indians barely slipped past the Yankees.

The Orioles claimed Game 1, 3–0, behind eight shutout innings from Erickson. Anderson, meanwhile, slugged Chad Ogea's first pitch of the game over the right-field fence.

Baltimore held a 4–2 lead in the eighth inning of Game 2 when Armando Benitez walked Sandy Alomar Jr. and Jim Thome. With two outs, Marquis Grissom, who replaced All-Star center fielder Kenny Lofton in Cleveland just before the season began, delivered a go-ahead three-run homer. That reversed the course of the series.

All of the wackiness came to a head in Game 3 at Jacobs Field. Despite Mussina's ALCS-record 15 strikeouts over seven innings, the Indians grasped a 1–0 advantage in the ninth inning when Jeffrey Hammonds sent a dribbler to second base. Fernandez gathered the baseball and attempted to tag Jeff Reboulet, who was running from first to second, but Reboulet dropped to the ground at Fernandez's feet and avoided the tag. Fernandez threw to first to retire Hammonds, but Reboulet advanced to second. Anderson then skied a fly ball to center field, and Grissom spread his arms to signal he didn't see it. The ball landed behind him, and left fielder Brian Giles sprinted over to corral it. Reboulet scored with ease to tie the game.

Grissom got redemption. He drew a one-out walk in the 12th inning and advanced to third on a single to right by Fernandez. On a 2-1 pitch, Omar Vizquel squared to lay down a squeeze bunt as Grissom bolted for the plate. Vizquel missed the ball as his momentum carried him up the first-base line. The ball skimmed off the glove of catcher Lenny Webster, who thought Vizquel had foul tipped it. Grissom crossed the plate as Webster leisurely picked up the ball and home-plate umpire John Hirschbeck motioned his arms to make a safe call. Vizquel jumped up and down, Orioles manager Davey Johnson rushed out of his dugout to argue, and the Indians spilled out of their dugout to greet Grissom, who had atoned for his lost ball in the ninth inning by winning the game with a controversial steal of home.

Another walk-off propelled the Indians to a 3–1 series lead, as Sandy Alomar Jr. delivered a decisive RBI single in Game 4, moments after the Orioles had tagged Jose Mesa with his second straight blown save. Baltimore staved off elimination with a 4–2 win in Game 5 to set up a pivotal Game 6 in Baltimore. Mussina and Charles Nagy dueled past sunset, albeit in different styles. Mussina piled up another 10 strikeouts and limited Cleveland to one hit—a David Justice leadoff double in the fifth—over eight scoreless frames. Nagy scattered eight hits and three walks across 7⅓ innings, retiring the Orioles in order only once.

The scoreless tie persisted until the 11th inning, when Fernandez faced Benitez with two outs. The Indians had Benitez solved that series. They knew that when he positioned his glove a certain way once he set on the mound, he would deliver a particular pitch. Fernandez waved his bat behind his head as he stood in his slightly opened stance. As Benitez reared back, Fernandez—sporting calf-high blue socks to accent his gray uniform—rocked back and executed his high leg kick. He offered a smooth stroke at a hanging slider over the heart of the plate. Right fielder Jerome Walton watched the baseball sail into the front row of fans perched atop the tall fence. The Indians' dugout erupted. Score delivered his famous line—and addendum.

Before the Indians departed for Miami the next morning for the World Series, they held a private party at the team hotel to toast to their second Fall Classic appearance in three years. Geneva, Ohio, native Brian Anderson, whose scoreless 10th inning earned him the win in Game 6, sat with his parents and recounted the time he told them he would help a Cleveland team win a championship some day after he watched Earnest Byner fumble away Cleveland's hopes at a Super Bowl berth in January 1988.

The team's broadcasters wandered through the streets of downtown Baltimore in search of a late-night meal, as they delayed their sleep until the morning plane ride and an afternoon on the beach. As the clock pushed 3:00 AM, they finally stumbled across an open diner. They walked in and received unwavering stares. Two police officers were sitting down in the establishment. One asked them what they were doing. They replied that they worked for the Indians.

"Oh yeah? You broke our hearts tonight," the officer said. He glanced at an employee working behind the counter. "I don't know if she'll serve you."

Comeback for the Ages

The Mariners ruled the regular season in 2001. Lou Piniella's bunch won a major league record-tying 116 games. The Athletics had to settle for the American League Wild Card because they tallied *only* 102 victories.

The Indians entered their tilt on August 5, 2001—a Sunday Night Baseball national telecast on ESPN—riding a three-game losing streak, a skid that dropped them to second place in the American League Central. Charlie Manuel's club hosted Seattle at Jacobs Field before a sellout crowd of 42,494. Many of those fans bolted for the exits once the Mariners amassed a 12–0 advantage in the third inning.

The Mariners mounted an eight-run, seven-hit attack in the third, one inning after they plated four runs. Dave Burba departed before he could record an out in the third.

"I was going through a rough spell," Burba said. "I couldn't get past the third inning. I was just hoping that I'd have a good game and pitch deep into the game and give my team a chance to win. Obviously, that didn't work out so well."

Mike Bacsik didn't fare much better.

"The reason I had gotten called up was we had just gotten killed by the Oakland A's [17–4]," Bacsik said, "and we used a lot of the bullpen, so we needed a fresh arm.... Usually, you don't see guys making big-league debuts against the best team in baseball with the bases loaded and nobody out on the national game of the night.... I came into the game and [catcher] Einar Diaz had no clue who I was. He had no clue what I threw. He didn't know my name."

By the time the seventh inning rolled around, the Mariners staked claim to a 14–2 lead. Both teams had pulled most of their starters. Center fielder Kenny Lofton recalled that he "wanted to stay in the game for some reason. Maybe I had a girlfriend there."

Russell Branyan began the bottom of the seventh with a solo home run. Two outs followed. Then, the floodgates opened. Einar Diaz singled to center, and Lofton and Omar Vizquel walked. Jolbert Cabrera unloaded the bases with a two-run single. A three-run seventh closed the deficit to 14–5.

Eighth-inning home runs by Jim Thome and Marty Cordova shaved Seattle's lead to 14–8. Vizquel's RBI double made it 14–9. Still, the Indians needed five runs in the ninth to extend the affair. The Mariners' bullpen, anchored by closer Kazuhiro Sasaki and setup men Arthur Rhodes and Jeff Nelson, rarely crumbled. Rhodes went 8–0 with a 1.72 ERA in 71 appearances, with 83 strikeouts in 68 innings. Nelson compiled a 2.76 ERA with 88 strikeouts in 65⅓ innings. Sasaki logged 45 saves.

"[Sasaki] used to have a *really* good split-finger," Vizquel said.

Eddie Taubensee led off the ninth with a single to center. Seattle's Norm Charlton retired Thome and Branyan, but Marty Cordova doubled and sent the southpaw to the showers. Nelson entered and walked Wil Cordero and served up a two-run single to Diaz. Lofton singled to left to load the bases.

Vizquel's five-year-old son, Nico, was spending his first day as the team's bat boy. Now, his father was coming to the plate with the bags packed with two outs in the ninth and his team trailing 14–11.

"Charlie told me in the fifth inning, 'Get ready, because you're going to win this game,'" Vizquel said. "I'm like, 'Yeah, right. Am I going to hit a 10-run homer or something?'"

The diminutive shortstop worked a full count and on the eighth pitch of the at-bat, he grounded a ball down the right-field line. The baseball trickled into the corner, past right fielder Charles Gipson. Cordero, Diaz, and Lofton all scored. Vizquel glided into third base and slapped hands with coach Joel Skinner, who then smacked Vizquel on the back of the helmet. Lofton repeatedly pumped his fists as he circled back to the dugout. It was delirium inside Jacobs Field.

"I never played in a World Series or anything," Bacsik said, "but for your first game ever, when he hits the ball down the line for a game-tying triple—I remember our dugout was going nuts. The people who stuck around were going nuts. It was an awesome feeling.... I remember thinking, 'Why weren't they playing the line? Why did Seattle let a ground ball get down the line?' Usually, you make sure that doesn't happen there. As the ball gets down there and we tie the game, I'm thinking, 'This can't be happening. There was no way we were coming back from 14–2.'"

Vizquel approached his manager and reminded him, "Man, remember what you told me in the fifth inning?"

"I remember watching Lou," Thome said. "When we tied it, he was like, 'What just happened?'"

The game proceeded until the 11th inning, when Lofton and Vizquel registered consecutive one-out singles. Cabrera then splintered his bat on the first pitch from Jose Paniagua as he sent a soft liner into left field. Lofton sprinted around third and snuck his hand onto home plate before catcher Dan Wilson could apply

Eddie Taubensee hoists Kenny Lofton over his shoulder during a celebration after the Indians overcame a 12–0 deficit to beat the Mariners 15–14 on Sunday Night Baseball.

the tag. Wilson stepped on Lofton's hand as the center fielder slid head-first across the dirt. Taubensee, who had been on deck, lifted Lofton over his shoulder as the Indians came pouring out of the dugout. The two had actually been traded for each other a decade earlier. The club congregated on the infield and went crazy. Vizquel lifted up Nico onto his shoulder as Lofton and Cabrera endured the celebratory wrath of their teammates.

In one controlled area of the ballpark: disbelief, shock, disappointment. Everywhere else: bedlam. The Indians became the first team in 76 years to overcome a 12-run deficit on their way to the 15–14 result. Over the final five innings, the Indians totaled 17 hits. Lofton and Vizquel each reached four times during that unfathomable stretch, with one walk and three hits apiece.

"I remember after the game, I'm in the clubhouse," Bacsik said. "I had never met Jim Thome or Travis Fryman or Roberto Alomar, guys you idolize. These guys are coming up to me and saying, 'Way to keep us in it!' I'm like, 'Man, I've never been congratulated for giving up seven runs in six innings.'"

Bacsik kept an article chronicling the game, as well as Manuel's lineup card from that night, which included an array of red marks noting each substitution in what appeared to be a blowout loss, until the Indians converted it into a historic win.

"It was one of the most exciting games I ever played in," Vizquel said. "I remember every minute of it."

30 'A Bad Stadium'

Cleveland Stadium played host to the Indians' home games for 60 years through the 1993 season. For much of that time period, it also served as the Cleveland Browns' home. When the Indians played, the diamond still showed signs of a football field, so much so that on a lazy fly ball, center fielder Rick Manning would raise his hand to signal for a fair catch.

Bob DiBiasio, the team's senior vice president of public affairs, once went for a run around the field on a Monday afternoon. The Indians had a home game that evening. The Browns had played there the previous day. As DiBiasio jogged around the track, he noticed the orange helmet logo still painted between the pitcher's mound and second base. DiBiasio sprinted back upstairs to the front offices, where he found team president Gabe Paul. DiBiasio begged his boss to venture outside and take a look at the field. It would not be the best look for the Indians to play on an orange infield with the logo of a team from a different sport.

Paul was angry. He yelled...at DiBiasio, for breaking the dress code by wearing gym shorts and a sweat-covered T-shirt around the office.

Ultimately, Paul agreed to see the field and he became even more livid upon seeing the Browns logo. So, the grounds crew cut a square at the location of the logo, removed it and re-sodded it. By the time first pitch rolled around, viewers could notice the patchwork fix, but at least infielders were not blinded by vibrant orange grass on ground balls.

Such was life for the Indians, who were just a tenant in a massive building they shared for decades. They played their first game at the venue on July 31, 1932, when hurler Mel Harder toed the rubber. Then, however, the team still played most of its games at League Park. The Indians truly transitioned to the shores of Lake Erie in the 1940s.

When the place was filled to capacity, it provided an overwhelmingly energized atmosphere. That did not happen often. For much of its existence, the cavernous building remained mostly deserted, as struggling teams played before, relatively speaking, a handful of fans. During its lifespan, it seated between 73,000–79,000 for baseball games. For that debut in 1932, it attracted 80,184, then a major league record. Gradually, the club played more and more games at Cleveland Stadium. First, it was only Sunday and holiday affairs. Then they shifted the important matchups to the larger stadium. When the league implemented night games into the schedule, the Indians shifted there when the sun went down, since League Park lacked lights. Once the 1940 campaign rolled around, the team played the vast majority of its schedule on the waterfront. It removed League Park from its plans after the 1946 season.

A Hope and a Prayer

After the final out of the 1993 season—the last ever recorded at Cleveland Stadium—Bob Hope sang a version of the song "Thanks for the Memory" on the field. The tune was filled with lyrics specifically written about the ballpark. Bob DiBiasio escorted the 90-year-old and his wife, Dolores, to the pitcher's mound, where Hope addressed the crowd.

Prior to the performance, DiBiasio had asked the longtime actor, singer, and comedian if he needed a podium upon which he could place his script. That way, in case he clutched the microphone in his hand, he would have a free hand to turn the pages.

Hope responded, "Young man, I've been doing vaudeville since I was 15 years old. I've never touched a microphone in my life."

As soon as Hope positioned himself in front of the mound, he grabbed the microphone from its stand. He held the mic in his right hand and his script in his left hand. When he needed to turn the page, he wouldn't be singing into the mic. DiBiasio described it as "a mess."

"All you heard was people going, 'We couldn't hear him!'" DiBiasio said.

He turned to Dolores and said, "We need to get that mic back into the mic stand."

She leaned over and replied: "You're on your own, kid."

And thus, Cleveland Stadium was laid to rest.

Because it also hosted football games, the outfield was vast and spacious. The stands were far removed from the field, so fans—when they showed up—were not as involved in the action. Its proximity to Lake Erie enticed swarms of pesky insects. Cleveland Stadium played host to four All-Star games (1935, 1954, 1963, 1981); a World Series championship in 1948; Ted Williams' 500th home run (June 17, 1960); Ten Cent Beer Night (June 4, 1974); and Len Barker's perfect game (May 15, 1981). It closed its doors to baseball on October 3, 1993, and remained the home of Browns football for two more years.

For a typical, sparsely attended game, broadcasters could hear every word muttered in the stadium. Catcher Sandy Alomar Jr.

recalled being able to hear fans shouting from the outfield bleachers as he crouched behind home plate. Jim Thome tried to ignore hecklers who badgered him about errant throws from third base. To offer perspective, Thome's dad would remind him of the legends who had also played at the venue: Williams, Babe Ruth, Bob Feller.

The building was damp and cold, "like a gigantic mausoleum," said longtime executive Dan O'Dowd. Alomar said playing there "was kind of demoralizing," especially when they moved the fences back in 1991, converting the field into "a graveyard" at least partially responsible for the club's league-worst run total and 105 losses. Employees kept space heaters at their desks and flickered the lights upon entering their offices to startle the mice who thought they owned the place.

"They were there all the time," O'Dowd said.

"They looked well-fed," said radio announcer Tom Hamilton. "They were chubby mice."

The locker rooms were cramped, with small spaces serving as kitchens and laundry rooms and training areas. Players would trudge through the concourse in their full uniforms and cleats to get to the batting cage under the bleachers. The bathrooms were grimy. The refrigerator held peanut butter and jelly sandwiches and cans of tuna fish and usually nothing else. The postgame spread typically included whatever leftovers the clubhouse staff could scrounge up from concession stands.

"The whole stadium was a bad stadium, to be honest," Kenny Lofton said. "But it's what Cleveland had."

31 Slim Jim

Even when the lanky, 21-year-old third baseman lifted Steve Farr's 1–0 offering into the deserted upper deck in right field at Yankee Stadium, no one could have envisioned what was to come for the kid sporting a No. 6 jersey. Jim Thome's first career home run, on October 4, 1991, the third-to-last day of the regular season, provided the last-place Indians with a victory against the Bronx Bombers.

"He didn't stand out like, 'This guy is going to be a Hall of Famer,'" said former team president Mark Shapiro. "He just clearly had incredible power. He was strong and much more athletic than people give him credit for."

Thome proceeded to club 11 career home runs at Yankee Stadium, one of 38 ballparks in which he trotted around the bases. He deposited 190 pitches over the fences at Progressive Field. Farr became the first of 403 different pitchers tagged by Thome for a tater. He teed off against Roger Clemens eight times and Justin Verlander seven times. He victimized Rick Reed on nine occasions in 27 career at-bats, including seven times in 16 at-bats during the 2002 campaign, in which he slugged a career-high 52 round-trippers.

He hit home runs for five different teams and against 30 different teams. He registered 48 multi-homer games, including a pair of three-homer affairs. Of his 612 career home runs, nine came with the bases loaded and 337 came with the bases empty. The fourth inning was his favorite (90 home runs), but he wasn't picky. He totaled at least 38 home runs in each of the nine innings. His final blast came against Toronto hurler Carlos Villanueva on September 26, 2012, a mere 7,664 days after his first career long ball. He swatted his 610th and 611th home runs against the Indians, the team with which he spent the majority of his career.

From his infamous batting stance, in which he pointed his bat to the sky above center field, he made a habit out of sending majestic drives into the stands. That stance is now permanently entrenched at Progressive Field in the form of a statue that stands tall beyond the center field wall.

For a while, such recognition of Thome near Lake Erie seemed implausible. Upon hitting the free agent market after the 2002 campaign and insisting that fans would have to "rip the uniform off of my back" for him to bolt Cleveland, Thome did just that. He ventured to greener pastures in Philadelphia, where the Phillies lured him with a six-year, $87 million commitment—a more enticing offer than the Indians' five-year, $62 million submission. The Indians, who had just initiated a rebuilding process, received a sucker punch to the gut with the loss of their offensive cornerstone.

"In life, you're always going to say things that ultimately you look back when you get older and say, 'You know what, maybe those weren't the right choice of words,'" Thome said. "I always envisioned that I was going to remain an Indian and when it didn't happen, it's not something that I look back on and say, 'I wish I would've made this decision or that decision.' When you make decisions, you move forward, but maybe some choice of words you do regret a little bit. I think you learn from them. You do make mistakes in life."

Thome contributed to the Indians' magical run of dominance from 1995–2001, a period during which the team claimed six American League Central Division titles and appeared in two Fall Classics. Thome himself earned trips to the All-Star Game in 1997, '98, and '99, as he shared the field with many of his Indians teammates.

Thome totaled 334 home runs during his 12 years in Cleveland. He provided power when it mattered most. He socked

Back at the Hot Corner

The night before the Indians' final home game in 2011, manager Manny Acta couldn't sleep. His racing mind spawned a creative notion. He presented his idea to the masses in the ninth inning of Cleveland's contest against Minnesota at Progressive Field on September 25.

Jim Thome, acquired one month earlier, pinch-hit for Shelley Duncan in the bottom of the eighth. In the ensuing frame, Thome's last at home as a member of the Indians, the 41-year-old trotted out to third base, the position he manned when he entered the league two decades earlier.

"I just felt that if this is the end—at least with our franchise—I thought it was proper that he end where he started—at third base," Acta said after the game.

Thome hadn't played third base since September 29, 1996. When the Indians traded for Matt Williams prior to the 1997 campaign, Thome shifted across the diamond to first. By 2011, Thome hadn't played the field at all in four years and hadn't played defense regularly since 2004.

"To get that opportunity to go back out there, it felt really good," Thome said. "Just like old times."

After one pitch by Joe Smith to Trevor Plouffe, Thome retreated to the dugout before a standing ovation. Acta had instructed Smith to toss a pitch out of Plouffe's reach to be safe, but he actually threw the Twins' third baseman a strike. Minnesota skipper Ron Gardenhire said he was hoping Plouffe would bunt the ball toward Thome.

The veteran, who was using infielder Jack Hannahan's glove, would have welcomed the action.

"I would have made the play," Thome said.

the go-ahead home run in Game 5 of the 1995 American League Championship Series against Seattle. He hit the game-tying home run in Game 1 and a pair of two-run home runs in Game 5 of the 1999 American League Division Series against Boston. In all, he totaled 17 postseason long balls.

Against Royals hurler Don Wengert, he clobbered a home run that traveled a ballpark-record 511 feet on July 3, 1999. The baseball landed in the plaza beyond center field and bounced onto Eagle Avenue, the street that runs adjacent to the left-field bleachers, behind the stadium.

"That will take two tape measures," radio announcer Tom Hamilton described on the broadcast.

He established a new club record with 52 home runs in his final season in Cleveland. He eclipsed Albert Belle's mark of 50, set in 1995, with his 51st blast on September 27, 2002.

"If you go to a game, you don't want to go eat when he's hitting," said former Guardians manager Terry Francona, "because those are majestic. He takes some pretty healthy swings."

Thome's career came to a close after he amassed 612 home runs over 22 seasons. He tallied 2,328 hits, 1,699 RBIs, 1,747 walks, 2,548 strikeouts, and five All-Star Game nods. He entered the majors with the Indians a week after reaching the legal drinking age as a skinny third baseman. He finished his career with the Orioles as a 42-year-old with a balky back, a guy limited to part-time designated hitter duties because of his body's limitations and the mileage accumulated over two decades in the league.

Before he finally called it a career, he mended a fence that had been hanging open in his mind for years. On August 25, 2011, the Indians paid the Minnesota Twins $20,000 to acquire Thome. Cleveland had surprisingly hung around in the American League Central race. Before the Detroit Tigers completely ran away with the division, the Indians opted to make one, final transaction in an effort to occupy a spot in an injury-riddled lineup, give the team a late-summer boost and fill Progressive Field with a month-long dose of nostalgia.

Thome arrived in Cleveland the following day, a Friday. He traversed every inch of the ballpark, reconnecting with old friends and colleagues. The Indians drew more than 100,000 fans to the stadium the weekend of his return. In his first game back, Thome batted fourth.

"The memories, the excitement of the fans, seeing them embrace me," Thome said. "I didn't know if I would ever get that opportunity to watch that again and see that excitement."

Thome said he doesn't have any regrets. He routinely imagined how a return to an Indians uniform would go over. He played out the scenarios, but never really considered them a possibility. When he knew he was Cleveland-bound in August 2011, he became overly anxious. He wasn't sure if the fans would embrace him.

"That first night when I got introduced and the crowd cheered me, it's something I'll never forget," Thome said. "You leave a place and ultimately you want to be accepted back. I appreciate the fact that they did accept me back and give me that opportunity and cheered."

The Indians celebrated Thome's birthday on August 27, 2011, as the man turning 41 played his second game with his old club. In the sixth inning, Thome slugged a game-tying home run off of Kansas City's Danny Duffy. The ball landed in the bleacher seats in left-center field. It marked the 602nd home run of his career.

"When you come in your rookie year," said second baseman Jason Kipnis, "you're already wide-eyed from the league itself and players around the league. Then you're talking to one of the guys you've emulated your swing after. He never let the success define who he is."

On August 2, 2014, the Indians unveiled a statue of Thome near Heritage Park in center field at the ballpark. The likeness displays the slugger amid his batting ritual, with his lumber pointed out into the abyss. Also on that cloudy Saturday afternoon, Thome signed a one-day contract with the Indians and officially retired as a member of the organization that had drafted him in the 13th round out of Illinois Central College a quarter-century earlier. In 2018, he became a first-ballot inductee into the Baseball Hall of Fame.

He left his mark with his teammates.

"He doesn't act like he's above anybody," said Sandy Alomar Jr. "It shows young players that you don't have to be this different type of guy to be a star player."

He left his mark on the league.

"He's a guy who has been so honest and truthful to the game," said Omar Vizquel. "He's the image people want to follow."

He left his mark with team executives.

"I have a different view of him in hindsight than I did when he was playing here," Shapiro said. "He is one of those guys that the longer you're in the game, the more you appreciate how special he is. Back then, he just seemed like an incredibly nice, genuine, innocent guy who was incredibly strong and had a lot of talent. Looking back, his humility and ability to treat people so incredibly well in light of the talent he had and what he was on the verge of accomplishing was pretty remarkable."

And he penned the final chapter of his career with the organization in which it all started.

"When the statue got closer, it was important for me to do this during this time," Thome said. "I wanted to retire an Indian. It's a dream come true."

The Curse of Rocky Colavito

Rocky Colavito just wanted the day to end. Not only did he go hitless with four strikeouts in six at-bats—the only four-whiff game of his 14-year big league career—but the tension and uneasiness were overwhelming. It was April 19, 1960. It was two days after Easter Sunday, two days after he switched allegiances, and two days after the latest show-stopping swap executed by Indians general manager Frank "Trader" Lane, a man who derived pleasure out of dealing star players.

Colavito led the American League with 42 home runs in 1959. A year earlier, he hit .303 with 41 home runs and 113 RBIs. In 1959, he earned a trip to two All-Star Games and finished in the top four in balloting for the American League Most Valuable Player award for the second consecutive season. That year, he set a franchise record (and tied the big-league mark) with four home runs in one game on June 10, 1959. Yet two days before the start of the 1960 regular season, Lane shipped Colavito to Detroit in exchange for Harvey Kuenn, the 1959 batting champion who had logged a .353 average for the Tigers.

Lane and Colavito had engaged in a contract squabble, but the powerful right fielder was the face of the franchise and a fan favorite. Kuenn was a nice player, a singles and doubles hitter and a perennial All-Star. He never whacked more than 12 home runs in a season, however. And Colavito was just reaching his prime, at the age of 26. Fans were not fond of the deal. They would support it even less as time went on.

Lane had built a reputation as a quick-trigger trader, an executive who once said the trades he did regret were the ones he did not make. He made 60 deals in a two-year span from December 1957–59. He dealt away Roger Maris in 1958. Three years later, Maris established a new major league single-season home run record. Lane acquired first baseman Norm Cash from the Chicago White Sox following the 1959 campaign. However, before Cash ever suited up for the Indians, he was sent to the Tigers. Cash proceeded to slug 373 home runs for Detroit. The player Cleveland received in return, Steve Demeter, totaled five hitless at-bats for the Indians. Five days before Colavito was traded to the Tigers, Cash joined the club. Cash, 25 years old at the time, would spend the final 15 years of his career with Detroit.

Kuenn played only one season in Cleveland before he, too, was traded. One month before Lane left his position, he dealt Kuenn to the San Francisco Giants for pitcher Johnny Antonelli and outfielder Willie Kirkland. Antonelli appeared in 11 games with the Indians and posted an 0–4 record and 6.56 ERA. Kirkland pieced together three forgettable years with the club, as he logged a .232 batting average and 63 home runs.

The Indians had amassed an 89–65 record in 1959, good for second place in the American League. Once they traded away Colavito, "The Curse of Rocky Colavito" began. For the next 34 years, the Indians finished better than fourth place just once: a third-place finish in 1968.

Gabe Paul wanted to make things right. Lane was gone and Paul, always one to fawn over and attempt to lure stars, ran the front office. So prior to the 1965 season, the Indians reacquired Colavito in a three-team deal involving the White Sox and the Kansas City Athletics. Cleveland parted with southpaw Tommy John, who had amassed a 2–9 record and 3.91 ERA as a 21-year-old the year before. He proceeded to pitch for another 24 years. By the time he retired, he had tallied 288 wins. The Indians also sent away 22-year-old outfielder Tommie Agee, who had played sparingly. He won the American League Rookie of the Year award with Chicago in 1966, made two All-Star teams and garnered a pair of Gold Glove awards. Catcher John Romano, a two-time All-Star for Cleveland, also departed.

Colavito came back to Cleveland and registered two more All-Star seasons. He was on the downside of his career, though. By 1967, he was washed up and the Indians traded him to the White Sox. The curse lived on.

33 In the Nick of Father Time

The Indians closed the 2013 campaign with 10 consecutive wins. They needed all 10 to earn the right to host the American League Wild Card Game. A handful of the victories came in dicey fashion, though none more demanding than a 5–4 triumph against the Chicago White Sox on September 24.

The Indians handed closer Chris Perez a 3–2 advantage in the ninth inning at Progressive Field, where a half-filled ballpark hoped to witness a fifth straight win. The polarizing pitcher surrendered a game-tying, solo home run to Dayan Viciedo on his third pitch. Three batters later, Alejandro De Aza took him deep to give Chicago the lead.

"We got the feeling of having the air taken out of us," infielder Mike Aviles recalled.

Jason Giambi approached the plate with two outs in the bottom of the ninth. Michael Brantley had singled and stolen second base. Giambi had tagged the White Sox for a walk-off home run two months earlier.

Giambi struck again.

On closer Addison Reed's third offering of the at-bat, Giambi socked a slider into the right-field seats to propel the Indians to a 5–4 victory. As soon as his bat struck the baseball, Giambi lifted the lumber high in the air with his right hand and flipped it aside. While his teammates crowded around home plate, anticipating the inevitable mob scene, Giambi slapped hands with third-base coach Brad Mills and spread his arms to brace himself for the celebratory drubbing. Jumping up and down, his teammates pounded him on the helmet and the backside and nearly yanked off his jersey.

"It's the stuff you dream about," Giambi said.

Shortstop Asdrubal Cabrera jumped into his arms. Jason Kipnis and Nick Swisher followed suit. Swisher and Aviles doused him with Gatorade. Michael Bourn was lying on a table in the trainer's room after leaving the game with a wrist injury. As soon as Giambi's bat met ball, he leapt off the table and excitedly grabbed trainer Lonnie Soloff.

"I almost broke Lonnie's neck," Bourn said. "That was a big moment for us. We needed that game."

"I remember it like it was yesterday, just absolutely losing it," Aviles said.

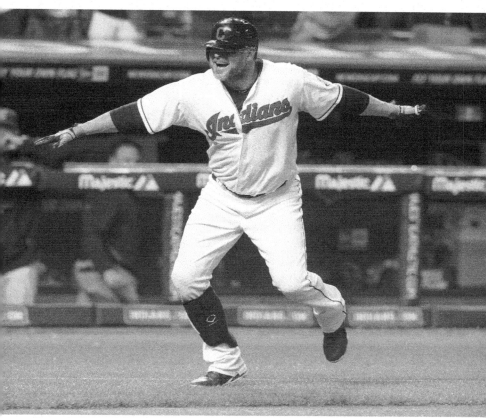

Jason Giambi celebrates the walk-off home run that propelled the Indians to a 5–4 victory over the Chicago White Sox on September 24, 2013.

"Coming down the stretch, trying to get a playoff berth," Giambi said, "it doesn't get any bigger than that. It really doesn't."

Giambi said he made Perez give him a hug, adding that the closer "was a little down" after blowing the lead. The 42-year-old became the oldest player in major league history to register a walk-off home run.

"None of us knew at that moment just how important it was," said team president Mark Shapiro. "When you look back, it was an incredible moment. For this to happen, for it to be a guy that our players felt that way about, just magnified what was already an unbelievable moment. Your range of emotions from Chris blowing the save to that happening, it was a pretty strong flop, just beyond belief."

The Indians forged ahead and won their remaining five games to clinch their first postseason berth since 2007. They capped the 10-game win streak—the longest such streak to end a regular season in franchise history—with a 5–1 victory at Target Field in Minnesota, as Twins outfielder Clete Thomas grounded out to second baseman Jason Kipnis to punch Cleveland's ticket to October baseball. Kipnis made a diving snag in the grass in short right field as pitcher Justin Masterson covered first, tagged the base and held the clinching baseball in his right hand, high above his head.

Players, coaches and team executives sprayed each other with champagne in the clubhouse after the game, the franchise's first taste of celebratory bubbly in six years. The Indians amassed a 21–6 record in September. They finished the season with a 17–2 mark against the White Sox and a 13–6 record against the Twins. They closed the regular-season slate with six wins against those division foes, including a four-game sweep in the Twin Cities.

"Things were falling in place for us," Aviles said.

In the '90s, it became routine and expected. Every October, sellout crowds filed into Jacobs Field to watch the drama, the duress and the desperation that come with postseason baseball. After an early exit in 2001, the club didn't qualify for the playoffs again for six years. And after a run to the American League Championship Series that fall, they went another six years—until that mad dash to the finish line in 2013—without a postseason appearance.

"I look back at it now and I still didn't appreciate it," Hamilton said. "When you're going through it, you're like, 'This will happen forever. These guys will never get old, and we'll go to the World Series every year.'"

After the 2007 run, the team fell far short of expectations the following season. They wound up trading away Cy Young Award winners CC Sabathia and Cliff Lee in successive seasons. They tallied 93 or more losses in 2009, 2010 and 2012. Manny Acta replaced Eric Wedge as manager and then, in 2012, the team sputtered through a 5–24 showing in August. Terry Francona entered the picture, and everything changed in 2013.

Now, their first taste of playoff baseball in six years lasted less than four hours, but those cherished minutes provided the championship-starved city with another reminder of the distinctiveness of October baseball. The ballpark was electric for that Wednesday night Wild Card Game matchup against the Rays, with the winner advancing to the AL Division Series to battle Francona's old team, the Red Sox.

"That vibe that night was just absolutely incredible," said Jim Thome.

Francona called upon a 23-year-old kid with 10 major league starts to his name to take the hill before a raucous crowd of 43,579 fans who squeezed into Progressive Field. When the Indians clinched a Wild Card berth on the final Sunday of the regular season, Francona informed Danny Salazar that he would start with the club's postseason fate hanging in the balance. The rookie right-hander became the third-youngest hurler in franchise history to start a playoff game.

It wasn't Salazar's first bout with pressure. In July, he tossed and turned the night before his big-league debut, so much so that he fell back asleep after his alarm clock went off in the morning. He ultimately woke in a panic, dashed to the ballpark, and arrived at the Indians' clubhouse less than an hour before his scheduled first pitch. He proceeded to carry a no-hitter into the sixth inning against the Blue Jays. He departed his debut after six frames, in which he limited Toronto to one run on two hits and a walk. He struck out seven.

Salazar was nervous and jittery only up until he resided upon his most comfortable setting.

"I asked him after his first start, 'How nervous were you?'" Francona said. "He was like, 'Not really.' And usually you get that from guys and you know they're lying. He explained it to me that, 'I've been through so much with my arm, being on the mound is the most comfortable place for me in the world.'"

After that outing, Salazar returned to Triple A. The Indians summoned him again in early August, and the right-hander remained in the team's starting rotation for the duration. He posted a 3.12 ERA in his 10 starts, a welcome boost to an injury-riddled group.

So on that Wednesday evening, Salazar stood atop the mound, with a house full of red-shirt-wearing, white-towel-waving backers howling at his near-untouchable heater. Fellow pitcher Joe Smith called the pitch a "lightning fastball." Salazar admitted to having a small dose of nerves at the start of the contest, but that only amped up his velocity. He capped a scoreless first inning when he blew away Tampa Bay's James Loney with a 100-mph fastball.

After Salazar set down the Rays in order in each of the first two frames, Delmon Young silenced the crowd with a solo home run into the left-field bleachers to start the third. Desmond Jennings then plated a pair of runs with a two-out double to left in the fourth. The Indians out-hit the Rays nine to eight in the contest, but Cleveland stranded nine runners and went 2-for-9 with runners in scoring position. Tampa Bay righty Alex Cobb scattered eight hits over 6⅔ scoreless innings. Salazar departed early in the fifth inning, having surrendered three runs on four hits.

Cleveland lost 4–0. The October experience was short-lived. A tease, almost. Still, the three hours—and the buildup the three days before it—served as a reminder of the magic of the postseason, a reminder that it's never a guarantee.

"Those moments, when you see this place like that and you look down and you see the parents and grandparents in the stands and the little kids, you're thinking, 'This building is multi-generational now,'" said Shapiro. "There are people who came here as little kids who are now here with their kids and have talked about what it was like to be here in the mid-'90s and now they're saying, 'This is what it was like.'"

The 180-Foot Dash

No one remembers Ruben Amaro scoring first. Kenny Lofton's mad dash around half of the diamond is all anyone recalls about the victory that propelled the Indians to their first World Series appearance in 41 years.

The Indians arrived at the Kingdome on October 17, 1995, grasping a 3–2 advantage over the Mariners in the American League Championship Series. Seattle sent southpaw Randy Johnson to the hill in an attempt to salvage its season. Cleveland countered with Dennis Martinez. The hurlers delivered a classic pitcher's duel that left the contest hanging in the balance until an unforgettable eighth inning.

Tony Peña opened the frame with a double to right-center. Amaro replaced him on the basepaths. Then Lofton put on a clinic and, in a short sequence, demonstrated the value of elite speed.

Lofton bunted to the right of the pitcher's mound and beat it out for a single. Amaro advanced to third on the play. On the next pitch, the first offering to Omar Vizquel, Lofton swiped second base. Two pitches later, Johnson's heater caromed off the mitt of catcher Dan Wilson and trickled past the visitors' on-deck circle.

Amaro jogged home with ease. Lofton dashed to third, but never hesitated or slowed down. He rounded the bag and bolted to the plate. The Mariners didn't anticipate his aggressiveness. Johnson was ill-prepared to cover home. Wilson couldn't retrieve the ball in a swift enough manner. Lofton scored from second on a passed ball. The Indians plated a pair of critical, late-inning runs without a swing of the bat. The passed ball turned the Indians' 1–0 edge into a seemingly insurmountable 3–0 advantage.

"You always advance with an aggressive turn just in case the guy bobbles it," Lofton said. "Sometimes guys kick a ball or something, you never know. But if you're lollygagging just to advance to one base, you can never advance that way. Once I looked up and Randy had his back turned and Dan Wilson was moping with his head down, I was like, 'Oh, shoot.' I just kept going. It's just instincts, reaction."

Not only did Lofton never slow down while rounding third base, he also never pumped his brakes after he crossed the plate. The visitors' dugout at the Kingdome was split into two halves, separated by an opening that led into a large space that fed into the clubhouse. In the large space sat batting tees and a cage. Lofton's dash took him through the opening and down toward the dugout. There he ran into traveling secretary Mike Seghi and vice president of public relations Bob DiBiasio, who pushed him back into the swarm of players who had followed him.

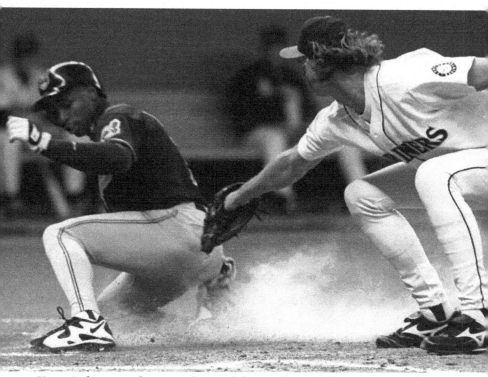

Kenny Lofton scores from second around the tag of Randy Johnson on a passed ball as the Indians secured a win in the 1995 ALCS and advanced to the World Series.

"We weren't afraid of doing anything," Lofton said. "I think that right there showed how aggressive we were throughout. We didn't take anything for granted."

After Vizquel lined out to left, Carlos Baerga tacked on one, final run with a solo home run. Cleveland captured a 4–0 victory and moved on to the Fall Classic to face the Atlanta Braves.

"I can see it in my mind like it was yesterday, Kenny Lofton dashing home from second base in the Kingdome," said radio announcer Tom Hamilton. "You knew then that they were going to win the World Series. First off, nobody scores from second on a passed ball. To do it against Randy Johnson—he didn't like Kenny

Lofton anyway and Kenny didn't like Randy Johnson—it was just poetic justice.

"You remember those kinds of moments."

35 The Dark Ages

From 1960 to 1993, the Indians finished better than fourth place just once—a third-place showing in 1968. They became the league punching bag, a perennial loser that played before sparse crowds at Cleveland Municipal Stadium.

So when Gabe Paul took charge of the front office, he fixated on adding star power to the roster. It did not always work. In fact, it did not ever work.

"He tried to make a trade for a name that people could latch on to," said Bob DiBiasio, Guardians senior vice president of public affairs, "whether it was Joe Carter, bringing Rocky Colavito back, getting Julio Franco, making blockbuster trades at the winter meetings, anything just to get people fired up and going."

It wasn't just Paul's follies, though. The Indians made a litany of poor signings and trades during the nearly four decades of dismal baseball.

After Wayne Garland posted a 20–7 record and 2.67 ERA for the Baltimore Orioles in 1976, the Indians signed the 26-year-old to a 10-year, $2.3 million contract. He could not believe a team valued him at that going rate, but he was not going to turn down the money. Garland went 13–19 with a 3.60 ERA and totaled 282⅔ innings in his first season with Cleveland. Then, he tore his rotator cuff. He won only 15 games over the next four seasons and

Mired in Mediocrity

The Indians were an average or below-average team for nearly 35 years, with a few extremely miserable seasons mixed in. Here are the club's five best and five worst season records from the dark period of 1960–93.

Five best:
87–75, 1965 (fifth place)
86–75, 1968 (third place)
84–78, 1986 (fifth place)
81–78, 1976 (fourth place)
52–51, 1981 (sixth place)

Five worst:
57–105, 1991 (last place)
60–102, 1985 (last place)
60–102, 1971 (last place)
61–101, 1987 (last place)
62–99, 1969 (last place)

the Indians released him after the 1981 campaign, halfway into his decade-long deal.

Dennis Eckersley won 14 games for the Indians as a 22-year-old in 1977. Then the club traded him to the Boston Red Sox for Ted Cox (batted .224 with five home runs in two seasons with Cleveland), Bo Diaz (batted .254 with 12 home runs in four seasons with Cleveland), Mike Paxton (won 20 games with a 4.97 ERA in three seasons with Cleveland), and Rick Wise (lost a league-high 19 games in his first of two seasons with Cleveland). Eckersley won 20 games with Boston in 1978, when he finished fourth in balloting for the American League Cy Young Award. He went on to become one of baseball's most celebrated pitchers, excelling both as a starter and a closer.

The team acquired hurler Gaylord Perry prior to the 1972 season. The spitballer captured the American League Cy Young Award in his first season in Cleveland. He spent three-plus years with the Tribe before the club dealt him to Texas. He was 36 years old at the time, but he proved he had plenty left in the tank. He tallied 63 wins over the next 3½ years and added more hardware to his mantle with the 1978 National League Cy Young Award. The three pitchers the Indians acquired in exchange for Perry combined for a 114–126 record during their tenures in Cleveland.

The Indians traded away 1971 American League Rookie of the Year Chris Chambliss in 1974. He blossomed into a cornerstone first baseman for the New York Yankees and Atlanta Braves. They dealt third baseman Graig Nettles to the Yankees in 1972. He was a steady force in New York's lineup for more than a decade, as he became a six-time All-Star. Following his trade to Texas in 1978, third baseman Buddy Bell won six Gold Glove awards and made four All-Star teams.

36 Manny Being Manny

Manny Ramirez's second career big league game provided the perfect foreshadowing for the rest of his career. In that contest in a mostly deserted Yankee Stadium on September 3, 1993, Ramirez flashed both his hitting potential and his, well, aloofness.

In the second inning, Ramirez struck a rising heater from Melido Perez toward the blue wall in left field. The ball took one bounce off the warning track and disappeared into the seats. Ramirez trotted around first base and cruised toward second. After all, he had hit a ground-rule double, his first major league hit. But he thought he had socked a home run. So he glided past second base and continued without hesitation on to third. Once he reached third, his base coach, Jeff Newman, directed him back to second. His teammates in the visitors' dugout laughed. Carlos Baerga stuck his hands out to make a "stop" signal. Candy Maldonado held up two fingers. Sandy Alomar Jr. convulsed with laughter.

Four innings later, Ramirez redeemed himself. Before a contingent of about 100 family members and friends, Ramirez, who attended high school in Manhattan, deposited a Perez offering into the left-field stands. This one did not one-hop its way into the seats. Ramirez tacked on another home run in the eighth inning to finish his second career game 3-for-4 with three extra-base hits, two home runs, and three RBIs.

"He was a hitting savant," said Dan O'Dowd, a longtime Cleveland front office executive.

"He was a professor at MIT in the batter's box," said former Cleveland general manager John Hart, "and a freshman at a junior college on the bases and in the outfield."

In 1991, Cleveland scouting director Mickey White discovered the shy kid with the mesmerizing swing just across the Harlem River. White hailed from Pittsburgh, and he vowed he would never pass up the chance to draft the next Roberto Clemente. He was right about Ramirez, who quickly developed into an offensive cornerstone in the center of some historically proficient Indians lineups.

And the tales of Manny being Manny…oh, they were plentiful. No one truly understood his quirks, but it didn't matter. He was Manny. Erratic and unpredictable, but harmless and lovable. A monster at the plate and a mystery anywhere else. Always aiming to spark laughter, but never willing to reveal whether he was in on the joke.

If a player were missing a piece of equipment or an article of clothing, he would dart directly to Ramirez's locker, a graveyard of teammates' possessions. During batting practice, he once donned the bullpen catcher's pants, which were five sizes too big and nearly swallowed him whole. No layer was off-limits. Closer José Mesa asked clubhouse attendants to boot Ramirez to the opposite end of the room so his gear wouldn't disappear.

"Guys would be looking for their underwear and Manny would be wearing it," said pitching coach Mark Wiley.

When Travis Fryman couldn't find his bat one day, he peered at the scoreboard to view the count on Ramirez, who was batting ahead of him in the order. Fryman was supposed to be on-deck. He was frantic. And then he noticed his bat, cocked above Ramirez's right shoulder. Ramirez ripped a double off the left-field wall. Even though he used them to tatter baseballs, bats were no sacred treasure to Ramirez. In one game, he "borrowed" four different bats from four different teammates and recorded four hits. In another, he slugged a home run with a broken bat—broken before he carried it with him to the plate. He shrugged when a reporter asked why he didn't select a stick that was fully intact.

He neglected to deposit his paychecks. He conveniently skirted on team dinner tabs. He'd forget to bring his luggage on road trips. He once was pulled over for an illegal U-turn moments after he pulled away from an officer who had just cited him for speeding. He thought it was his teammate Chad Ogea, not O.J. Simpson, riding in the infamous white Bronco on June 17, 1994.

Ramirez finished second in balloting for American League Rookie of the Year in 1994. In his first full season in 1995, he hit .308 with 31 home runs and 107 RBIs. He produced a similar season in 1996, batted .328 in '97, and totaled 45 home runs and 145 RBIs in 1998, including a two-game stretch in which he belted five home runs. In 1999, he hit .333 with 44 home runs and 165 RBIs, the most by any player since Jimmie Foxx in 1938. He proved clutch in the postseason, as well, as he tallied 13 home runs in 52 postseason games with Cleveland.

"I wasn't looking to be the best right-handed hitter ever," Ramirez said. "I was just playing and competing and knowing that if I fell, I could get up."

He collected Silver Slugger awards and All-Star Game nods and Man of the Year honors from the Cleveland chapter of the Baseball Writers' Association of America. But he never cared to take home his hardware, instead encouraging his teammates to pick up his awards or pawning them off on the team psychologist or clubhouse attendants.

"You know how many Player of the Month awards Manny won? Silver Sluggers?" Baerga asked. "I don't think there's a single picture of Manny grabbing a trophy at the ballpark."

As the 2000 campaign wore on, the realization set in that Ramirez, an impending free agent, might land a more lucrative contract elsewhere. In his final at-bat of the season, he crushed a home run off the green wall that bordered the picnic area beyond the center-field fence. As soon as his bat made contact with the thigh-high fastball from Toronto hurler John Frascatore, Ramirez dropped his lumber at home plate and, before he commenced his home run trot, he leisurely walked a few steps as he watched the ball sail out of the stadium. The fans stood and applauded the slugger. They held up signs pleading him to stay and begging ownership to pay him. Slider, the team's furry pink mascot, stood atop the home dugout and bowed to him as he retreated to the bench. Ramirez said that's his fondest memory from his time in Cleveland.

"We were the best offensive team in baseball for eight or nine years," Hart said, "and as great as Thome was, probably one of the best power hitters, Albert Belle, great power hitter, Robbie Alomar, Carlos Baerga, great hitters—the best hitter I've ever been around in my 50 years in baseball has been Manny Ramirez. I had Alex Rodriguez in Texas. The absolute best hitter I've ever been around is Manny. I'll go to my grave saying that."

After he posted a .351 average with 38 home runs and 122 RBIs in 2000, he signed an eight-year, $160 million pact with the Boston Red Sox, making him the sport's highest-paid player. The Indians had offered a seven-year deal worth about $119 million.

Ramirez proceeded to round out a career that was met with much critical acclaim. He continued to compile eye-popping statistics and execute bone-headed plays. He won a pair of World Series rings with the Red Sox. He endured trade rumors, made trade demands and was, at one point, traded. He was slapped with suspensions for testing positive for banned substances. He won a batting crown, a home run crown, an RBI title and made 12 All-Star teams. Even after his power display and his goof in his second career game, who could have seen it all coming?

"I think because people looked at him as kind of goofy at times," O'Dowd said, "that gets lost in the fact of how serious he was about his craft and becoming the best. Manny told me right to my face: 'I want to be the best hitter that's ever played this game.'"

37 Watch *Major League*

Hank Peters, the Indians' president, called Bob DiBiasio into his office one afternoon in 1988. On Peters' desk sat the script to a potential movie, *Major League*. Peters handed the document to DiBiasio, the team's public relations director, and said, "Here. For some reason, MLB is allowing Hollywood to do a movie on us. Here it is. Go for it. You're in charge."

DiBiasio had script approval. He presented the idea to the team.

"Our players had a lot of fun with it," DiBiasio said. "They loved it."

Some of the players, including knuckleballer Tom Candiotti, attended the premiere. Actors Charlie Sheen and Tom Berenger spent time with the club at Cleveland Municipal Stadium. Sheen and Mel Hall went out for a night in Cleveland.

"Who knows what *they* ended up doing," DiBiasio said.

The movie was officially released on April 7, 1989. Much of the film was actually shot in Milwaukee, but it was based on the woeful (both fictional and factual) Cleveland Indians, who needed a winning season to attract fans to the ballpark and prevent the team owner from relocating the franchise to Miami. A collection of goofy misfits starts the season slowly, but bands together and makes a run at the American League pennant.

There's pitcher Ricky Vaughn, played by Sheen, who boasts a blazing fastball but struggles to control it. Outfielder Pedro Cerrano, played by Dennis Haysbert, possesses a powerful swing but is constantly overmatched by curveballs, so he turns to voodoo to help his chances at the plate. Third baseman Roger Dorn, played by Corbin Bernsen, is a diva who is always concerned with his next contract. Catcher Jake Taylor, played by Berenger, has the knees of an 80-year-old and focuses on his ex-girlfriend. Hurler Eddie Harris, played by Chelcie Ross, has lost so much luster on his pitches that he resorts to doctoring the baseball. Center fielder Willie "Mays" Hayes, played by Wesley Snipes, flashes blistering speed on the base paths but can only hit pop-ups.

The group of oddballs ties the New York Yankees for first in the American League East, so the two clubs square off in a one-game playoff to decide the champion. Vaughn shuts down the Yankees in the top of the ninth with the score tied and Hayes scores from second on Taylor's bunt single in the bottom of the frame to win the game.

The movie grossed $50 million, debuted at No. 1 at the box office, and gave the real Indians their place in Hollywood lore. Bernsen said he signs Dorn jerseys all the time and is asked regularly if there will ever be another *Major League* film.

38 The First Taste of Victory

The fate of the 1920 World Series changed once Elmer Smith took a powerful hack in the first inning of Game 5. Charlie Jamieson, Bill Wambsganss, and Tris Speaker had all singled to load the bases. Smith then uncorked the first-ever World Series grand slam over the right-field fence at League Park, referred to at the time as Dunn Field.

Suddenly the Indians, who had trailed 2–1 in the series to the Brooklyn Robins, had a comfortable lead and the inside track at a 3–2 series advantage. The Indians forged ahead for an 8–1 victory in Game 5, a contest that oozed with baseball lore. In addition to Smith's feat, Wambsganss etched his name into the sport's history books.

Wambsganss snagged a line drive off the bat of Brooklyn pitcher Clarence Mitchell in the fifth inning. The runners on first and second base had taken off for their next destination, allowing Wambsganss to complete an unassisted triple play, the second ever recorded and the first in the postseason.

Jim Bagby, who set a franchise record with 31 wins during the regular season, pitched nine innings for the win and contributed a three-run home run. The Indians blanked Brooklyn in Games 6 and 7. Duster Mails tossed a three-hit shutout in Game 6 and Stan Coveleski clinched the series with a five-hit shutout in Game 7.

The Cleveland Press displayed a headline of "All Over—We win" with a subhead of "Atta boy, Tris" (a commendation of player/manager Speaker) in the following day's newspaper. A crowd of 200,000 lined Euclid Avenue to applaud the team in a victory parade.

Speaker once said, "The American boy starts swinging a bat about as soon as he can lift one." He would know. He burst onto the big-league scene as a 19-year-old in 1907. He batted .388 for the Indians in 1920 and, during the World Series, he hit .320 and scored six runs. In 11 seasons with Cleveland, Speaker batted .354 with a .444 on-base percentage. He led the league in doubles six times, batting average once and on-base percentage three times.

Some say it may never have happened if not for the Black Sox Scandal. Chicago—in contention with Cleveland for the American League pennant—had three games to play in 1920 when it was revealed that eight players had thrown the 1919 World Series, which the White Sox dropped to the Cincinnati Reds. The seven players still remaining on the team were suspended for the final three games in 1920. The White Sox lost two of the three and the Indians finished with a two-game cushion in the standings at the end of the regular season.

39 Handsome Lou

Bob Feller referred to Lou Boudreau as the Indians' on-field leader, even as a 21-year-old shortstop in his rookie season. Feller also frequently commended his teammate for his boyish looks. Still, Boudreau, who played for the franchise from 1938 to 1950 and managed the team from 1942 to 1950, commanded the respect of a team littered with veterans. It was not always easy. Older players did not always give in. Eventually, though, Boudreau and the Indians were rewarded for their efforts. The kid from Illinois guided the team to a World Series title in 1948.

When the Indians made the 24-year-old Boudreau a player/ manager prior to the 1942 season, they supported him with a staff of experienced coaches. That did not stop the skeptics. Other players had auditioned for the position and were less than pleased to learn a kid with only two full major league seasons under his belt received the job. Boudreau met resistance when making pitching changes. He was badmouthed by teammates. He helped assimilate Larry Doby, the first African American player in the American League, into the Indians' clubhouse, where not all teammates were accepting. He clashed with owner Bill Veeck. He was second-guessed by teammates, media and upper management. And he had to figure out how to balance his own responsibilities on the diamond with those that included overseeing the rest of the team.

The Indians were an average team under Boudreau from 1942 to 1947. Boudreau himself was an All-Star from 1940–44 and again in 1947 and '48. He finished in the top 10 in balloting for American League Most Valuable Player in all but one season from 1940–48. He led the league in doubles three times and in batting average once. He developed a reputation as one of the slickest fielding shortstops in baseball.

Most Wins by a Cleveland Manager

Terry Francona: 921
Lou Boudreau: 728
Mike Hargrove: 721
Tris Speaker: 617
Al Lopez: 570
Eric Wedge: 561
Roger Peckinpaugh: 490
Nap Lajoie: 377
Lee Fohl: 327
Pat Corrales: 280

In 1948, the Indians battled with the New York Yankees and Boston Red Sox throughout the summer for American League supremacy. Cleveland fell four games off the pace in mid-September before rallying for 11 wins in 12 games to take a slight lead. Boudreau submitted the most productive season of his career. He batted .355 with a .453 on-base percentage, 34 doubles, 18 home runs, and 106 RBIs. He walked 98 times and struck out on only nine occasions. His efforts earned him the MVP award and the Indians topped the Red Sox in a one-game playoff to advance to the World Series against the Boston Braves, which Cleveland claimed in six games.

Boudreau played for and managed the Indians for two more years before wrapping up his career with the Red Sox. He ended his 15-year playing career with a .295 lifetime average. He racked up 1,162 wins as a manager, with a .487 winning percentage in 16 seasons in charge. He was inducted into the Baseball Hall of Fame in 1970.

Upon his induction, Commissioner Bowie Kuhn said: "There are hitters in the Hall of Fame with higher batting averages, but I do not believe there is in the Hall of Fame a baseball man who brought more use of intellect and advocation of mind to the game than Lou Boudreau."

40 Hold Up

It might not have made a difference. After all, the Red Sox surged to an 11–2 victory and advanced to the World Series, a clash with the Colorado Rockies that ended in four games.

It probably will never be forgotten, though.

Would Kenny Lofton have scored? Would the momentum have turned the tide in the decisive game? Would the Indians have bested Colorado in the Fall Classic as handily as Boston did?

The Indians grabbed a commanding 3–1 series lead in the 2007 American League Championship Series, thanks to strong starting pitching by Jake Westbrook and Paul Byrd and a slew of timely hitting. Josh Beckett pitched Boston to a Game 5 victory at Jacobs Field with eight dominant innings and 11 strikeouts.

The series shifted back to Fenway Park for Game 6, a contest in which the Red Sox breezed to a lopsided win. That set the table for Game 7, with Cleveland reeling and the Red Sox salivating about the thought of a second World Series appearance in a four-year span after finally ending their 86-year title drought in 2004. Instead, it's Cleveland saddled with the league's longest drought.

Boston staked claim to a 3–2 lead as the teams reached the seventh inning. Hideki Okajima retired Jhonny Peralta on a fly out to right field. Kenny Lofton reached first and advanced to second on an error. Franklin Gutierrez then roped a base hit over the third-base bag. The baseball caromed off the green wall that juts out in foul territory in shallow left field. As Manny Ramirez trotted in to corral the loose ball, Lofton scurried around the third-base bag.

But there stood third base coach Joel Skinner, both of his arms raised, his body sending a forceful message to Lofton, instructing the speedster to stop in his tracks.

Lofton slammed on the brakes and retreated to third base. Skinner shook Lofton's hand, patted him on the back with his left hand and pointed to where the ball had ricocheted as he explained his reasoning for holding him.

Initially, Skinner had waved Lofton toward home, his left arm rapidly spiraling like a pinwheel. As Lofton approached the base, with Ramirez bearing down on the stray baseball, Skinner changed his mind. At the moment Lofton rounded third base, Ramirez was four steps shy of the ball. He eventually scooped it up with his bare hand and tossed it into the infield. By then, however, Lofton had been denied a chance to score.

The give and take between announcers Joe Buck and Tim McCarver conveyed the element of surprise about Lofton being held at third.

Buck: "Lofton will round third. He's STOPPED. And it's first and third, one out."

McCarver: "What is that all about?.... There is no way that Manny, in my judgment—and Joe, evidently in yours—that he even would have had a play. He'd probably go to second base with the ball."

Sing Along

The Indians stood one win away from a ticket to the World Series. They had one game remaining at Jacobs Field. If the Boston Red Sox captured Game 5 of the 2007 American League Championship Series, the series would shift back to Fenway Park.

So the Indians pulled out all of the stops for Game 5 in an attempt to deliver their fans a postseason series victory at home. It was all unintentional, of course. Or so the Indians claimed.

Singer Taylor Swift was slated to sing the National Anthem prior to Game 5 but backed out. The Indians replaced her with country singer Danielle Peck. Shortly after the announcement of the musical revision, the Indians learned Peck was the ex-girlfriend of Red Sox pitcher Josh Beckett, who just so happened to be Boston's starter for Game 5.

Peck grew up in Coshocton, Ohio, about a two-hour drive from the Indians' ballpark. She was a Cleveland fan. And she watched her ex-boyfriend pitch a gem. Beckett tallied 11 strikeouts in eight innings, as the Red Sox recorded a 7–1 triumph. They would proceed to win the remaining games of the series and sweep the Colorado Rockies in the Fall Classic.

The Indians pleaded ignorance with regards to Beckett and Peck's prior relationship. Beckett thanked the Indians for flying a friend to the game so she could watch his performance free of charge.

On the first pitch of the ensuing at-bat, Casey Blake grounded into an inning-ending, momentum-squashing, series-altering double play.

"It's tough to read if it's ricocheting back to the shortstop or to left-center," manager Eric Wedge said after the game. "I think it was just a tough read for [Skinner]."

Skinner never received publicized blame from anyone on the Indians or anyone involved with that game, though many agree Lofton would have undoubtedly scored.

"I think it gets overblown," said Mark Shapiro, then the club's general manager. "You could argue Kenny could see that on his own or know the ballpark. There's not any one player or one moment that is single-handedly responsible for us winning or losing."

The Red Sox eventually tagged reliever Rafael Betancourt for seven runs (six earned) to remove any doubt from the outcome.

Terry Francona served as Boston's manager for that enthralling seven-game series. In October 2012, he took over the reins as the Indians' skipper. He was once asked about Skinner's decision.

"Being a third-base coach in Boston is probably the most unfair job in the world," Francona said, "because you're making a split-second decision, and you're the only one in the ballpark who can't see the whole field, because you get that blind spot down the left-field line, and the ball caroms off the wall like it did in that instance—I think what you have to hope for is you have to make that split-second decision. What we used to tell our runners was, 'Keep your head up, like on a swivel, so you can be your own coach.' Because that happens more often than people realize.... If the runner keeps his head up, then he can score on his own and you don't run into that problem, because the third-base coach is in a real bind there."

That play doesn't claw at Shapiro any longer, but the series as a whole still stings.

"Certain things are less and less over time. That one is more and more," Shapiro said. "They were the best team in baseball, but we had them on the ropes. We had them down 3–1 and we had CC [Sabathia], Fausto [Carmona], and Westbrook pitching and we couldn't get a win. You kind of felt like once we went back into their place, anything could happen. That one is tough to get past. Getting in the World Series would have been great, and in these jobs, you don't spend a ton of time dwelling on it, but that one doesn't get easy to get past."

41 Visit League Park

It originally opened its doors on May 1, 1891, a day in which Cy Young pitched the Cleveland Spiders to a 12–3 victory against the Cincinnati Reds. (Surely you remember some of Young's teammates from that season, such as Cupid Childs, Spud Johnson and Patsy Tebeau.) It hosted the Indians' only World Series-clinching win at home in 1920, the same year in which second baseman Bill Wambsganss registered the first Fall Classic unassisted triple play and Elmer Smith slugged the first Fall Classic grand slam. It served as the site for Babe Ruth's 500th home run, a towering shot to right field—a fence not far from home plate, but one that was tall, menacing, and not so easy to clear. It hosted the Cleveland Buckeyes of the Negro League, who won the organization's World Series in 1945.

League Park, home to the Indians from 1901–46, played host to plenty of baseball history. It was where Addie Joss tossed his perfect game against the Chicago White Sox in 1908. It was where 17-year-old Bob Feller made his first major league start, a dazzling 15-strikeout performance against the St. Louis Browns.

The Indians, though, eventually moved to Cleveland Municipal Stadium, leaving behind the venue in an area that succumbed to socioeconomic hardship. The building itself deteriorated over time, becoming a shell of its former showy self. The Hough neighborhood, where it was situated, transitioned into a poverty-stricken community.

An article in *The Plain Dealer* on May 2, 1891, the day after the original debut of League Park, described it as "a magnificent opening in Cleveland—there never was one like it and there never may be again."

There was.

In August 2014, the city unveiled a refurbished League Park, at the same location, the corner of E. 66ᵗʰ Street and Lexington Avenue. The project, spearheaded for years by councilwoman Fannie M. Lewis, required $6.3 million in renovations. Artificial turf spans the field. A new building houses bathrooms and concessions and includes the park's original dugout steps. An original wall displays artwork of some of the legends who played at the stadium. There is a heritage museum and a statue of Lewis, who passed away before her vision was completed. In addition to serving as a beacon of Cleveland baseball history, the site hosts local teams' games and recreational contests.

On the afternoon of the grand re-opening, a sun-splashed summer day, former Indians sluggers Andre Thornton and Travis Hafner represented the franchise before a large gathering of fans and baseball heads. Hafner took part in a home run derby contest.

"Baseball is a game that spans generations and we are a city that has a historic franchise and that has had three stadiums," team president Mark Shapiro said at the grand reopening. "To stand in the exact spot where the first professional and Major League Baseball was played in the city of Cleveland, to know that little kids will be able to play on this field that has been so incredibly restored and pristine in a neighborhood that I think will just really cherish it and take care of it—that historic link of baseball is just incredible."

42 Center of the Baseball Universe

A baseball icon, and former Indians slugger, tossed out the first pitch. Another Indians slugger swatted the most important pitch of the night to decide the entire event. The 1997 All-Star Game, played at Jacobs Field in the heart of downtown Cleveland in front of a sold-out crowd that had long desired the spotlight, showcased the best of Cleveland baseball.

It started with the annual Home Run Derby, an event won by Yankees slugger Tino Martinez. Cleveland first baseman Jim Thome participated but failed to swat any pitches over the fence.

Country singer LeAnn Rimes performed the National Anthem prior to the 68th edition of the Midsummer Classic. Earlier in the year, the 14-year-old won Grammy Awards for Best New Artist and Best Female Country Vocal Performance.

Five months earlier, Cleveland hosted the NBA All-Star Game at Gund Arena, next door to Jacobs Field. The Eastern Conference walked away victorious, as Cavaliers guard Terrell Brandon contributed 10 points and eight assists. Another hometown star helped his team in a national exhibition in the MLB contest.

But first, the game had plenty of antics. In the second inning, Mariners southpaw Randy Johnson sailed a pitch high above the head of Rockies slugger Larry Walker, who was known to fear the 6-foot-10 hurler. The baseball was so off the mark—and intentionally so—that it hit the backstop. Colorado's right fielder dropped to one knee, paused for a moment of contemplation as his life seemingly flashed before his eyes, stretched out his back, stood back up, flipped his helmet around backward, switched to the opposite side of the batter's box, and dug in to hit righty against the flamethrower. The sequence was reminiscent of a similar altercation between Johnson and Phillies first baseman John Kruk in the 1993 All-Star Game. After another fastball out of the zone—though not nearly as astray as the first offering—Walker retreated to the other side of the plate and flipped his helmet forward. He eventually drew a walk.

The American League grabbed a 1–0 lead in the second inning when Seattle's Edgar Martinez clubbed a leadoff home run off of Braves right-hander Greg Maddux. The National League responded in the top of the seventh, as Atlanta catcher Javy Lopez deposited a pitch from Kansas City lefty Jose Rosado over the wall. Then, the hometown hero was anointed.

Yankees outfielder Bernie Williams drew a one-out walk in the seventh and advanced to second on a wild pitch with two outs. Indians catcher Sandy Alomar Jr. then struck a pitch over the outside part of the plate from San Francisco hurler Shawn Estes. The ball landed in the left-field bleachers as the Jacobs Field crowd went into a frenzy. The two-run shot provided the American League with a 3–1 advantage, one it would not relinquish. New York closer Mariano Rivera shut the door in the ninth inning, as Florida's Moises Alou lined out to Minnesota second baseman Chuck Knoblauch to end the game.

Cleveland has hosted the All-Star Game on six occasions, more often than any other city: 1935, 1954, 1963, 1981, 1997 and, most recently, in 2019. After the '97 affair, Alomar delivered a message to the fans.

"They've been hungry for this situation, for the All-Star Game," Alomar said on the national broadcast. "They've been talking about this the whole year. This is a gift from God. The whole year, they've been outstanding."

100 Things Guardians Fans Should Know & Do Before They Die

The Indians hosted the 1981 All-Star Game at Cleveland Stadium on August 9. The exhibition had been pushed back because of a players' strike, which forced the cancellation of nearly two months of the season.

Len Barker, the Indians' ace, had compiled a 5–3 record and 2.08 ERA prior to the All-Star break. He tallied seven complete games (including two shutouts) in his 10 starts. On May 15, Barker threw the eighth perfect game in Major League Baseball's modern era. He blanked the Blue Jays in a 3–0 win and registered 11 strikeouts.

Given Barker's early-season success, the Indians believed the right-hander deserved to start for the American League in front of his home crowd. Instead, Detroit's Jack Morris, who posted a 9–3 record and 2.56 ERA in 13 first-half starts, was tabbed to take the mound first. Morris tossed a pair of scoreless innings, as he limited the National League to two hits and one walk. Barker then took over and retired all six batters he faced. Pete Rose, Dave Concepcion, Dave Parker, Mike Schmidt, George Foster, and Andre Dawson—who combined for 58 career All-Star Game appearances—all made outs against Barker.

The club hosted the festivities again in 2019, and a slew of former Cleveland players and coaches returned for the events, including Thome, Kenny Lofton, Omar Vizquel, Carlos Baerga and Charlie Manuel. Carlos Santana, in a homecoming season and his lone All-Star campaign, participated in the Home Run Derby, but fell short against eventual champion Pete Alonso, who swatted pitches from his friend, Cleveland native Derek Morgan.

Shane Bieber—who five years earlier walked on at UC Santa Barbara, who only snagged a roster spot because Tyler Mahle opted to sign with the Reds and forgo college, who wasn't named an All-Star until a few days before the exhibition, who thought the reason manager Terry Francona summoned him to his office was to tell him he was being optioned to Triple A—pitched the fifth inning for the American League. He struck out Ketel Marte, Willson Contreras and Ronald Acuña Jr. in succession. In front of his home crowd, in his first full big-league season, he captured All-Star Game MVP honors.

"I didn't know what to think," Bieber said. "I kind of lost all feeling in my body."

But the most moving moment of the week came after the fifth inning, when Carlos Carrasco's All-Star teammates stood beside him, holding up signs that read "I stand up for 'Cookie'" to show support of his leukemia battle during the annual Stand Up 2 Cancer showcase. Carrasco's placard simply read, "I stand."

"Letting him know, 'Cookie, we're all right next to you, brother,'" Francisco Lindor said. "'We stand up for you. We're all right next to you. You're a family member. We love you.'"

43 Meet Slider, Guardians Mascot

As Carlos Baerga socked Bob Wells' offering into left field for a single, a strange creature hobbled along the warning track in right-center. Slider, the Indians' furry, fuchsia—umm, well, what species is he exactly?—mascot with a bushy yellow beak and eyebrows instantly gained nationwide recognition. During Game 4 of the 1995 American League Championship Series against the Seattle Mariners, the tubby critter tumbled off the outfield wall while dancing, plummeting to the field below.

"Meanwhile, the umpires don't see it. Slider is on the field," announcer Bob Costas said on the national telecast, expressing disbelief. "The mascot fell out of the stands and he is hobbling toward the bullpen."

Slider, the Indians' fuchsia-colored, furry mascot, dances on the dugout.
(AP Images)

Slider entered the open bullpen door and immediately dropped to the ground, writhing in pain in the bullpen dirt. It had been a rainy day in Cleveland and the top of the wall was slick. Slider, the Indians' mascot since 1990, fell victim to the conditions. Indians personnel, including relief pitcher Julian Tavarez, surrounded the character—and the man playing him, Dan Kilday, who actually did suffer injury.

"What if Baerga had hit a ball to right-center field?" Costas wondered aloud. "The mascot is on the field and you've got a couple of outfielders converging on the ball. How bizarre would that have been?"

Kilday blew out his right knee, and when he returned to the costume the next day with a cast on his real leg, he added a pair of crutches and some bandages to Slider's get-up. He received a standing ovation when he entered Jacobs Field prior to Game 5.

Despite that snafu, Slider has been a steady face at Indians home games. He burst onto the scene at Cleveland Municipal Stadium, then a pink body in a sea of mostly empty seats. The team then shifted to Jacobs Field, it started winning and Slider became an integral part of the entertainment.

He became the fourth Major League Baseball mascot to be elected to the Mascot Hall of Fame when he was inducted on September 29, 2008, joining his counterparts the Phillie Phanatic, Mr. Met, and the San Diego Chicken.

44 K-Love

He was feisty on the diamond, always aggressive on the base paths, and undeterred in the outfield. He was feisty away from the field, never afraid to speak his mind or offer his opinion, even when unsolicited.

Kenny Lofton was a core piece of the Indians glory teams in the '90s. He was the table-setter at the top of the lineup, a speedy center fielder who regularly flashed his wheels. He was a part of the purge of personalities prior to the 1997 campaign, as GM John Hart traded him and reliever Alan Embree to the Atlanta Braves for David Justice and Marquis Grissom. For one year, Lofton felt out of place. He had spent five statistically sound seasons with Cleveland. He didn't hold a grudge, though. He understood the business. And after the Indians fell one scoreless frame shy of a

World Series title in '97, he re-signed with the organization that gave him his chance to shine.

His honesty was brutal, yet sometimes refreshing and commendable. Lofton never buried his true beliefs. After closer Chris Perez challenged fans for not filling the seats of Progressive Field in 2012, Lofton objected and chimed in with a perspective about what it took to fuel 455 sellouts from 1995 to 2001. When the Indians qualified for the 2013 American League Wild Card Game, which they lost to the Tampa Bay Rays, Lofton contended that they had not truly made the playoffs. Lofton argued that a postseason series requires more than just one game. Nick Swisher took issue with Lofton's comments and the two engaged in a face-to-face dispute about how to fairly measure the Indians' campaign.

Ask Lofton about the strike zone during the 1995 World Series or how he was unfairly booted from the Hall of Fame ballot after only one year and he'll deliver a convincing rant he's rehearsed hundreds of times.

The Indians were October regulars during Lofton's tenure in Cleveland. He was part of five of their six American League Central championships from 1995 to 2001. When he returned via midseason trade in 2007, he helped the team to a division crown for the first time since he departed six years earlier. With the Indians, Lofton made five American League All-Star teams. He led the league in stolen bases for five consecutive seasons and his 452 steals rank first in franchise history.

"In a sport of professional athletes, where they're all the best at what they do, he was head and shoulders above the rest in pure athleticism," said former team president Mark Shapiro. "That athleticism, combined with his competitiveness, fueled incredible performance."

Lofton attended the University of Arizona on a basketball scholarship. He teamed with eventual NBA stars Steve Kerr and

Sean Elliott in guiding the Wildcats to the Final Four in 1988 and the Sweet Sixteen a year later. During his junior year, Lofton tried out for Arizona's baseball team.

When he first joined the Houston Astros' farm system, he struggled at the plate. Charlie Manuel, Lofton's hitting coach in the minors and majors with the Indians, taught him to "know thyself," and play to his strengths by utilizing his speed and instincts. By the time he stepped into the batter's box with the Indians, he wreaked havoc on opposing pitchers. He hit .310 or better each season from 1993–97. He won four Gold Glove awards. He routinely scaled the center-field wall at Jacobs Field to rob the opposition of extra-base hits or home runs.

In 1994, he finished fourth in the American League Most Valuable Player award voting, with a .349/.412/.536 slash line and a league-leading 160 hits and 60 stolen bases in only 112 games, thanks to the strike. He finished behind three sluggers entering their primes: Frank Thomas, Ken Griffey Jr. and teammate Albert Belle.

"He had a chance to be the AL MVP that year," said former Cleveland executive Dan O'Dowd. "He was simply dominating games on both sides of the ball, but no one remembers that or talks about that. I wonder if that strike didn't happen, if Kenny did win the MVP that year, if the whole Hall of Fame situation for him would have changed. He was like a human highlight film."

Lofton knew he was talented. He knew his on-field production could be considered elite. That's what made his shortcomings on the Hall of Fame ballot so disheartening. Despite finishing his career with 2,428 hits, a .299 batting average, .372 on-base percentage, 622 steals and 1,528 runs, Lofton received only 18 votes on the 2013 ballot. He failed to garner the 5 percent of votes necessary to remain on the ballot another year.

"I really got penalized," Lofton said. "I felt like I wanted a chance for people to look at my numbers and look at what I did

"Can't Beat That"

Kenny Lofton points to a Sunday afternoon in early September 2000 as the best day of his career. He can accurately recite every numeral in his stat line from the 12–11 win against the Baltimore Orioles.

The speedy center fielder finished with four hits, four runs scored, and a franchise record-tying five stolen bases. He also won the game on a walk-off home run in the 13th inning.

"Can't beat that," Lofton said.

Lofton singled and stole second in the first inning. He scored on a Jim Thome single, as he tied the American League record with a run scored in 18 consecutive games. When the statistic was displayed on the scoreboard, fans lured him out of the dugout for a curtain call.

In the third inning, Lofton singled and stole both second and third. On his swipe of third, he scored on an errant pickoff throw by Baltimore catcher Brook Fordyce to first base. He notched a bunt single and stole second again in the fourth. He reached on a fielder's choice and swiped second in the seventh. He was intentionally walked in the 11th.

With one out in the 13th, he deposited a pitch from Mike Trombley into the visitor's bullpen. He kept the bat raised in his right arm as he watched the baseball soar over the fence.

"It was my second walk-off," Lofton said. "I was pretty proud of that."

year after year after year. But now you get off the ballot your first year, it's like you're just kicked to the curb now."

Perhaps Lofton's name was overshadowed on the ballot by the presence of known or suspected users of performance-enhancing drugs. No player was elected in the 2013 class. Lofton admitted he wished he would have debuted on a different year's ballot, rather than one that included names such as Barry Bonds, Roger Clemens, Sammy Sosa, and Mark McGwire.

"The focus was not on myself and others," Lofton said. "It was only on whether they should put in cheaters."

In typical Lofton fashion, he was not shy about expressing his feelings on the topic.

"I can't be sour at the game per se," Lofton said. "I'm sour at the people who could have made certain decisions and didn't."

Nonetheless, Lofton remains one of Cleveland's most celebrated players. He was inducted into the Indians Hall of Fame in 2010.

"Kenny was a special player," said former teammate Sandy Alomar Jr. "He was an every-nighter, full of energy. He came ready to play every day."

45 The SI Jinx Strikes...Twice

Joe Carter's smile seemed natural. Cory Snyder's seemed more forced. The two sluggers stood in a makeshift batting stance, their pieces of lumber pointed toward the large Chief Wahoo logo hovering above them. "Indian Uprising," the *Sports Illustrated* cover read on April 6, 1987. "Believe it! Cleveland is the best team in the American League," the issue claimed. It projected Cleveland for 94 wins and an American League pennant.

The Indians won 84 games under manager Pat Corrales in 1986, their highest win total in nearly two decades. They had guys who hit for average in Pat Tabler, Tony Bernazard, and Julio Franco. They had a guy who hit for power in Snyder. They had guys who hit for both average and power in Carter, Brook Jacoby, and Mel Hall.

The offense performed up to expectations in 1987. Pitching is also important, though. Tom Candiotti, Phil Niekro, and Scott Bailes tied for the team lead in wins...with seven. Candiotti, a knuckleballer, finished with 18 losses and a 4.78 ERA. Niekro, a 48-year-old knuckleballer, posted a 5.89 ERA. Steve Carlton, an eventual Hall of Famer who was 42 at the time, fashioned a 5.37 ERA in 23 outings. The pitching was a disaster. The team logged a 5.28 ERA and surrendered 957 runs.

On April 18, the Indians lost 16–3 to the Baltimore Orioles to fall to 1–10. Not even two full weeks into the regular-season slate, the club had fallen 10 games back in the American League East. By the end of the dismal season, the Indians, at 61–101, sat in the division cellar, 37 games out of first place.

Corrales was canned after the team hobbled into the All-Star break with a 31–56 record. The team lost 33 games by five or more runs. It did not finish with a winning record in any month and in April, May, June, July, and September, it finished at least five games below .500.

It was not an Indian Uprising. The Indians were not the best team in the American League. Whether a result of the *Sports Illustrated* jinx or simply a severe miscalculation, the magazine cover did not prove clairvoyant. The Indians did not finish with a winning record again until 1994.

In late June 1987, *Sports Illustrated* ran a story titled "It Won't Be An Indian Summer." The author admitted that *SI*'s prognosticators were "maybe a tad off" in their projection on that year's Cleveland squad.

History repeated itself 27 years later, though without such drastic results. This time, ahead of the 2014 season, Corey Kluber and Michael Brantley graced the cover that displayed the title, "Wait Till This Year." It was a similar premise, banking on an upstart team that had learned how to win the previous year to take another leap and end the franchise's title drought. Instead, the 2014 club finished with an 85–77 record, good for third place in the AL Central.

46 Stick a Cork in It

Few pitchers are recognized more for a covert operation than for a complete game. Few pitchers are known because of their stealthy ways and not their four-seam fastball. Jason Grimsley is not a household name for bouncing around the league for nearly two decades or for winning 42 games or for leading the league in hit-by-pitches in 1996. Any familiarity with his name likely stems from his participation in one of baseball's most bizarre tales.

Albert Belle corked his bats. His teammates knew it. Opponents thought it. White Sox manager Gene Lamont was tipped off to it before a game on July 15, 1994, at Comiskey Park. So in the first inning of the tilt between the top two teams in the American League Central, Lamont approached umpire Dave Phillips and disputed the legality of Belle's lumber. Phillips stored the bat in his locker in the umpires' dressing room. Grimsley had to make his move. The pitcher had the night off anyway, so why not set out on an adventure?

Grimsley retreated to the clubhouse to survey the scene and plot his route to the umpires' room to replace Belle's bat. He described the deed as a puzzle. He stepped up onto the desk in the office of manager Mike Hargrove, removed a ceiling tile and lifted himself up into a narrow passageway. Grimsley brought a flashlight and an uncorked bat from teammate Paul Sorrento. Why not replace Belle's bat with another one of Belle's bats? All of his were corked, as Omar Vizquel would attest eight years later in his autobiography.

At one point along his dark travels, Grimsley removed a ceiling tile for what he believed was the umpires' room. It was not. A groundskeeper sat on a couch below. Grimsley tried again. His heart racing, he removed another tile. This time, he was correct.

Had anyone entered the room, Grimsley would have been in serious trouble. The door to the room had been locked and the bat was somewhat shielded in Phillips' locker. Grimsley descended onto the top of a refrigerator and lowered himself to the ground. He identified Belle's bat and switched it with Sorrento's used model, which bore the name of the first baseman. The swap could not have been more obvious. Grimsley re-entered the ceiling, made his way back to the Indians' clubhouse and spread the word with his teammates that the bats had been switched.

Upon the conclusion of the game, a 3–2 Cleveland victory, the umpires quickly noticed the misconduct. Phillips was certain someone had broken in. White Sox owner Jerry Reinsdorf referred to the exchange as a "serious crime." Commissioner Bud Selig asserted that the league, which immediately launched an investigation, would "get to the bottom of this."

The league eventually worked out an agreement with the Indians. The intruder would not be sentenced if the team provided Belle's original bat to the American League office. The team complied. Belle received a 10-game suspension, which, after an appeal, was whittled down to seven games. Grimsley's identity remained a secret until he revealed his journey through the bowels of the ballpark some five years later.

The End of an Era

Mark Shapiro knew months in advance that he would be taking over as the Indians' general manager in November 2001. He also knew that his reign as the team's chief roster decision-maker would likely begin with some unpopular choices, ones that signaled an end to the franchise's most successful era, ones he felt were necessary if the organization was to ever again reach a similar standard.

Shapiro informed his bosses, owner Larry Dolan and his son, Paul, the team president, that a shift in strategy was required. He warned them of the impending seismic transition. The Indians' near-decade of talent accumulation—executed, after years of deft drafting and development, through spending on the free-agent market and trading minor league prospects for proven performers—left the farm system barren.

"I couldn't necessarily chart a clear path back," Shapiro said.

A month after his promotion to the GM position became official, the Indians traded perennial All-Star second baseman Roberto Alomar to the Mets. In return, Cleveland acquired prospects Alex Escobar, Billy Traber, and Earl Snyder; pitcher Jerrod Riggan, and veteran outfielder Matt Lawton. Six days later, as an accompanying move, the club signed 31-year-old infielder Ricky Gutierrez to a multi-year contract to replace Alomar. Those transactions, to Shapiro, weren't completed with enough commitment. If the Indians were going to dive head-first into a rebuilding plan, they needed to part with veterans and stockpile promising young talent.

"That was a flawed execution because it was in the middle," Shapiro said.

He corrected that so-called "flawed execution" with a heist of the Montreal Expos in an exchange that included ace pitcher Bartolo Colon.

"Colon was kind of the flip of the switch," Shapiro said, "like, 'Hey, we have to be on.'"

The Indians dealt Colon and fellow right-handed hurler Tim Drew for veteran first baseman Lee Stevens and three minor league prospects: center fielder Grady Sizemore, left-handed pitcher Cliff Lee, and second baseman Brandon Phillips.

Shapiro remembers the exact date of the swap: June 27, 2002.

"Think about how early that is," Shapiro said.

There are reasons the Indians dashed to the front of the transaction line more than a month before the non-waiver trade deadline. The Indians were desperate, in need of organizational replenishing. The Expos were more desperate, in jeopardy of being contracted. Montreal GM Omar Minaya eventually became a close friend of Shapiro's, but in 2002, he had not been on the job very long. Thus, he did not have extensive knowledge of the Expos' minor league system. Meanwhile, the Indians employed Montreal's former farm director. Minaya was tasked with improving his big-league club in order to make a run at the postseason, attract more fans to Olympic Stadium, and attempt to stave off contraction.

"He was highly motivated with the short-term horizon," Shapiro said. "We knew that. That's why we made the trade on June 27 instead of waiting."

Sizemore was a 19-year-old outfielder whom the Expos had selected in the third round of the amateur draft two summers earlier. The teenager did not display much power at the Expos' lower ranks, as he clubbed only three home runs in 253 games in their organization. He did demonstrate patience at the plate and an ability to reach base consistently, rare traits for such an inexperienced kid. He posted a .380 on-base percentage as a 17-year-old in the rookie league and a .381 on-base percentage the following year at Class A Clinton. When he joined the Indians' organization, the power arrived as well. Sizemore earned his way onto three American League All-Star teams while with Cleveland. He totaled at least 22 home runs, 76 RBIs, 22 stolen bases, 34 doubles, and 101 runs scored in each season from 2005–08. He won a pair of Gold Glove awards and finished in the top 12 in American League Most Valuable Player balloting on three occasions. He tallied a league-high 53 doubles and 134 runs scored in 2006.

Lee, then a 23-year-old southpaw, was a fourth-round draft choice in 2000. He made his big-league debut for the club in 2002, posting a 1.74 ERA in two starts. He proceeded to win 46 games for the Indians from 2004–06 and captured the American League Cy Young Award with a 22–3 record and 2.54 ERA in 2008.

Phillips spent his 21st birthday on June 28, 2002, packing his bags for Buffalo, New York, the site of the Indians' Triple-A affiliate. Montreal's second-round draft pick in 1999, the middle infielder had already established himself as one of the league's premier prospects. He burst onto the big-league scene that season, though he never attained solid footing with the Tribe. He bounced between Buffalo and Cleveland until the start of the 2006 campaign, when the Indians dealt him to Cincinnati, where he flourished.

All three blossomed into All-Stars and all three had unceremonious exits from Cleveland. Injuries derailed Sizemore's career. The club traded Lee amid yet another rebuilding process in 2009. Phillips sparred with manager Eric Wedge and was exiled to Cincinnati in a lopsided exchange that left Cleveland with reliever Jeff Stevens. Still, the Colon trade is one of the more one-sided executions in league history. It allowed the Indians to jump-start their roster transformation.

"Is there any way to do it non-traditionally? Traditionally is eight, nine, 10 years," Shapiro said. "You lose enough to pick at the top and those guys get to the big leagues and you do that for three or four years. It takes a long time for that to happen.

"We decided we wanted to expedite that, because this place had been used to winning for a long time. So Colon represented that rare opportunity to infuse three top-level talents into our farm system and do it at the upper levels where you sped up that timeframe."

Cleveland hit rock bottom in 2003, when the Indians amassed a 68–94 record, but they won at least 78 games each season from 2004–08, including 93 in '05 and a league-high 96 in '07. The stretch did not quite resemble the one from the '90s—the ballpark wasn't sold out every night and they didn't field a team of household names and All-Stars—but it was a start.

"I don't think any of us realized how incredible an achievement it would be to turn an entire team over and get back to 93 wins in three years," Shapiro said. "When you look back at that, that was pretty good. But at that point, you're saying, 'Anything is possible. We can do that.'"

48 Snow-pening Day

In 2007, Milwaukee's Miller Park played host to Cleveland's "home" opener. The team had Mother Nature to thank for that.

An early-April snowstorm wiped out a four-game set against the Mariners that was intended to take place at Jacobs Field. The record books display no evidence of competition at Cleveland's ballpark that weekend, but the Indians were actually one out away from notching a victory—not to mention a truncated no-hitter.

The Indians and Mariners endured a light but steady snowfall as they braved the Friday afternoon conditions. Cleveland staked claim to a 4–0 lead before Mariners manager Mike Hargrove—nicknamed "The Human Rain Delay" during his playing days for his lengthy, time-stalling at-bat rituals—griped that his batter, Jose Lopez, could not see the baseball through the falling flakes. Umpire Rick Reed opted to delay the game, but Mother Nature never relented. Eventually, the game was called and Indians hurler Paul Byrd's 4⅔ innings of no-hit baseball went out the window.

The game was initially rescheduled as part of a split double header the following day, but the snow did not relent. Weather wiped out the entire series and forced the Indians to relocate to Milwaukee, where they hosted a three-game set against the Angels.

The words "Welcome to Opening Day 2007" conjure images of a sunny April day, but in fact the Jacobs Field Opening Day game against the Mariners had to be called due to a snowstorm.

The Brewers sold tickets to each contest for $10 apiece and the series attracted more than 52,000 fans.

Slider, the Indians' mascot, made the trip. So, too, did drummer John Adams, who banged on his 26-inch bass drum at nearly every Indians home game from 1973 through 2019. Adams received a call from a woman in the Indians' front office on Monday, April 9. She asked if Adams could travel to Milwaukee on Tuesday.

Adams replied, "No. There's a baseball game. I can't go to Milwaukee."

"She goes, 'Oh, you haven't heard?'" Adams said. "'We've decided, because of the snow, we're going to play the series with the Angels in Milwaukee.'"

Adams reached out to his boss at his day job at a local phone company and got people to take on his work shifts for the following three days. He called back the Indians employee and committed to drumming at the series at Miller Park. Adams needed a case to tote his drum north. He met a man halfway and picked up a 28-inch case that protected his old instrument.

The Indians claimed two of three games from the Angels. In the rubber match, Travis Hafner slugged a game-winning, three-run home run in the eighth inning to erase a 2–1 deficit. The club returned to Cleveland and hosted the White Sox at Progressive Field on Friday, April 13, a week after its originally scheduled home opener.

To make up the four games with the Mariners, Seattle traveled to Cleveland to play games on May 21, June 11, and August 30. Due to logistical challenges, the teams made up the fourth tilt at Safeco Field in Seattle as part of a twin bill lodged in the center of a four-game series in late September. In the first game, the Indians served as the home team and batted last. In the nightcap, the Mariners returned to their role as the home team in their home ballpark.

Snow Days

For two years, Progressive Field morphed into a winter wonderland. From late November into January, the Indians filled the ballpark with the constructions required to host cold-weather activities.

Atop the left-field bleachers sat the Batterhorn, a 10-lane snow tubing hill. Along the outfield warning track rested an ice-skating path dubbed the Frozen Mile. A small ice-skating rink was tucked away in the left-field corner near Slider's Snow Mountain, a kids' play area. They placed a fire pit on the home run porch and a walking trail with winter lights through the outfield. They hosted hockey games on the Frozen Diamond. On January 15, 2012, the ballpark hosted a hockey game between Ohio State University and the University of Michigan. The matchup, the first-ever outdoor college hockey game in the state, was dubbed The Frozen Diamond Face Off.

The Indians hosted the event in 2010–11 and 2011–12 but ceased production after two years because of low attendance, not helped by an unusually warm winter the second offseason.

"You knew in the back of your mind that this was going to create a challenge for us," said Mark Shapiro, then the club's general manager. "We were going to end up having to play a lot of games in a row. We were going to lose a lot of off days. We just lost a home series. In the end, what became apparent was that that team was not going to accept that. They weren't going to take the excuses. They were just good from day one on and defied the odds."

49 Visit the Player Statues

Perhaps one day, alongside the bronze likenesses of Jim Thome, Larry Doby, Bob Feller and Frank Robinson, will stand a statue of Albert Belle in an intimidating pose, his finger pointing to his flexing bicep as he offers a menacing glare. That statue would probably come best as a package deal with one of former pitcher Jason Grimsley crawling on all fours, as he did to retrieve Belle's corked bat from a locked room in Comiskey Park in Chicago in 1994. Perhaps they could be joined by a statue of Fausto Carmona, as he was then named, standing atop the mound, his glove in front of his face, midges crawling up and down his skin as he resists the temptation to submit to their pestering ways. How about a statue of Jose Canseco rubbing his noggin? Canseco never played for the Indians, but Cleveland Stadium was the site in which Carlos Martinez's fly ball bounced off of his dome and over the fence for a home run. Or a depiction of José Ramírez with his helmet at his feet?

For years, a statue of Feller, rocking back in his windup with his front leg extended high in the air, stood alone outside of Progressive Field. The Indians unveiled one of Thome, in his patented stance

Indians fans admire the statue of Hall of Fame pitcher Bob Feller outside Progressive Field.

with his bat pointed out into the abyss, on August 2, 2014. His lumber is wrapped with tape. His helmet is slapped with pine tar. Thome appreciates the intricacies.

"I love it. I absolutely love it," he said. "You don't really ever think of getting a statue at all. It's humbling, it's honoring, and it's something I think my family will love every day the rest of their lives."

The Robinson statue, unveiled on May 27, 2017, stands in the center of the upper level of Heritage Park and depicts him exchanging his lineup card before his first game as the first African American

Lineup Exchange

Progressive Field was filled with nostalgia on September 22, 2011. Before the first pitch between the Indians and White Sox, Jim Thome—Cleveland's 41-year-old designated hitter—and Omar Vizquel—Chicago's 44-year-old utility infielder—exchanged lineup cards.

The two spent nine years as teammates with the Indians. They accounted for eight All-Star appearances, 11 Gold Glove awards (all won by Vizquel), 692 home runs (most of them belonging to Thome), and more than 5,000 hits.

"They've accomplished a lot of things that many other players haven't accomplished," said their former teammate, Sandy Alomar Jr.

Both Thome and Vizquel played one more year in the big leagues, but neither with Cleveland.

"To be able to still play and to be able to take the lineup card and have him do it as well," Thome said, "is very special, especially here in Cleveland, where we played during the golden years of our careers. To have fun with that is great."

manager in league history on Opening Day 1975. The lineup card he's clutching in his hands is detailed enough to include the nine starters (plus pitcher Gaylord Perry) from that day: Oscar Gamble, Robinson himself, George Hendrick, Charlie Spikes, Boog Powell, John Ellis, Buddy Bell, Jack Brohamer and Ed Crosby.

The statues offer a glimpse into the history of the franchise, as they stand tall above anyone who ventures to look at them.

"I don't think anyone could be comfortable getting a statue, and I mean that respectfully," Thome said. "You play the game as a kid, you progress and go to high school, you get drafted and you go through the minor leagues. Nobody ever dreams of a statue. I certainly didn't."

50 Veeck's Trek

When Rick Bay was the club's president in 1992, the Indians held a weekly radio show. Fans could write in questions and Bay would answer them on air. This was a relatively new concept, an untapped form of transparency. It was a tribute to former owner Bill Veeck.

Veeck was not a conventional owner. No one was more open, quirky, eccentric, or over-the-top. He introduced outrageous promotions and unearthed never-before-considered techniques to engage fans. He purchased the Indians in 1946 and immediately boosted the franchise's attendance figures. He moved all of the team's home games to Cleveland Stadium, which could seat 50,000 more fans than League Park could.

"He came out of the war and brought a fun and joy and a little bit of a carnival atmosphere to the world of baseball," said Bob DiBiasio, Guardians senior vice president of public affairs. "A remarkable guy."

Veeck served in the Marines for three years during World War II. He suffered an injury that cost him his right leg. He had it amputated and used a wooden leg. As owner of the Indians, he would sit in his office and smoke. He burrowed a little ashtray in the wooden leg, and he would bury his cigarette in the small hole that he carved. While he did this, he would leave the door open to his office.

"Any fan, anybody, could walk into Gate A at Cleveland Stadium and walk in and talk to him about the team," DiBiasio said.

Veeck was always trying to be a trendsetter with his gimmicks, his personnel decisions, and his modus operandi. In

History of Cleveland Indians Ownership

Charles W. Somers: 1900–16
Jim Dunn: 1916–22
Estate of Jim Dunn: 1922–27
Alva Bradley: 1927–46
Bill Veeck: 1946–49
Ellis Ryan: 1949–52
Myron H. Wilson: 1953–56
William R. Daley: 1956–62
Gabe Paul: 1963–66
Vernon Stouffer: 1967–72
Nick Mileti: 1972–76
Ted Bonda: 1977–78
Steve O'Neill: 1978–83
Estate of Steve O'Neill: 1983–86
Dick Jacobs: 1986–2000
Dolan family: 2000–present

1947, he signed Larry Doby, who broke the color barrier in the American League. The following year, he signed Negro Leagues star pitcher Satchel Paige, who contributed to the team's run to a World Series triumph. In 1949, he presided over a funeral at the ballpark to symbolize the end to Cleveland's chances of repeating as champion. After that season, he sold the team to help finance his divorce.

Veeck was inducted into the Baseball Hall of Fame in 1991. He was elected to the Indians' Distinguished Hall of Fame in 2009.

Said DiBiasio, "He was always bringing the fun and excitement."

51 The Ultimate Trade Tree

Jerry Dybzinski spent three seasons with the Indians from 1980–82. He batted .234. He hit one home run. He slugged .290. He spent most of his time at shortstop, though he moved around the infield. And he is responsible, in a way, for the franchise landing fireball-tossing closer Emmanuel Clase some 42 years after the Indians drafted Dybzinski in the 15th round out of Cleveland State.

Welcome to the trade tree, the almost unfathomable string of wheeling and dealing that serves as a tour guide through franchise history. It began with Dybzinski and his unassuming Cleveland career. The Indians traded him to the White Sox in 1983 for Pat Tabler, who spent six mostly productive seasons with the club, posting a .294 average. In June 1988, Cleveland flipped Tabler to the Royals for pitcher Bud Black, his first of two stints with the team. Black was a steady hand in the Indians' rotation—well, at least until they traded him to the Blue Jays in September 1990 for Mauro Gozzo and a pair of players to be named later. Gozzo totaled four appearances for the franchise, and they didn't go well. Steve Cummings, one of the players named later, never pitched for the big-league club. And then there's Alex Sanchez, the last puzzle piece to the late-season swap. He never pitched for Cleveland, as Hank Peters and John Hart sent him back to the Blue Jays that winter for pitcher Willie Blair.

Blair made 11 appearances for the dreadful 1991 Indians, who packaged him and catcher Eddie Taubensee that December in a deal with the Astros for utility man Dave Rohde and a young center fielder named Kenny Lofton. That trade, um, paid dividends, though it's worth noting Taubensee did piece together a solid career, mostly with the Reds. He also returned to Cleveland in

2001 and, ironically, lifted Lofton over his shoulder after the team's implausible comeback against the Mariners.

"It was kind of surreal being there in 2001," Taubensee said. "When I was there in '91, I was the one traded to Houston for Kenny Lofton. Then that happened."

Lofton represented Cleveland on five All-Star teams, won four Gold Glove Awards and led the league in stolen bases for five consecutive seasons, as he emerged as one of the league's premier leadoff hitters, the catalyst for Cleveland's relentless lineups and a borderline Hall of Famer. Oh, and Rohde went 0-for-7 with a couple of walks as a member of the Indians.

A week before Opening Day in 1997, though, Hart dealt Lofton and reliever Alan Embree to the Braves for outfielders David Justice and Marquis Grissom. And that's how this trade tree keeps growing. Both Grissom and Justice played a role in Cleveland reaching the World Series that season, but the club moved on from Grissom the following winter, in part to create space for Lofton to return as a free agent. Justice enjoyed a few strong seasons in the center of the Indians' lineup, but the club dealt him to the Yankees in late June 2000 for pitchers Jake Westbrook and Zach Day and outfielder Ricky Ledee. Justice said the trade "stunned" him. Hart called the trade "simple economics."

Cleveland flipped Ledee to the Rangers a month later in exchange for veteran masher David Segui. They later sent Day to the Expos for outfielder Milton Bradley. Westbrook was the key; Cleveland's front office liked how often his sinker-slider combination resulted in harmless ground balls. Westbrook blossomed into an All-Star in 2004, and he spent a decade with the franchise. Then, at the 2010 trade deadline, the club dealt him to the Cardinals in a three-team swap that landed Corey Kluber with the Indians.

Kluber was a lottery ticket. The front office was encouraged by his strikeout rate, but his name didn't appear on any top prospects list. The rest of his statistics fell somewhere between pedestrian and alarming. And, well, he developed into a two-time Cy Young Award winner, the ace of the staff, one of the best starters in franchise history and one of the peak performers in the league for a five-year stretch.

In December 2019, with Kluber's contract nearing its end and his ability beginning to decline, the Indians traded him to the Rangers for outfielder Delino DeShields and...Clase.

It started with Dybzinski in 1977. The organization received helpful contributions from Tabler and Black, elite production from Lofton and Justice, solid performances from Westbrook, award-winning efforts from Kluber and, most recently, lockdown ninth innings from Clase. It's the tree that keeps on giving.

52 Decisions, Decisions

There was the veteran—the 30-year-old, the two-time All-Star, the guy who had seen the growth of the franchise from a doormat to a championship contender. And then there was the kid—the hot-shot rookie, the 21-year-old who had been in the big leagues for all of four months.

Mike Hargrove had a decision to make. Outwardly, he acted as if there were no decision. Veteran Charles Nagy would be his starter if the Indians and Marlins reached a Game 7 in the 1997 World Series. Inside his mind, however, a storm was brewing. The wheels were spinning. A manager in a postseason series has no choice but to plan ahead and prepare for all contingencies.

Nagy started Game 3 and allowed five runs in six innings. He exited with the Tribe on top 7–5, but the Marlins roared back for a 14–11 win. Jaret Wright held Florida to three runs in six innings in

Game 4, which Cleveland claimed 10–3. After that contest, reporters started pressing Hargrove for his Game 7 plan. Orel Hershiser and Chad Ogea would start Games 5 and 6, respectively, either way. Would the reserved veteran Nagy get the call for Game 7, or would it be Wright, the chubby-cheeked kid, on three days' rest?

Before Game 5, Hargrove insisted Nagy was his choice.

"As of right now it's Charles Nagy," Hargrove said. "I think we may have a decision to make, but as of right now it's Charles Nagy."

After Game 5, Hargrove's tune changed slightly.

"Officially, right now, it's Charles Nagy in Game 7, if we go that far," Hargrove said. "There are a lot of things that we're going to look at going into that, and the fact of how Jaret can bounce back enters into it. But Game 7, everybody is available for that. So that's why I'm saying that."

Hargrove backed Nagy again before Game 6.

"If we get to Game 7, as of right now we have Charlie penciled in for the start," Hargrove said. "Again, it depends on what happens tonight and who we have to use tonight, whether that happens, but Charlie is, as of right now, the starter for tomorrow."

As he continued to talk, however, he again hedged his bets.

"It depends on if we have to use Charlie Nagy tonight. We may have to use Charlie Nagy, may have to use Wright, [Brian] Anderson, may have to use [Jeff] Juden. It depends on who we use tonight as to who is going to start tomorrow night. As of right now, it's Charles Nagy. I say that leaving my options open. It may not be Nagy, also, but as of right now it is."

The Indians breezed to a 4–1 victory to force Game 7. After Game 6, the second question directed at Hargrove asked for his final decision. The skipper cut to the chase.

"We will start Jaret Wright tomorrow night.

"The performance we got out of him in Game 4 led me to believe that he still is effective and so we will go with Jaret on three days. Last time he had thrown on three days was against the

Yankees in the divisional series, and he threw the ball well. We've got everybody available as will the Marlins, too."

Hargrove said he arrived at his decision the day before Game 6, and the way that game unfolded—Ogea and three relievers seamlessly pieced together nine strong innings—solidified his choice. Hargrove had mentioned the idea to Wright a few days earlier and the rookie had little reaction.

"He doesn't let you see him get very excited," Hargrove said. "He has a tremendous will to win. I don't want to get all philosophic, but he handles things real well."

Nagy was disappointed. It was his regular day to pitch. He had been a constant on the team for the entire decade. And now he lost the opportunity of a lifetime to a pitcher with 20 career starts on a big-league mound.

Wright, on the other hand, was living out a dream.

"When you dream, you don't dream to pitch in the playoffs, like the first round," he said. "It's always Game 7 of the Series."

Wright authored the best start of his young career. He held the Marlins scoreless on one hit through six innings. In the seventh, Bobby Bonilla took him deep for a leadoff home run. Wright rebounded to punch out Charles Johnson before he walked Craig Counsell and he departed with Cleveland ahead 2–1.

"Being young was a huge advantage for me in that situation," Wright said. "You feel like you're on top of the world."

He would not factor into the decision, of course. The Marlins sent the game into extra innings and tagged Nagy for the winning run in the 11th after a Tony Fernandez error.

"It doesn't eat at me," Wright said. "Life goes on. I was so fortunate to do what I did. It's just a chapter of my life."

That was the peak for Wright in Cleveland. He battled injuries and inconsistency for the rest of his tenure, which lasted through the 2002 season. In 98 games with the club, he posted a 5.50 ERA. He later pitched for the Padres, Braves, Yankees and Orioles.

53 Once in a Lifetime

Duane Kuiper said if players used walk-up music during his playing days, he would have chosen Three Dog Night's "One Is the Loneliest Number."

There stood Kuiper, in the batter's box, completing his daily practice rituals before a game against the Angels when surly slugger Reggie Jackson yelled loud enough for everyone to hear.

"If I only had one home run, I'd fuckin' quit," Jackson shouted.

Said Kuiper, "That's kind of what I had to live with."

Jackson finished his Hall of Fame career with 563 home runs. Kuiper deposited exactly one ball over the fence in his 3,754 trips to the plate.

So it goes for those with the lanky, lonely digit in the home run column on the back of their baseball cards. Kuiper, who played second base for the Indians from 1974–81, said he wished he would have socked more than one long ball, but he receives more recognition for his lone round-tripper than he would if he had a less distinguished total.

"What's the perfect number after one?" Kuiper said. "Twenty? Would I have rather hit 10 or 20 instead of one? At a certain stage in your life, after it's all said and done, you get mentioned more for hitting one than you did for hitting five."

Plus, the rarity of the event provides Kuiper, now a broadcaster for the San Francisco Giants, with the ability to remember every detail about the night of August 29, 1977. The Indians hosted the Chicago White Sox at Cleveland Stadium in a national telecast that included Al Michaels on play-by-play duties. Michaels is known for his line uttered during the 1980 Olympics: "Do you believe in miracles?" Kuiper, though, said he jokes with Michaels that the line initially earned its acclaim from Kuiper's improbable power stroke.

Cleveland native Steve Stone took the hill for Chicago, with his parents occupying their season seats along the third-base line near the dugout and on-deck circle. With one out in the bottom of the first, Kuiper turned on a pitch and lifted it to right field. He remembers running to first and seeing the No. 15 on the back of right fielder Wayne Nordhagen's uniform. He wasn't accustomed to that sight, since he rarely hit the ball over an outfielder's head.

"I thought, 'You know what? This maybe has a chance to get out of the park,'" Kuiper said.

The baseball landed on the other side of the right-field fence. Kuiper had never engaged in a home run trot before, so he sprinted around the bases.

"If I could do something different," Kuiper said, "I would have definitely slowed it down a little bit."

Buddy Bell, the next batter and one of Kuiper's favorite teammates, greeted him at home plate.

Kuiper never clubbed another pitch over the outfield wall, but he tagged Stone again three years later. On September 9, 1981, at Memorial Stadium in Baltimore, Kuiper belted a pitch off the right-field fence. The ball bounced back into the field of play and Kuiper ended up on second base with an RBI double.

"At the time, I was really disappointed," Kuiper said. "I would've loved to have a home run."

After the ensuing hitter, Mike Fischlin, singled to left to give the Indians a 3–0 lead, Dave Ford replaced Stone on the mound. As Stone retreated to the Orioles' dugout, he passed Kuiper, who had advanced to third base on Fischlin's base knock. Kuiper intentionally avoided making eye contact with Stone. Instead, he turned his back to the sauntering pitcher and peered toward the outfield.

"I liked him," Kuiper said. "He was a good guy. I didn't want him to have to say anything to me and I didn't want to have to say anything to him."

When he was not facing Stone, Kuiper did not have much of a power stroke at the plate. Manager Frank Robinson stressed that Kuiper not attempt to hit the ball in the air on any occasion. Kuiper contends that the skipper's mandate only reinforced what the infielder already knew: power was not his game.

"Guys around the league respected me, whether I hit one or whether I hit 30," Kuiper said. "I always said I was a regular player for all those years and only hit one home run, so I was doing something right."

54 Bye Bye, Cy

Victor Martinez sat at his locker, tears streaming down his face.

Earlier that day, 4-year-old Victor Jose had asked his father, "Daddy, are we still an Indian?"

Martinez told his son, "So far." But so far only lasted so long.

After coming within one victory of a trip to the World Series in 2007, the Indians fell so hard, so fast, that two years later, the club started from scratch. The tears shed by the father and son in the Indians' clubhouse resembled what many inside—and outside—the Indians' organization felt about trading away one of the franchise's centerpieces and about how close the team had come to a championship but how far it now stood from one, less than two years later.

It started with CC Sabathia. The burly left-hander was slated to become a free agent after the 2008 campaign. He was destined for a big market and was operating on borrowed time in Cleveland. So when the Indians stumbled out of the gate in '08, dealing Sabathia seemed to be their most sensible strategy.

The Indians selected Sabathia in the first round of the 1998 amateur draft out of high school. He debuted at the start of the 2001 campaign, when he was a 20-year-old rookie. That season, he amassed a 17–5 record and 4.39 ERA, with 171 strikeouts in 180⅓ innings, as he finished second in the balloting for American League Rookie of the Year. He eventually blossomed into the anchor of the club's starting rotation, as evidenced by his three All-Star Game selections and his 2007 American League Cy Young Award, earned after a 19–7 showing, 3.21 ERA, and league-high 241 innings.

Once the team sputtered at the start of the '08 season, the writing on the wall became clear. The Indians were going to lose Sabathia in a matter of months, anyway. They needed to get something in return while they could. After weeks of speculation, the club shipped him to Milwaukee for powerful first base prospect Matt LaPorta, pitchers Zach Jackson and Rob Bryson, and a player to be named later, which became eventual All-Star left fielder Michael Brantley. Jackson and Bryson never amounted to much at the major league level. LaPorta, the crown jewel of the deal from Cleveland's perspective, fizzled in the big leagues. Brantley's inclusion—only made possible because Sabathia carried the Brewers to the playoffs on his massive shoulders—salvaged the trade for Cleveland.

The exchange signaled the end of the brief window of contention the Indians had initiated the previous season. They sunk lower a year later.

"Those things are difficult because they defy your competitive nature," said Mark Shapiro, then the organization's general manager. "You operationally understand the challenges and you start to say, 'I guess this is the model that we're going to have to always be in, that churn cycle where we play the window out and if we feel like the window might be closing, we need to be opportunistic to get assets back in and players back in so we're not losing for eight to 10 years.' We really wanted to stay out of those long-term valleys and try to turn things around as quickly as possible."

Shapiro continued wheeling and dealing in 2009. Cliff Lee spent his first eight big league seasons with the Indians following his relocation from Montreal in the Bartolo Colon trade in 2002. In 2008, the southpaw compiled a sparkling stat line, with a 22–3 record, a 2.54 ERA, and a pair of complete-game shutouts. All of the production merited him the distinction of starting the All-Star Game for the American League squad and earning the league's Cy Young Award. As the Indians struggled through the 2009 season, however, his name came up in trade rumors. He was scheduled to hit the free-agent market after the 2010 campaign. Two days before the July 31 non-waiver trade deadline, the team dealt Lee and outfielder Ben Francisco to the Phillies for minor league pitchers Jason Knapp and Carlos Carrasco, infielder Jason Donald, and catcher Lou Marson.

The Indians considered Knapp the prized acquisition in the exchange. There was one problem—the righty's pitching shoulder was in shambles. Knapp was on the disabled list at the time of the trade. He ended up needing two operations and never advanced past Class A ball before the Indians released him in August 2012. Knapp went nearly four years without pitching professionally before he returned for the Texas Rangers' Class A affiliate in 2014.

Lee and Sabathia opposed each other on the mound in Game 1 of the 2009 World Series, when Sabathia's New York Yankees squared off against Lee's Phillies.

Two days after the Lee trade, the Indians' front office struck again. Martinez—whom the organization had signed as a 17-year-old shortstop out of Venezuela in 1996—had spent parts of eight seasons in the middle of the team's batting order and earned three trips to the Midsummer Classic. He was moved to Boston for pitchers Justin Masterson, Nick Hagadone, and Bryan Price. Martinez was not shy about his adoration for the Indians' organization. He became the heart and soul of the clubhouse and the lineup. Now he had to leave the only franchise he had ever known. Martinez called it the toughest day of his career. Cleveland lost 97, 93, 82 and 94 games from 2009–12.

"We were trading a lot of those guys who were great guys, guys like Victor who meant so much to us personally, guys we had believed in so completely and totally," Shapiro said. "That's hard. You never get past the personal nature of trading a player that you care about and believe in."

55 Grover

Mike Hargrove, or Grover, had the task of making sure a clubhouse full of ticking time bombs didn't explode. He had to oversee a group of confident players who carried themselves with a palpable swagger, guys who admitted that they knew they were going to win when they stepped onto the field.

The winning part wasn't the most demanding facet of the manager's job. Not during the regular season, at least. The Indians captured five consecutive American League Central Division crowns from 1995–99 with Hargrove at the helm. The talent on the roster alone translated into victories. But Hargrove had to guarantee that that talent didn't interfere with daily business. He had to ensure that a clubhouse oozing with ego didn't collapse.

"He doesn't get anywhere near the accolades he deserves for keeping that collection of personalities together," said Bob DiBiasio, Guardians senior vice president of public affairs.

Hargrove spent the second half of his playing career with the Indians, from 1979–85. He hit .292 with Cleveland and logged a .396 on-base percentage. He batted .300 or better in each of his first three seasons with the Tribe. He also developed a reputation as a hitter who capitalized on the game's timelessness. Hargrove often stalled by stepping out of the batter's box to readjust his batting gloves, helmet, or any other gadget that could possibly require realignment. That attribute earned him the nickname "The Human Rain Delay," a gimmick that wouldn't fly with the advent of the pitch clock.

Perhaps all of that fine-tuning foreshadowed a successful managerial career. Hargrove oversaw a roster of young players who blossomed into All-Stars. He took over at the helm for John McNamara in 1991. In the spring of 1993, Hargrove steered the organization through the boating tragedy that claimed the lives of relief pitchers Steve Olin and Tim Crews.

"We had a team full, a locker room full of very, very young players that had not been through anything like that," said former general manager John Hart. "This was a club that had been together for two or three years. There was not a free agent on that ball club in '93. These were all kids. And I think it allowed Grover to perhaps do some of the things he does best, which is allow his character, his caring, to show."

After a pair of 76–86 seasons, the Tribe made the leap in 1994. Unfortunately, the player's strike cut the season short. In 1995, however, as the Indians established themselves as baseball's most loaded and dangerous team—and the players in the clubhouse knew it—Hargrove pushed the right buttons. Cleveland finished with a league-best 100–44 record and pushed the Atlanta Braves to six games in the World Series, the franchise's first appearance in the Fall Classic in four decades.

"[Hargrove] not winning the Manager of the Year award in '95 was a travesty," DiBiasio said. "Our guys won 100 out of 144. And he doesn't win Manager of the Year? It makes no sense. Just because we're a talented team? It wasn't something where you and I could have managed that team to 100 wins."

The Indians qualified for the postseason in each of the final five years of Hargrove's tenure in Cleveland. He was dismissed after the 1999 American League Division Series, in which the Indians blew a 2–0 series lead and bowed out, again falling short of a league title, despite five straight division championships.

During Hargrove's time as skipper, he captained a roster full of hotheads, divas, and personalities. His relaxed temperament helped mesh a group of All-Stars who carried All-Star egos. He challenged the collection of star power to etch its name into franchise lore. When people look back at the most prolific stretch of Indians baseball, they note that Hargrove served as the lead man for those teams.

"He was a big part of it," said former team president Mark Shapiro. "I'm not sure any one person gets credit, but Mike was a guy who understood the personality and nature of the team and understood how to keep a calm, steady hand on the rudder and kept the team going in the right direction and did what he had to do. Some of that is making sure the talent actually produces and plays. Maybe that gets overlooked, but there is talent in that, too."

56 Web Gems

They made it look so easy, so effortless. Gloves weren't always required. Neither was eye contact. Ground balls didn't skip through the middle of the Indians' infield from 1999–2001. That was the domain of second baseman Roberto Alomar and shortstop

Omar Vizquel. For three years, the Gold Glove award hoarders teamed up to provide perhaps the most dazzling display of defense in franchise history.

They were flashy and flamboyant and resplendent. No baseball trickled past them and into the outfield. They seemed to turn every double play, no matter the degree of difficulty.

"That was the greatest duo I've witnessed, in regard to range, acrobatics and athleticism," said former catcher Sandy Alomar Jr. "It was easy to sit back there and call a game knowing that if the ball was hit on the ground to those guys, a play is going to be made."

Vizquel had already earned Gold Gloves in 1993, 1994, 1995, 1996, 1997, and 1998 before he teamed with Alomar, who had earned Gold Gloves in 1991, 1992, 1993, 1994, 1995, 1996, and 1998. They both garnered the distinction in all three years they played together. Combined, they totaled 21 Gold Gloves between them.

"There probably wasn't a better middle infield than those two guys," said former second baseman Jason Kipnis. "Definitely from what I've seen, it was unbelievable watching those two."

Vizquel's teammates initially needed some convincing, though. On April 16, 1994, in his ninth game with his new team, Vizquel committed three errors.

"Nobody knew me in Cleveland," Vizquel said. "I made three errors in a game. Three errors."

Vizquel vividly remembers each miscue. He misplayed consecutive balls in the top of the third inning. He missed a grounder off the bat of Kansas City's Greg Gagne with one out. Two pitches later, Vince Coleman hit a grounder toward Vizquel, who corralled the baseball and, while attempting to initiate a double play, threw the ball away. Both runners were safe and later scored. In the eighth, with the Indians unraveling and the bases loaded in a 9–9 game, Vizquel booted a pop fly. Two runs scored.

The Diving Stop

Ask Omar Vizquel for his choice on the greatest play he ever made in the field, and he will hem and haw for a moment before opting for the one with the best timing. His manager, Mike Hargrove, was getting a drink of water when the ball was hit to the shortstop.

"I saw Omar dive and make the play and I almost choked," Hargrove said.

It came in Game 6 of the 1997 World Series. On a hazy night in South Florida, the Indians grasped a 4–1 lead in the sixth inning. The Marlins had runners on second and third with two outs and Mike Jackson was pitching with Charles Johnson at the plate. Johnson pulled Jackson's offering into the hole between short and third. Vizquel laid out, his chest smacking the grass beyond the infield dirt. He stretched out his left arm to corral the sharply hit grounder. At that time, Gary Sheffield was waltzing toward the plate. Jim Eisenreich was more than halfway to third. Had the ball skirted past Vizquel, two runs would have scored.

Instead, the limber shortstop propped himself up with his left knee and fired the baseball across his body toward first base. When he let go, his back foot was in the outfield grass. His front foot was gracing the edge of the infield dirt. His throw struck Jim Thome's glove on a line drive to retire Johnson and end the inning. The Indians maintained their 4–1 advantage.

"Nothing that Omar does with his glove surprises me," Hargrove said after the game. "Nothing he does with his bare hands surprises me. This guy has got the guts of a burglar. And he's very, very good at what he does and is very cool and collected. He's a player."

Vizquel took off his hat as he jogged off the field. His teammates and coaches left their spots on the bench to greet him upon his return to the dugout.

On the national telecast, Hall of Fame second baseman Joe Morgan, who won five Gold Glove Awards himself, said, "You don't win Gold Gloves if you can't make the great plays under pressure."

"Three errors," Vizquel repeated, almost amazed, years later, that he could have been responsible for such a litany of mistakes. "I remember a guy from the stands said, 'Send this guy back to Seattle!'"

It wasn't the ideal first impression to make on his new teammates.

"The first thing we said was, 'Who is this guy?'" said center fielder Kenny Lofton.

Vizquel didn't make another error until August 3, a span of 52 games. He committed six all season and earned his second consecutive Gold Glove Award. He would proceed to capture the honor for nine straight seasons—one with the Mariners and eight with the Indians. He tacked on two more to his collection later in his career with the San Francisco Giants.

"He made us a better defensive team," said second baseman Carlos Baerga. "I remember the first day he came up and he said to us, 'I watched you guys play the last few years and you guys make a lot of errors. For us to win, we need to play better defense.'"

Bill Plummer, one of Vizquel's first coaches in pro ball, said Vizquel made it look like he "never got a bad hop." "You just can't teach it," Plummer said.

"How many times did you turn the TV on and see Omar making a play that made you gasp?" said former Cleveland manager Terry Francona. "He was pretty incredible."

Lofton marveled at the way Vizquel chased pop-ups into the outfield grass.

"The thing that I'll always remember is it would be 100 degrees out there, the sun is so bright. We all need our shades on to catch a fly ball. But Omar is the only guy on the field with no shades on. I'm trying to figure out what the heck he's doing. All of a sudden, a fly ball hits, and we look and say, 'What is Omar going to do?' He's the only guy I know who turns his back to the hitter and catches the fly ball over his shoulder. I'm still amazed by that. It's something that I tell people about all the time, to look at tape of Omar doing that."

Vizquel was a stable force at shortstop for the Indians for 11 years, from 1994–2004. Alomar filled a void created when they traded Baerga to the New York Mets in 1996. That crater resurfaced when the Indians traded Alomar to the Mets after the 2001 campaign. Over the next 10 seasons, 34 players started a game at second base for the Indians: Ricky Gutierrez, John McDonald, Jolbert Cabrera, Bill Selby, Greg LaRocca, Brandon Phillips, Zach Sorensen, Angel Santos, Ronnie Belliard, Lou Merloni, Alex Cora, Ramon Vazquez, Jose Hernandez, Joe Inglett, Hector Luna, Aaron Boone, Josh Barfield, Mike Rouse, Asdrubal Cabrera, Chris Gomez, Luis Rivas, Jamey Carroll, Jorge Velandia, Tony Graffanino, Luis Valbuena, Mark Grudzielanek, Jason Donald, Anderson Hernandez, Jayson Nix, Drew Sutton, Orlando Cabrera, Adam Everett, Cord Phelps, and Kipnis.

Not only were Vizquel and Alomar stalwarts in the field, but they batted next to each other in the lineup as well, with Vizquel typically in the No. 2 hole and Alomar often slotted third. An All-Star in all three of his seasons in Cleveland, Alomar batted .323 with a .920 OPS, 362 runs scored, and 106 stolen bases with the Tribe. His hits often plated Vizquel, who tallied 297 runs scored from 1999–2001.

57 Mini

The clock was ticking toward the deadline—an artificial one, but one both sides understood they needed to respect, given that the 2022 season was about to start and the front office had to consider trade offers if they couldn't strike a deal.

Team president Chris Antonetti was in Goodyear, Arizona. General manager Mike Chernoff was on a flight back to Cleveland after leaving spring training in the desert. Team owner Paul Dolan was in Cleveland. José Ramírez's agent was in California. Ramírez, the man of the hour, was set to play five innings in his final spring tune-up at Chase Field in Phoenix. And the Guardians' team translator, Agustín Rivero, was coaching first base in Scottsdale, the site of the club's other game on a split-squad day.

Not, uh, the ideal arrangement to hammer out a contract extension before the buzzer.

Antonetti drove to Chase Field, arriving when Ramírez exited the game. Rivero, in full uniform, directed a Lyft driver to Chase Field and tagged in Justin Toole to coach first. Ramírez finished his duties, showered, changed into his street clothes and met with Cleveland's brass in the manager's office. There, they nailed down the framework of a franchise-altering, season-changing contract extension. Ramírez left tens of millions of dollars on the table, but he was adamant he remain in Cleveland for the balance of his career, even after a couple weeks of contract talks didn't inspire a ton of confidence that something would materialize.

Ramírez has always bet on himself, always gone about things his own way. No one would have predicted his ascent, aside from himself. He dropped out of middle school to focus on baseball. There was no backup plan. He tells kids not to follow his path, to stay in school, to make sure they're resourceful enough to carve out a career in something secure.

"One in a million," he once said to students in the library of Thomas Jefferson International Newcomers Academy in Cleveland. "I was that [one]."

Even in the minors, evaluators projected the pint-sized infielder as a utility player. He broke into the majors in September 2013 as a 20-year-old pinch-runner lending a hand for the club's postseason push. Terry Francona jokingly called him "Little Shit" for the way

José Ramírez has been the heart and soul of the Guardians since signing a long-term extension with the club ahead of the 2022 season.

he irritated the opposition on the bases. For a few years, teammates called him "Mini." But those who played with or coached him always describe him as acting as though he's the most imposing player on the field, no matter his stature.

"Nothing scares him," said Ramon Peña, who signed Ramírez in 2009 as the Indians' director of international scouting.

"Don't judge a book by its cover," said catcher Austin Hedges. "He's just a little guy, but he's probably better than you at everything."

Veterans Mike Napoli and Juan Uribe helped Ramírez turn a corner in 2016. He struggled for his first couple seasons in the big leagues during his bid to lock down a regular spot on Cleveland's infield. Ramírez and Napoli played cards in the center of the clubhouse every day that season, even though they didn't speak the same primary language.

Ramírez didn't say much his first couple years in the majors, and he's still relatively quiet, but he does plenty of chirping in the dugout and on the field, he picks his spots to deliver the perfect line to spark laughter, he keeps things loose in the clubhouse before games and he developed into more of a leader in 2022. He made connections with every teammate, whether randomly joining the background of reliever Trevor Stephan's FaceTime calls or taking rookie outfielder Oscar Gonzalez on a Michigan Ave. shopping spree in Chicago or asking rookie outfielder Will Benson for the first-pitch time as if everyone arrived at the ballpark at 10:00 AM for a night game or challenging young players earning the league minimum to million-dollar Mario Kart matches, even though everyone in the room knows he's the unconquerable king of the game.

He's known for that, certainly. He's known for his helmet flying off whenever he scampers along the baseline. He's also known for his confident strut, with his arms swinging like pendulums and the weight of his body shifting from side to side with each step.

"Try to do it," reliever Dan Otero once said. "It's freaking hard work. Gets the obliques going."

Franmil Reyes noticed that strut while auditioning for scouts in the Dominican Republic a decade before he and Ramírez became teammates in Cleveland. Peña said Ramírez had that same strut in 2009, when he signed him, even though the teenager who then measured 5-foot-8, 140 pounds wasn't the player he was tasked with scouting.

"There are a lot of kids with tools and ability," Peña said, "but they don't have it inside them. I said to myself that day, 'This guy is going to play in the major leagues.'"

Pitcher Shane Bieber called Ramírez the team's heart and soul. Assistant hitting coach Victor Rodriguez called him "a miniature David Ortiz," and Rodriguez would know—he was Ortiz's right-hand man in Boston for five years.

Ramírez's seven-year, $141 million contract extension was the most lucrative in franchise history, even if it undersold Ramírez's true market value. He has never offered a reason to believe he won't make it worthwhile.

"When you talk about confidence," Peña said, "that's José Ramírez."

58 Rally Alley

The Indians were dejected. The flight back to Cleveland from Atlanta was long—much longer, it seemed, than the hour and a half it actually took. After a 100-win regular season, the Indians came up short against the Braves in six games in the 1995 World Series. They mustered only one hit off Tom Glavine and Co. in the series-deciding contest, a 1–0 loss. To come so close, after a 41-year World Series (and postseason) drought, was agonizing. The accomplishments accumulated throughout a magical season were placed on the back burner.

Then the plane landed.

The team received a police escort from the airport back to Jacobs Field. Cars pulled over on I-71. People exited those cars and applauded the team busses as they whizzed past. Hordes of fans greeted the team downtown and at the ballpark. They were not dwelling in the demoralization of a Fall Classic defeat. They were proud of the leaps forward taken by a franchise that had been mired in dreadfulness for four decades.

"We were disheartened," said Jim Thome, then the club's third baseman. "We wanted to win a World Series. I think what put it in perspective is how our fans showed up."

Two days after Game 6, the city of Cleveland hosted a rally to celebrate the Indians' season. Thousands of fans poured out into Public Square, the center of downtown, where a giant stage was set up for players, coaches, and executives. Player banners adorned every light post in front of the Terminal Tower. Fans brought signs and donned Indians garb for the chilly, overcast Monday afternoon celebration.

A group of police on motorcycles first carved a path down Superior Road, adjacent to Public Square. A row of police on horseback followed. Next came a line of cars, followed by a series of high school marching bands and cheerleaders. Band members had players' names and numbers inscribed on their instruments. One tuba bore the name Belle and the No. 8. A few trucks drove past. One displayed a banner that read "Wahoo, what a season! Wahoo, what a finish!! Wahoo, what a TEAM!!!" There was persistent screaming and chanting and ringing of cowbells.

As the players took the stage, fans jockeyed for position to get the best possible view. One person even climbed a cylinder post to stand atop the crosswalk sign. Others stood atop newspaper stands, all to catch a glimpse of their heroes of the diamond. It was the start of what blossomed into the golden era of Cleveland baseball. It was a telltale sign of an attachment between the fan base and team. On this day, no one could tell that the Indians had actually lost the World Series. Everyone was just appreciative of what had been achieved. The team generated that kind of response just by reaching the Fall Classic. Now they had a taste of what the ensuing years would bring.

"It was overwhelmingly positive, the feeling," Thome said. "I think at that point, we as players knew, 'Wow. Our fans are really behind us and we have something special here.'"

Mark Wiley, the pitching coach for the '95 team, bumped into Sandy Alomar Jr. nearly a quarter-century after that season. The conversation immediately darted to the magic of that year.

"It's my favorite season," Wiley said. "No doubt. By far.... It's like it's etched in our minds, exactly what happened. I can remember, I coached for 17 years in the big leagues. It's hard for me to figure out who [was] on what teams. But I know every player that was on that '95 team."

Super Joe

They told stories that built up his legendary status, tales about him opening beer bottles with his eye socket, swallowing lit cigarettes, yanking his own tooth with pliers, removing an unwelcome tattoo with a razor blade, and consuming alcoholic beverages through a straw shoved up his nostril. There were whispers about pet alligators and rhinoceros rides and bare-knuckle boxing matches.

"I was a little different," Joe Charboneau said. "I enjoyed being a little different."

They marveled at his hitting prowess. This kid, who turned 25 mid-season, stood toe-to-toe with the American League's pitching elite and racked up numbers that earned him the Rookie of the Year award.

The ride on which Charboneau took Cleveland in 1980 ended rather abruptly. The rush and the jolt he provided the team and the city swiftly fizzled. Charboneau never duplicated that unforgettable rookie campaign. In fact, after just a few short years, he never even had the chance to come close.

Charboneau burned bridges with the Philadelphia Phillies, who had selected the outfielder in the second round in 1976. The Indians took a chance on him, and he batted .352 for Double-A Chattanooga in 1979. The following spring, a litany of injuries paved the way for him to make the Opening Day roster, even though a fan in Mexico stabbed him in the side with a pen knife while he signed autographs before an exhibition in early March.

Charboneau quickly won over the media and the fans in Cleveland. His bat did much of the talking—he hovered near the .300 mark for most of the season before finishing with a .289 average, 23 home runs, and 87 RBIs. His crazy, unfathomable stories did the rest. At one point, the legend of the phenom grew so large that a song, titled "Go Joe Charboneau," reached No. 3 on the local music charts.

Who's the newest guy in town?
Go Joe Charboneau
Turns the ballpark upside down
Go Joe Charboneau
Who do we appreciate?
Go Joe Charboneau
Fits right in with the other eight?
Go Joe Charboneau
Who's the one to keep our hopes alive?
Go Joe Charboneau
Straight from the seventh to the pennant drive?
Go Joe Charboneau
Raise your glass, let out a cheer
Go Joe Charboneau
For Cleveland's Rookie of the Year
Go Joe Charboneau

Charboneau soaked up the attention. He did not care for the "Super Joe" nickname or the hyperbolizing of some of the tales of his eccentric ways, but the support was overwhelming. The positive recognition was short-lived, however.

After Charboneau garnered the Rookie of the Year award for his performance in 1980, he injured his back sliding into second base the ensuing spring training. He played through pain, but after he batted just .210 with four home runs through 48 games, the Indians demoted him to Triple-A Charleston. There, he hit just .217 in 14 contests. He underwent a procedure on his back after the season. In 1982, he needed another operation after re-injuring his back.

Had he suffered from the dreaded Sophomore Jinx? Was he merely a flash in the pan to begin with? Had his off-the-field antics caught up to him? Was he simply the victim of a handful of career-debilitating injuries?

"I always wonder," he said, "if I didn't get hurt, if I could have been pretty good, or played 10 years, or hit .300, or hit 40 home runs. You just don't know."

Charboneau's last major league at-bat came on June 1, 1982, less than two years after he took home hardware as the American League's top rookie. The Pittsburgh Pirates gave him an opportunity in 1984, but he hit just .224 in 15 games at Triple-A Hawaii. While there, he appeared in the movie *The Natural* as an extra (he played one of Roy Hobbs' teammates on the New York Knights).

Charboneau has tried as hard as possible to keep baseball in his life. He coached in independent leagues, gave lessons, and ran clinics. He served as an alumni ambassador for the Indians. He also maintained his presence in Cleveland as a hitting coach for the Lorain County Ironmen, a summer collegiate team in the Prospect League. In February 2014, the Lake Erie Crushers of the Frontier League hired him as a hitting instructor.

"You can't live off one season, obviously," Charboneau said, "but it was a tremendous asset in my life. I was afforded a big luxury that I'm thankful for every day."

60 Hard-Headed

Twenty-one years after it happened, Jose Canseco posted a message on his personal Twitter account.

"Poor ball was never the same," he wrote.

Canseco laughed at it at the time, and he poked fun at himself years after the matter. With video evidence available for all to see, what else is he to do?

On May 26, 1993, in the Indians' final season at Cleveland Stadium, designated hitter Carlos Martinez skied a fly ball to right field in the bottom of the fourth inning. As Canseco rushed back toward the wall in right field, he looked up to locate the baseball and it promptly bounced off the top of his head and over the fence. Martinez was awarded a home run, a solo shot that narrowed the Texas Rangers' lead to 3–2. The Indians eventually emerged with a 7–6 victory.

The following day, *The Plain Dealer* ran the headline, "CONK! The Tribe Wins By A Head." As the ball struck Canseco's dome, the right fielder stumbled into the blue-padded wall and fell to the ground. Once he returned to his feet, he surveyed the area and tried to figure out how such a comical series of events had unfolded. He laughed it all off. Canseco said after the game that he did not know what had happened.

At one point in 2013, Major League Baseball's website, MLB. com, posted a slow-motion video of the play when its pages

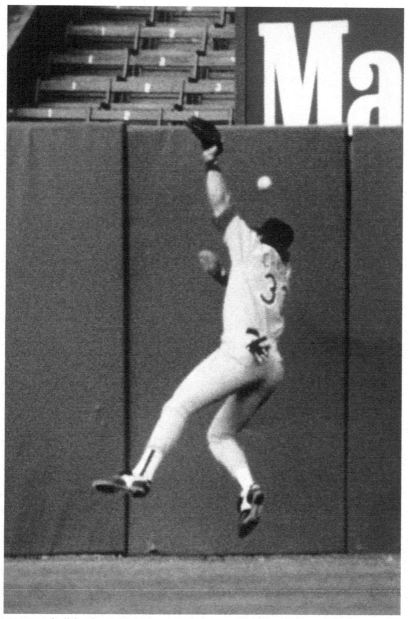

1993: A ball hit by Carlos Martinez bounces off the head of outfielder Jose Canseco and over the wall at Cleveland Stadium, which resulted in an Indians home run.

malfunctioned, to symbolize an error with the site. The play has lived on as the top selection on just about every baseball blooper reel.

From the moment the baseball caromed off of his cranium, Canseco knew the play would live in infamy. He quipped that he would be on the highlight shows for the ensuing month and said, "I guess I'm just an entertainer."

The Indians proceeded to score twice more in the fourth inning on a two-out, two-run single by Felix Fermin. They increased their 4–3 lead with three more runs in the sixth and they hung on, as the Rangers tacked on a run in each of the final three innings. Cleveland won by one run. Was Canseco's blunder the difference? His hard-headedness certainly did not help.

61 A Banner Season

The 2007 season was a banner year for the Indians. It did not end with a World Series banner, but the team came awfully close, and the widespread organizational success signified the culmination of what the club had been working toward since it initiated a rebuilding process five years earlier.

Center fielder Grady Sizemore won a Gold Glove award. Southpaw CC Sabathia took home the American League Cy Young Award. Eric Wedge was named American League Manager of the Year. General manager Mark Shapiro was recognized as Executive of the Year.

The Indians had improved their win total in 2004 and again in 2005. They tumbled, however, in 2006 when they finished fourth in the American League Central and dropped from 93 wins to 78.

The 2007 season was the perfect storm. At first, it was a literal snowstorm, one that wiped out the team's first home series and forced the club to host three games against the Los Angeles Angels in Milwaukee, of all places. But by the time summer heat swept through Cleveland, the Indians had ascended to the top of the division, the American League and, in the end, all of baseball. Their 96 wins tied them with the Boston Red Sox for most in the league.

They got off to a blazing start, with a 14–8 mark in April, an atypical first month for Wedge's Cleveland teams. For much of the summer, they jockeyed back and forth with the Detroit Tigers for possession of first place in the division. They used an eight-game winning streak at the end of August to attain a 5½-game lead over the Tigers. When the clubs met at Jacobs Field for a three-game set beginning September 17, Detroit all but needed a sweep to have any shot at displacing the Tribe.

In the first game of the series, the Tigers took a 5–2 lead into the eighth inning. Cleveland carved into the deficit when Victor Martinez plated a run with a groundout. Jhonny Peralta then swatted an opposite-field blast to right off of Joel Zumaya to tie the contest. The Indians won the game on a Casey Blake walk-off home run in the 11th. The deflating loss crushed Detroit's hopes. The Indians proceeded to sweep the series and build an insurmountable division lead.

On September 23, Rafael Betancourt struck out Oakland's Mark Ellis for the final out before a Sunday afternoon crowd of 40,250. The outfielders sprinted in toward the pitcher's mound. Players poured out of the dugout and onto the infield. Martinez jumped into Betancourt's arms. Streamers and fireworks filled the sky. The Indians had clinched the division and their first playoff berth in six years.

62 The Quest for 200

Carlos Baerga and Sandy Alomar Jr. argued back and forth during a moment of reminiscing.

"Three days," Alomar said. "Not a week."

"A week!" Baerga insisted.

"Three days."

"A week."

"I have to refresh your memory," Alomar said.

To Baerga, the memory is crystal clear. It is one of a few that stands out the most in his major league career. Baerga was stuck on 199 hits for the season in 1993. More pertinent, he was stuck in a hospital bed with an infection in his leg, acquired after fouling a ball off of his ankle with about a week remaining in the regular season. Baerga begged his way out of the hospital and back onto the field for Game 160, the first contest of the Tribe's final series at Cleveland Stadium.

Mike Hargrove slotted Baerga into his usual No. 3 spot in the batting order. The second baseman—who served as the designated hitter that night—went hitless in his first three at-bats. In his fourth and final trip to the plate, he noticed the White Sox third baseman was playing back so, with runners on first and second, he dropped a bunt down the baseline. Baerga sprinted down the line, safely crossed first base, and crumpled to the ground in pain.

"The thing about Carlos," said former teammate Kenny Lofton, "we always talk about why Carlos ran so slow. He swears he runs fast. When you run, you go forward. Carlos is the only guy in major league history that runs and he goes sideways."

No matter his running style, Baerga had enough speed on his gimpy limb to leg out his 200th hit. It marked the second consecutive year he reached that plateau. Granted, he had to return to the hospital and did not play again that season.

"I had to get 200 hits," Baerga said.

Baerga earned three trips to the All-Star Game during his tenure with the Indians. He contributed to one of the league's most potent offenses. He batted .312 with 20 home runs and 105 RBIs in 1992. He followed that up with a .321 average, 21 home runs, and 114 RBIs in 1993. He became the first player at his position with consecutive seasons of 200 hits, 20 home runs, 100 RBIs, and a .300 batting average since Rogers Hornsby seven decades earlier. Baerga hit .314 in each of the next two seasons until Cleveland traded him during the 1996 campaign. The Indians cycled through second basemen for three years before luring Roberto Alomar to the lakeshore.

Cleveland Players with 200+ Hits in a Season

Nap Lajoie: 208 hits in 1904, 214 hits in 1906, 227 hits in 1910
Shoeless Joe Jackson: 233 hits in 1911, 226 hits in 1912
Tris Speaker: 211 hits in 1916, 214 hits in 1920, 218 hits in 1923
Charlie Jamieson: 222 hits in 1923, 213 hits in 1924
Joe Sewell: 204 hits in 1925
George Burns: 216 hits in 1926
Lew Fonseca: 209 hits in 1929
Johnny Hodapp: 225 hits in 1930
Ed Morgan: 204 hits in 1930
Earl Averill: 209 hits in 1931, 232 hits in 1936
Hal Trosky: 206 hits in 1934, 216 hits in 1936
Joe Vosmik: 216 hits in 1935
Dale Mitchell: 204 hits in 1948, 203 hits in 1949
Al Rosen: 201 hits in 1953
Joe Carter: 200 hits in 1986
Carlos Baerga: 205 hits in 1992, 200 hits in 1993
Kenny Lofton: 210 hits in 1996
Michael Brantley: 200 hits in 2014

The 200-hit story—no matter how much Baerga exaggerates it or his teammates downplay it—is one of which he is quite proud. So, too, is he about a couple of other feats he accomplished.

On April 8, 1993, Baerga became the first player in big league history to slug a home run from both sides of the plate in the same inning. He tagged New York Yankees hurlers Steve Howe and Steve Farr during a nine-run seventh at Municipal Stadium. In a 9–5 loss to the Detroit Tigers at Tiger Stadium on June 17, 1993, Baerga socked a career-high three home runs, all off Detroit right-hander Mike Moore. Baerga drove in all five Cleveland runs that afternoon.

"That was a day that I'm never going to forget," Baerga said.

Even Alomar cannot argue with that.

Honoring a Legend

Anne Feller stood atop the mound before a sold-out Progressive Field crowd on a chilly April afternoon. She then knelt down in front of the white No. 19 scribbled in the dirt behind the rubber, where she placed a baseball before walking off the field.

One day after her husband, Hall of Fame hurler Bob Feller, was memorialized at a service in Cleveland, Anne capped a pregame ceremony honoring the Indians' all-time wins leader. During the team's pregame routine, each player sported a No. 19 uniform adorned with a patch displaying the hurler in his patented high-leg-kick windup motion. The patches remained on the club's jerseys throughout the 2011 campaign.

About an hour before first pitch, the team hung a pair of banners and a giant Feller uniform over the left-field wall. One

Surprising Ending

The Indians hosted the Detroit Tigers at the end of the 1940 season. Cleveland needed to sweep the three-game series to clinch the American League pennant. The Tigers needed one win to eliminate the Tribe and capture the pennant themselves.

Cleveland turned to Bob Feller for the first game. The right-hander had amassed 27 victories, including an Opening Day no-hitter. The Tigers countered with relatively unknown hurler Floyd Giebell, who had made 10 career appearances, nine out of the bullpen. Tigers manager Del Baker wanted to save his aces—Bobo Newsom and Schoolboy Rowe—for the two games in which Feller was not taking the hill.

Giebell twirled a six-hit shutout. Feller allowed only three hits in nine innings, but he served up a two-run home run to Rudy York for the only scoring in the contest. The Tigers' 2–0 triumph propelled Detroit to the World Series. The final two games of the three-game set at Cleveland Stadium meant nothing. The Indians won both.

Feller won another 184 games during his prestigious Hall of Fame career. Giebell never won another major league game.

of the banners showed a portrait of a young, smiling Feller in his military uniform. The day after the Japanese bombed Pearl Harbor in 1941, Feller put his baseball career on hold and enlisted in the Navy. He served for four years. The other banner showed Feller in that windup, his body arched back, his right arm reaching toward the dirt on the mound, his left leg lifted high in the air, ready to deliver one of his 100-mph fastballs, a blazing pitch known as the "Heater from Van Meter," named after his hometown in Iowa.

"Bob gave his life and soul to the Cleveland Indians," said manager Manny Acta. "No one will ever be associated with the Cleveland Indians the way Bob has been."

On March 31, 2011, at a memorial service for Feller—attended by four Cleveland players, a host of Indians brass, and hundreds of others—team owner Paul Dolan, Governor of Ohio John Kasich, and Jeff Idelson, president of the Baseball Hall of Fame, shared anecdotes about the man who racked up 266 wins in an Indians uniform. Feller died on December 15, 2010, at the age of 92. The day after the memorial service, after Anne Feller deposited the baseball in the dirt, Fausto Carmona scooped it up, and another Opening Day was under way. The timing was fitting, given that Feller stakes claim to the most heralded Opening Day feat in baseball history.

On April 16, 1940, a 21-year-old Feller tossed the only Opening Day no-hitter in major league lore, as he blanked the Chicago White Sox in a 1–0 win at Comiskey Park. Feller walked five. Another reached base when center fielder Roy Weatherly misplayed a fly ball in the second inning. Other than that, the right-hander proved unflappable.

64 Great Sock-cess

The Indians' surge to the World Series in 1997 often overshadows their pedestrian showing during the regular season. Mike Hargrove's bunch wobbled to an 86–75 mark, as the club captured the American League Central crown by a six-game margin. The division title was in doubt until early September. The Indians finished with the fewest wins of any division champion in the American League. They finished with 10 fewer wins than the New York Yankees, who earned the American League Wild Card berth.

Cleveland treaded water until late August. The team needed a spark. First baseman Jim Thome was known to hike up his pant legs and display his high socks when he played. So, on Thome's 27th birthday on August 27, shortstop Omar Vizquel spearheaded

A Triumphant Homecoming

The whispers circulated throughout the Indians clubhouse on the afternoon of August 26, 2011. The club had re-acquired Jim Thome a day earlier. Initially, his new teammates tossed about the idea of sporting high socks—in honor of Thome's patented look—on his birthday, August 27.

In 1997, the Indians began wearing high socks on Thome's birthday. They won that day and, subsequently, rode the fashion wave to a World Series appearance.

They couldn't wait until his birthday in 2011, however. According to reliever Joe Smith, certain players whined, "I don't look good in high socks" and "I have 'cankles.'" Still, the players pulled up their red socks as they took the field.

"I thought it looked great," Smith said. "Everybody, coaches included, did it. Maybe it means something, maybe it doesn't, but I thought it was pretty cool. He definitely deserves that for what he's done for the game."

The wardrobe adjustment worked; the Indians won on August 26. They won again the next day, as Thome launched a home run on his 41st birthday.

Thome appreciated the gesture.

"It was very nice," he said. "It was similar to '97."

a clubhouse movement that required everyone to make a collective fashion statement.

The players all sported their high socks that night against the Angels at Anaheim Stadium. A 10-run inning—fueled by Matt Williams' three-run home run and three-run double—provided the club with a 10–4 win. Ironically, Thome had the night off. As superstition mandates, the Indians could not ditch the wardrobe choice after such an offensive outburst. So the team maintained its fashion stance in its next game two days later against the Cubs. The Indians won 7–6. The socks stuck around. After a loss, the team rattled off a couple more victories. Another loss was followed by a five-game winning streak. After the implementation of the dress code, the Indians won nine of 11. The stretch enhanced their lead in the American League Central by three more games. By the second week of September, they sat somewhat comfortably atop the division.

The team marched all the way to the World Series, an enthralling, seven-game bout that the Florida Marlins claimed in dramatic, gut-wrenching fashion. It was fashion itself, though, that spurred the club in the home stretch of the 1997 campaign. Frankly, the Indians seemed relatively average that season. The roster underwent a litany of modifications. The lineup lost its most powerful punch when Albert Belle cashed in on a hefty pay day with the White Sox in November 1996. It added veteran third baseman Matt Williams, which forced Thome to relocate to the other side of the infield. One week before the start of the regular season, the team traded reliever Alan Embree and All-Star center fielder Kenny Lofton to Atlanta for outfielders Marquis Grissom and David Justice. Grissom and Williams struggled for much of the regular season while growing accustomed to the American League.

"We did make some very difficult decisions," said general manager John Hart. "I think some very probably controversial calls, starting with the Carlos Baerga trade, the decision to let Albert Belle go, and then obviously the Kenny Lofton trade. And we knew that we were bringing in some different types of players, very talented players that were changing leagues."

Aside from April, when they posted a 12–13 mark, the Indians finished every month with a winning record. But the best record they amassed in any month was May's 15–11 showing. They certainly were not the well-oiled machine they were a year earlier, when they registered a 99–62 mark. They barely resembled the team that rolled to a 100–44 record two years prior. In fact, between 1994–2001, the Indians' .534 winning percentage in 1997 represents their worst such mark for any season.

"This club won 86 games," Hart said, "I think without a consistent starting rotation throughout the year, and without a consistent bullpen."

Still, the club flaunted its newfound fashion sense all the way to a World Series appearance.

65 The Score

To one generation, Herb Score was a gifted storyteller and broadcaster. To another, he was a talented left-handed pitcher whose career was cut short by injuries and misfortune. He is remembered by some as the hurler who was struck in the eye by a line drive. He is remembered by others as the guy who declared the Indians were headed to the World Series—even though they still needed to record three outs. No matter the perspective on the man, the player, the announcer, Score is widely regarded as an integral piece of Indians lore.

"He was an icon," said Tom Hamilton, his radio play-by-play partner for nearly a decade.

Score was the American League Rookie of the Year in 1955, when he went 16–10 with a 2.85 ERA and tallied 245 strikeouts. He bettered those numbers to 20–9 with a 2.53 ERA and 263 strikeouts the following year. He made the All-Star team in both seasons. But in his fifth start in 1957, tragedy struck.

In the first inning of a contest against the New York Yankees at Cleveland Stadium on May 7, Gil McDougald lined a 2-2 pitch back toward the mound. Score lifted his head, saw the white blur buzzing toward him and attempted to move his glove into position in time, but the baseball sailed past his fingers and drilled him in the right eye. He grabbed at his face, stumbled and dropped to the dirt. At first, he thought his eye popped out of its socket. Blood streamed down his face. He endured severe hemorrhaging in the eye and suffered a swollen retina and a broken nose. He might as well have paid rent at the hospital.

Score typically preferred not to rehash the events of that game and he was adamant that the accident did not trigger the downfall of his career. He was once billed to be the next in line in a slew of legendary Cleveland pitchers, following in the footsteps of Bob Feller and Bob Lemon. He eventually returned to the mound in the 1958 season, but arm troubles plagued him, and he was never the same. He won only 19 games after 1956 and he pitched his last game before he turned 29.

Score transitioned into a broadcasting career. He called Indians games from 1964–97.

"The two best mentors I could have ever had were Herb and Mike Hegan," Hamilton said.

When Hamilton joined the fold before the 1990 season, Score wanted to do only five innings of play-by-play and he wanted nothing to do with the first two frames of each game. That was fine with Hamilton.

"Whatever Herb wanted to do," Hamilton said, "he could have done."

Vote for Pedro

At some point in the '90s, the Indians had to break through. The players' strike prevented them from a potential postseason berth in 1994. The Atlanta Braves' stout pitching staff kept them from a title in 1995. The Baltimore Orioles sent them packing in the first round of the 1996 playoffs. The Florida Marlins crushed the city's dreams in the 11th inning of Game 7 of the 1997 World Series. The New York Yankees, winners of 114 games in the regular season, emerged triumphant against Cleveland in the 1998 American League Championship Series.

The Indians had seen it all by 1999. They had fallen short as the underdog and as the favorite. They had fallen short because of poor pitching, poor hitting, and poor fortune. How long can a franchise remain near the top without winning a championship? The Indians resembled a dynasty, just without the hardware validation.

The Indians, Yankees, Boston Red Sox, and Texas Rangers all qualified for the postseason in 1999. Cleveland had compiled just a 10–22 record against their three American League playoff counterparts, including a 4–8 showing against Boston, its first-round opponent. Still, the Indians seemed poised to make another run at the Fall Classic.

In 1999, the Indians were an offensive force. They compiled a 97–65 mark in the regular season, despite league-average pitching. Any team that was going to stop them in October needed some talented arms. The Indians scored 6.23 runs per game, nearly a half-run more than any other team. They totaled 1,009 runs, the first team since 1950 to top the 1,000-run plateau and only the seventh overall since the turn of the 20th century. They were shut out only three times all season.

They batted .289 as a team, second-best in baseball. Manny Ramirez hit .333 with 44 home runs, 165 RBIs, and 131 runs scored. Roberto Alomar batted .323 with 24 home runs, 120 RBIs, 138 runs scored, and 37 stolen bases. Jim Thome totaled 33 home runs, 108 RBIs, and 101 runs scored. Omar Vizquel batted .333, swiped 42 bases, and scored 112 runs. Kenny Lofton hit .301, stole 25 bases, and scored 110 runs. Even Richie Sexson clubbed 31 home runs and drove in 116. It was a lineup full of players producing video game numbers.

The odds took a turn in Cleveland's favor when Red Sox ace Pedro Martinez left his start in Game 1 because of a strained back. With the dominant right-hander sidelined, the Indians erased a 2–0 deficit and captured a series-opening victory when Travis Fryman delivered a walk-off single with the bases loaded. They breezed to victory in Game 2 behind their record-setting offense. Harold Baines blasted a three-run home run and Thome clubbed a grand slam in Cleveland's 11–1 win. Boston stormed back with a 9–3 triumph at Fenway Park in Game 3. Dave Burba departed after four scoreless innings because of a strained forearm. Rather than turn to his bullpen, manager Mike Hargrove, aiming to put the series away, summoned scheduled Game 4 starter Jaret Wright. The young righty unraveled, and Boston scored nine times over the ensuing three innings, including six times in the seventh.

With Wright unavailable for Game 4 the following night, the Indians turned to Bartolo Colon on three days' rest. That plan flopped. Boston scored multiple runs in seven of its eight innings at bat, including the first five. The Red Sox had seven runs after two innings, 10 after three, 15 after four and 18 after five en route to a 23–7 romp. Colon did not make it out of the second.

Charles Nagy and Bret Saberhagen both started Game 5 on three days' rest. Martinez warmed up briefly before the game and was deemed available if necessary. He spent the early innings draped in a blue Red Sox jacket, stretching and staying loose in the dugout. Nomar Garciaparra socked a two-run home run to center in the top half of the first, but Thome responded with a two-run shot to center—after Vizquel registered an RBI double—to provide the Indians with a 3–2 advantage. An inning later, Fryman sent Saberhagen to the showers after a two-run shot off the railing perched above the left-field wall.

Boston shaved its deficit to 5–3 in the third and Nagy—after a discussion with Hargrove—intentionally walked Garciaparra to load the bases for Troy O'Leary, who promptly slugged a grand slam to right-center on the first pitch of the at-bat. The Indians responded yet again, as Ramirez contributed an RBI double and Thome launched another two-run shot to center in the bottom of the third for an 8–7 edge. Once Thome circled the bases and retreated to the dugout, Martinez dug his cleats into the dirt in the bullpen and began warming up.

The Red Sox knotted the game at 8–8 in the top of the fourth and they called upon Martinez in the bottom half of the frame. Martinez had logged a 23–4 record and 2.07 ERA, with 313 strikeouts in 213⅓ innings during the regular season, statistics that earned him his second Cy Young Award. The pain in his back forced him to throw a bevy of curveballs and hampered his command a bit. He still persevered through the final six innings and did not allow a hit.

In the seventh, with first base open, the Indians again walked Garciaparra intentionally. That placed two aboard for O'Leary, who deposited Paul Shuey's first offering into the Boston bullpen in right field. The three-run home run handed the Red Sox an 11–8 lead and provided more than enough backing for Martinez. With two outs and Boston holding a 12–8 advantage in the ninth, Martinez struck out Vizquel on an off-speed pitch that dove toward the dirt. He raised his arms, his left fist clenched and looked toward the sky. Catcher Jason Varitek, lacking sympathy for the pitcher's troublesome back, rushed him and squeezed him tight. The rest of the Red Sox raced toward the mound, circled around Martinez and lifted him in the air as the Indians stared with disbelief from the dugout.

Four days later, the Indians fired Hargrove. It was yet another postseason with dreams unfulfilled. A pain worse than the one Martinez felt in his back? Cleveland could have employed Martinez atop its rotation. The Indians discussed a trade for the ace with the Expos in 1997, but they were reluctant to part with a package that included young hurlers Wright and Colon. Instead, Montreal dealt Martinez to the Red Sox, with whom he signed an extension and wound up spending the bulk of his Hall of Fame career.

67 From Lottery Ticket to Ace

Members of Cleveland's front office shuffled through every top prospect list they could get their hands on, but they couldn't locate the name of the moderately intriguing right-handed pitcher for the Padres. In July 2010, the Indians assigned a pair of scouts to monitor Corey Kluber's outings with Class AA San Antonio. His minor-league numbers weren't anything noteworthy, but they at least liked his strikeout rate, and they knew in this budding three-team arrangement, they couldn't ask for a ton. Cleveland was parting with the final two months of soon-to-be 33-year-old Jake Westbrook's contract, an impending free agent on a team headed nowhere.

Kluber was a lottery ticket. And Cleveland hit the jackpot.

When he learned of the trade, Kluber, who rarely spoke above a whisper, called his parents and relayed the news in typical Kluber fashion: stoic, nonchalant, emotionless. His father, on the other hand—a graduate of Mayfield High School on the east side of Cleveland—couldn't contain his excitement. "You're kidding," Jim said to his son, laughing.

That robotic persona followed Kluber to the top. You could never tell if he had just spun a complete-game shutout, collected a Cy Young Award or been sprayed by a skunk. There was no better example than when Kluber joined an in-game TV broadcast for an interview, with his teammates pelting him with sunflower seeds, water and baby powder. He refused to crack the slightest hint of a smile. Whenever he retreated to the dugout following a start worthy of a standing ovation, Kluber would remain unfazed and unwavering, in such a zone, he would say, he wouldn't even notice the fans showering him with applause.

From 2014–18, Kluber won a pair of Cy Young Awards and twice finished third in the balloting. All five seasons, he topped both the 200-inning mark and 200-strikeout mark, the only player in franchise history to eclipse those totals in five consecutive seasons. In that stretch, he ranked second in the majors in innings pitched (1,091), fourth in the majors in ERA (2.85), third in the majors in strikeouts (1,228) and third in the majors in pitcher WAR (30.3). He stands atop the team's all-time leaderboard in strikeouts per nine innings and strikeout-to-walk ratio. He ranks third in team history in strikeouts, behind only Bob Feller and Sam McDowell, who stuck around far longer than Kluber's nine seasons and 208 outings.

No start better encapsulates Kluber's peak effectiveness than his outing on May 13, 2015, when he tied Feller's club record of 18 strikeouts, a feat that had gone unmatched for 77 years. Kluber piled up those 18 punchouts in only eight innings, and he did it while carrying a no-hitter into the seventh against the Cardinals. That just so happened to be the same day Feller's widow, Anne, visited Progressive Field to snip a red ribbon to unveil a Terrace Club display full of her late husband's keepsakes that had been relocated from the defunct Bob Feller Museum in Van Meter, Iowa.

During the Indians' march to the World Series in 2016, Kluber unleashed cutter after cutter and two-seam fastball after two-seam fastball and devastating curveball/slider thing after devastating curveball/slider thing until his right arm begged for mercy. With Cleveland's rotation in tatters, Kluber pitched repeatedly on short rest. He pitched deep into games. He pitched even though his tank had run empty. In his first five playoff starts in 2016, he logged a 0.89 ERA.

There's an alternate universe in which the team finishes off the Cubs in that Fall Classic and Kluber's run becomes the stuff of legend in Cleveland sports lore.

"You can obviously go look at it and say, 'I want to pitch like him,'" Josh Tomlin once said about his locker mate. "Of course, everybody does. But what a lot of people don't understand is it's the things he does prior to that start. It's mirrored every fifth day. Every day, it's the same thing. He knows how his body is going to feel that fifth day. Guys notice that. They start to get in a better routine, better preparation, and once you do that, you're set up for success.... A bunch of guys follow him. And rightfully so. They should."

68 Kenny's Catch

Only the horizontal bar of green padding suffered a worse fate than Baltimore's B.J. Surhoff. Pitcher Paul Shuey, after a sigh of relief, made out just fine. The fans were treated to perhaps the most impressive spectacle they had ever witnessed live. And, of course, the star of the moment, Kenny Lofton, garnered the spotlight he eternally craved.

The Indians clenched a 3–2 lead against the Orioles in the top of the eighth inning at Jacobs Field on August 4, 1996, a sunny, warm Sunday afternoon. Shuey had registered one out in the frame with Rafael Palmeiro aboard via a single. Surhoff worked a 3–0 count before he socked a fastball down the middle deep to center field.

Flipping Over

There was Austin Jackson, upside down in the Red Sox bullpen, feet in the air, pointed at the Boston sky. Record scratch. Freeze frame. Yep, you're probably wondering how he ended up in this situation.

When Hanley Ramirez sent Dan Otero's pitch to deep center in the fifth inning of a game between Boston and Cleveland at Fenway Park on August 1, 2017, Jackson took off for the fence. He jumped. He caught it. And then he realized he was about to take a tumble. He grabbed onto the wall as he flipped over into Boston's bullpen. And as he hung upside down, he thought about a similar effort his old Tigers teammate, Torii Hunter, made during the 2013 ALCS. Hunter couldn't haul in David Ortiz's grand slam, but Jackson did rob Ramirez of a home run.

"That will go down as one of the best catches of all-time," said fellow Cleveland outfielder Brandon Guyer, who raced over to the fence and started to climb it to check on Jackson. "At first, I didn't think he would even catch it. The ball just kept carrying and I was like, 'Oh, man.' For him to catch it and hold on and stick the landing and everything, I've never seen anything like it."

Boston fans gave Jackson a standing ovation.

"That was awesome," he said. "I was just so pumped up, it's like I didn't even hear them. I was just pumped up for us. I'm glad I was able to hold onto it, especially going over like that. I could have easily dropped it. I was able to hold onto it and get the out."

Yes, but...

"I thought it was going to look a little better, me flipping over," he joked. "I thought I'd land it a little better than that."

As the ball sailed through the air, Lofton, after giving chase, tiptoed toward the warning track to achieve ideal timing on his eventual jump. He accelerated up into the wall and stuck his right foot onto the padding to prop himself up even higher. With both feet on the ledge, he stretched his right arm over the fence and twisted his body into position to make the catch. As he peered down at Eric Plunk and the rest of his colleagues in the bullpen, the baseball settled into the webbing of his glove. His cleats slipped off the padding, but he landed on both feet, took two quick steps and fired a throw back toward the infield as Palmeiro retreated to first.

"I said, 'Holy shit!'" said catcher Sandy Alomar Jr., who had a front-row seat while warming up Plunk. "No way that just happened. That's impressive."

"I thought that ball was going to be a homer. Period," said shortstop Omar Vizquel. "I dropped my head and I said, 'Damn, man.'"

The awe-inspiring grab prevented the Orioles from grabbing a 4–3 lead. The Indians would strike for an 11-run eighth to cruise to a 14–2 victory. As the fans showered Lofton with gratitude, he stood in center field, his left hand on his hip, his sunglasses shading the bright sun and he curled his lips and shook his head, as if to—in a tongue-in-cheek manner—act as if it were just another day at the office.

"It's just an instinct play," Lofton said. "It's just something that happens."

Lofton felt that kind of sterling defensive effort—the kind that helped him earn four Gold Glove awards in his career—was his job as a speedy center fielder.

"It has to take an understanding of who you are," Lofton said. "As a person, I knew that was my job and that's what I do. I'm a leadoff hitter. I look at what a leadoff hitter is supposed to do, and that's what I do. I look at what a center fielder is supposed to do, and I do it. I look at what a guy who is considered a speedster on a team is supposed to do."

In 2010, the Indians released a bobblehead that depicted Lofton making the catch. Lofton, clad in his white uniform, is seen scaling a green wall as he reaches over the yellow line to secure the catch.

"For me, no doubt, I think it was one of the greatest catches I ever saw," Jim Thome said. "Literally, I thought he was going to jump over the wall."

"I always ran hard and went after balls at the wall, because you never know," Lofton said. "You can't catch it if you're not up there."

69 Carnegie and Ontario

In February 1990, Tom Hamilton arrived at Indians spring training in Tucson, Arizona, wide-eyed and naively optimistic.

"I thought in spring training, 'Damn. We're going to win the pennant,'" Hamilton said.

Not exactly.

The Indians had registered only two winning seasons over the previous decade. During that stretch, they never placed better than fifth in the American League East. Herb Score, the former Cleveland pitcher and longtime broadcaster whom Hamilton joined in the radio booth, set the rookie announcer straight.

"No," Score said to Hamilton, "we're not."

Then Score offered Hamilton a piece of advice he still reminds himself on a daily basis.

"He goes, 'This is a bad team,'" Hamilton said. "'But that can't have any impact on the broadcast. The record of the ball club can never impact how you prepare for a game or how you broadcast that game. There are too many people depending on you to hear that game and it might be the highlight of their day, listening to an Indians game, and you owe them your very best. It doesn't matter what their record is.'"

Hamilton never expected to last in Cleveland, in his first real job, in the field he selected once he accepted that his dreams of playing professionally were far-fetched. When the Indians first hired him to pair with Score in 1990, Hamilton and his wife, Wendy, purchased a house in Bay Village, Ohio, because homes in the area "had such good resale value."

"You didn't know if you were going to last a year or two years or what," Hamilton said.

Especially given Hamilton's lack of a filter off the air.

"I'm just lucky the booth wasn't miked up during commercials, or my career might have lasted five years," Hamilton said.

His career has persisted much longer than that. The Indians recognized Hamilton on August 1, 2014, for his 25th season as the club's play-by-play voice. He has been a finalist multiple times for the Baseball Hall of Fame's Ford Frick Award, handed out annually to one broadcaster for excellence in the booth.

"He's iconic," said former team president Mark Shapiro. "He's not just iconic because he's been here a while. He's really good. He's legitimately among the best at what he does."

Hamilton's signature lines resonate with anyone who has tuned in to a game over the last 35 years.

"And we're underway from the corner of Carnegie and Ontario!"

"Swing and a drive, awayyy back. Gone!"

"Strike! Three! Called!"

"Ballgame!"

Shapiro said Hamilton brings the club to life.

The Indians posted a 77–85 record in 1990. They did not, to Hamilton's surprise, win the pennant. They sank to 57–105 the following year. Hamilton needed that reality check, though, especially given what lay ahead.

From 1994–2001, the Indians recorded eight consecutive winning campaigns, captured six AL Central crowns and twice reached the World Series.

"I'm lucky that in my first four years, we weren't very good," Hamilton said. "So I had an appreciation for how tough it was for them to get good and begin to win. I wouldn't have had as much of an appreciation for that if I would've been hired in, say, '94. They won from '94 on. But '90, '91, '92, '93, we were not a good team and in '91, it was the worst season in franchise history. So because of that, you have a greater appreciation for what winning meant."

Hamilton can pinpoint a few memories from that era—Kenny Lofton's dash to the plate in Game 6 of the 1995 American League Championship Series, the celebration in Baltimore after the 1997 American League Championship Series, walking around Miami prior to the 1997 World Series—as some of the fondest in his career. He worked with Score and then Mike Hegan, a Cleveland native, and, since 2007, has partnered with Jim Rosenhaus.

His eyes well up when he reflects upon his most cherished memory, one that unfolded during spring training in 2014. As camp wound down, the Indians and Reds were set to square off one late March afternoon at Goodyear Ballpark, the complex they share in the Arizona desert. Cincinnati was deemed the home team and, originally, the Reds opted to dismiss the designated hitter and play by their National League rules. So the Indians sent Nick Swisher—scheduled to serve as the DH that day—home. Shortly before the first pitch, however, the Reds granted the Indians permission to use a DH. Manager Terry Francona opted to pencil Nick Hamilton—Tom's son, who had been added to the roster that day as an extra—into the starting lineup.

"It was the perfect storm," Hamilton said.

For Hamilton, it was really just perfect.

The Indians had selected Nick in the 35th round of the 2012 first-year player draft. He overcame a hearing impairment and his short stature, played in the College World Series with Kent State, and signed a professional baseball contract. When Hamilton first took the job with the Indians, Nick was two months old. Now here he was, suiting up for the Indians on a balmy spring day with his father still in the booth.

The game was not broadcast on radio that day, but Rosenhaus provided play-by-play on the webcast on the Indians' website. Hamilton sat beside his colleague and watched his son. As Nick grounded out in his first at-bat, tears streamed down Hamilton's face.

"You couldn't script it any better than that," Hamilton said, choking up. "We'll never forget Tito and the Indians for making that happen."

Hamilton lives for those kinds of moments. He downplays his longevity in the booth, and he termed his ascension to a big league gig a "long shot." Hamilton, a kid who grew up on a dairy farm near Milwaukee, never thought he would last this long in the first place.

"For me, it was like winning the lottery," Hamilton said. "The impossible dream came true."

70 Visit Guardians Spring Training

In the middle of a row of palm trees beyond the left-field fence at Goodyear Ballpark stands a run-of-the-mill scoreboard. It is not any elaborate video board with showy graphics or fiery displays intended to lure visitors to the venue. The atmosphere and the climate already take care of that. The scoreboard does, however, occasionally post a message that makes many of those in attendance appreciate their surroundings.

Cleveland, Ohio: 29 degrees
Goodyear, Arizona: 75 degrees

Any Cleveland native in search of a reprieve from a harsh winter or longing for the start of the baseball season ought to visit Goodyear. The Indians moved into the facilities in 2009; the Cincinnati Reds, in 2010. The club had spent spring training in Winter Haven, Florida, since 1993. Before that, the club played in Tucson, Arizona. The primary benefit to spring training in Arizona: Unlike the Florida setup, any trek to another team's stadium is under an hour. No matter if the Guardians play in Scottsdale or Tempe or Mesa or Surprise or Peoria, the drive isn't unreasonable for fans wanting to see an away game. Plus, there are plenty of mountain ranges within a short drive for an off-day hike.

The setting is serenity. The temperature in Goodyear in February and March typically ranges from 70 to 90 degrees during the day. Clouds are a rarity. Rainfall is foreign.

Goodyear Ballpark sits on a flat strip of land, with the Estrella Mountain range visible in the distance. The surrounding area is newly developed and populated with plenty of restaurants. Both the Guardians and the Reds have complexes down the street from the stadium, with multiple practice fields and minor league diamonds. They use the facilities year-round for their youngest minor leaguers, as well as players rehabbing from injuries.

Before the snow melts away on the streets of Cleveland, the Guardians' clubhouse attendants load a pair of semitrucks with player jerseys and pants, exercise machines, bicycles, golf clubs, hundreds of cases of bottled water, and a collection of ballpark mustard. The trucks make a cross-country trip to Goodyear, where the staff completes a two-hour unloading process.

It may take the equipment 30 hours to travel by truck from Cleveland to Arizona, but a fan flying from Ohio can be sitting in the sun at practice in as little as four hours.

71 The Namesake of Pitching

Cy Young won more games than any other pitcher in baseball history. He lost more games, started more games, and completed more games than any other pitcher in baseball history, too. His longevity, durability and, of course, ability have gone just about unmatched. Certainly, the sport has changed, as has the way hurlers are handled. Young, however, remains a pitching icon, as evidenced by the award bearing his name that is handed out annually to the top pitcher in each league.

Born in eastern Ohio, Young spent the first nine years of his professional career with the Cleveland Spiders. He routinely logged upwards of 400 innings and won 25–35 games per season. In 1892, he won 36 games, posted a 1.93 ERA and totaled 453 innings. What a different universe. At the tail end of the 19th century, the Spiders had crumbled as an organization and fed their premier talent to the St. Louis Perfectos. The new Cleveland franchise started up in the American League in 1901, but by that time, Young had moved on to St. Louis and then to Boston, where he trimmed his ERA even though he had grown old in the tooth. In his final season with the Red Sox, 1908, a 41-year-old Young posted a 1.26 ERA.

In 1909, the Cleveland Naps acquired Young via trade for Charlie Chech, Jack Ryan, and a sum of cash. Young pitched in Cleveland for two and a half years and recorded a 2.50 ERA. The right-hander amassed a 511–316 record during his 22-year career. His 511 wins are 94 more than any other pitcher in baseball history. He pitched in 906 games, including 815 starts. He tallied 749 complete games and 76 shutouts, racking up 7,356 innings and facing 29,565 batters.

For the sake of comparison, in 2018, Corey Kluber, the reigning Cy Young Award winner, led the league with 215 innings and faced 842 batters. To match Young's totals, Kluber would need to take that heavy workload and repeat it for 35 seasons.

Young is credited with three no-hitters, including one perfect game. He was elected to the Baseball Hall of Fame in 1937. The Cy Young Award was created in 1956, the year after his death.

72 World Series Walk-Off

The 1995 campaign was like a dream. Cleveland fans did not want to pinch themselves for fear of feeling nothing and realizing that it was all a mirage. The Indians had been so bad for so long. This could not be real. When the Indians claimed Game 3 of the World Series, that pinch became admissible. There was feeling there, and plenty of it.

The Indians rolled into the World Series an offensive juggernaut, winners of a league-high 100 contests in the 144–game regular season. The Braves' dynamic starting pitching carved them down to size in the first two games at Atlanta-Fulton County Stadium. Greg Maddux, who earned his fourth consecutive National League Cy Young award for his 19–2 record and 1.63 ERA, tossed a complete game in the Braves' 3–2 Game 1 victory. Tom Glavine, who posted a 16–7 record and 3.08 ERA during the regular season, stymied Cleveland in a 4–3 win in Game 2.

Cleveland mustered only eight total hits in the first two tilts. The Indians collected 12 in Game 3. None was more significant than Eddie Murray's liner to center.

Murray approached the plate with the score tied 6–6 and no outs in the 11ᵗʰ inning. He had gone 0-for-5 with three strikeouts, but he had a chance to erase that from everyone's memory banks. Alvaro Espinoza stood at second base after pinch-running for Carlos Baerga, who started the inning with a double to right-center. Albert Belle stood at first following an intentional walk.

Murray attacked the first offering from Alejandro Peña, a fastball at the letters. Marquis Grissom's outfield throw sailed up the third-base line. Espinoza slid toward home and brushed the plate with his right hand.

"The Indians are back in the World Series!" Bob Costas shouted on the national telecast.

Six years after capturing a championship, the Indians were swept by the New York Giants in the 1954 World Series. Four decades of mostly misery ensued. Even after a magical regular season and first two rounds of the playoffs in 1995, the first two games of the Fall Classic seemed to serve as a reality check. Murray's walk-off single proved otherwise. Cleveland could exhale. This was no fantasy. It was real.

73 Streak Snappers

It is an achievement that might never be topped, a feat that has stood the test of time, of generations, of eras of baseball that have catered to the skill set required to even consider a chance at such a hallowed mark. Joe DiMaggio's 56-game hitting streak, a major league record and a historical anomaly, did, however, come to an end at Cleveland Stadium.

Longest Hitting Streaks
Here are the longest hitting streaks in franchise history.
1. Sandy Alomar, 30 games (1997)
2. Hal Trosky, 28 games (1936)
3. Bruce Campbell, 27 games (1938)
   Tris Speaker, 27 games (1916)
5. Casey Blake, 26 games (2007)
6. Matt Williams, 24 games (1997)
7. Mike Hargrove, 23 games (1980)
   Ray Fosse, 23 games (1970)
   Johnny Temple, 23 games (1960)
   Al Rosen, 23 games (1953–1954)
   Dale Mitchell, 23 games (1951)
   Charlie Jamieson, 23 games (1923, 1924)
   Tris Speaker, 23 games (1923)

The Yankees and Indians met on the evening of July 17, 1941. A crowd of 67,468 filed into the massive structure to watch first-place New York battle second-place Cleveland and, more pressing, to witness the possible extension of DiMaggio's streak. Since he delivered an RBI single that scored Phil Rizzuto in his first at-bat of a 13–1 loss to the White Sox on May 15, DiMaggio had notched at least one hit in each contest. The Yankees went 41–13 during the streak (two games ended in a tie because of curfew rules). During the stretch, DiMaggio collected 91 hits, as he batted .408 with a .463 on-base percentage, .717 slugging percentage, 15 home runs, 16 doubles, 55 RBIs, 56 runs scored, and only five strikeouts.

Then, Ken Keltner, a classic case of kryptonite, entered the picture. The third baseman made a pair of diving stops to keep DiMaggio off the basepaths on July 17. He robbed the Yankee Clipper of a hit in the first inning. DiMaggio walked in the fourth and again grounded to Keltner in the seventh. In the eighth, with the bases loaded and New York holding a 4–1 lead, DiMaggio grounded a pitch to Indians shortstop Lou Boudreau, who initiated a 6–4–3 inning-ending, streak-ending double play.

Had the Indians stormed back and forced the game to extra frames, DiMaggio could have had another at-bat. Larry Rosenthal delivered a two-run triple with no outs in the bottom of the ninth, but Hal Trosky grounded out and Soup Campbell bounced one back to the pitcher, who threw Rosenthal out at home. Roy Weatherly grounded out to end the game.

74 Off the Scoreboard

Jim Thome's 511-foot majestic shot that bounced out of the ballpark and onto Eagle Avenue is the longest-measured home run in the history of Progressive Field. It might not be the most impressive power display, though. That standard was established by Mark McGwire on April 30, 1997.

McGwire socked an Orel Hershiser offering off of the Budweiser sign on the ballpark scoreboard. The baseball sailed over the 19-foot-high wall in left field. It zipped past the 23 rows of bleacher seats. It struck the red sign near the letter "I" and caromed back into the stands. The two-run home run was estimated at 485 feet. Upon impact with the scoreboard, fans let out oohs and aahs. Some applauded McGwire for the feat.

"It was still going up when it hit it," said Jason Giambi, a member of that Athletics team. "I remember distinctly watching it. It was pretty unbelievable."

Giambi estimated that, had it not been for the scoreboard, the baseball would have landed on the roof of a parking garage that sits adjacent to the ballpark.

Powerful People

The following Cleveland players hit 40 or more home runs in a season.

52: Jim Thome (2002)
50: Albert Belle (1995)
49: Jim Thome (2001)
48: Albert Belle (1996)
45: Manny Ramirez (1998)
44: Manny Ramirez (1999)
43: Al Rosen (1953)
42: Travis Hafner (2006)
42: Rocky Colavito (1959)
42: Hal Trosky (1936)
41: Rocky Colavito (1958)
40: Jim Thome (1997)

"It's one of the hardest balls I've ever seen hit," Giambi said.

The swat provided McGwire's Oakland Athletics with a 5–2 lead in the third inning. At the time, it was the longest home run in ballpark history, eclipsing Juan Gonzalez's 460-foot blast in July 1994.

"I can't believe that a man hit a ball that far," one of the Athletics' broadcasters quipped.

McGwire and fellow A's slugger Jose Canseco had spent batting practice targeting the scoreboard, but neither hitter was able to dent the structure. Hershiser paced around the mound before stepping back onto the rubber and taking a deep breath. McGwire would tack on a go-ahead home run to lead off the 10th inning. The A's won the game 11–9.

75 Selby vs. Rivera

Tom Hamilton's voice could have shattered glass.

The Indians' radio play-by-play man erupted as Bill Selby lined one of Mariano Rivera's cutters to right field. The Indians had narrowed a 7–0 deficit to 7–6 on July 14, 2002, and it was up to Selby to provide the knockout punch against the most celebrated closer in Major League Baseball history.

He did. Or so it seemed. An ecstatic Hamilton shouted as Selby socked Rivera's offering, but there was one problem: the supposed walk-off hit landed in foul territory.

"It looked like a game-winner," Hamilton said. "I thought it was a fair ball. You always remember your mistakes."

Hamilton apologized, though who could blame him? There hadn't been much to scream about in excitement during the 2002 campaign. The moment came during the first season of the Indians' rebuilding process, one that abruptly halted the greatest stretch of baseball in franchise history.

After a seven-year period in which the Indians captured six American League Central Division crowns, advanced to a pair of World Series, and filled the ballpark to capacity on a nightly basis, this was a new era. It was uncharted territory, and the initial results were tough to swallow.

On this particular Sunday afternoon, the Indians had mounted a respectable comeback against the titans of the American League. A moral victory amid a murky season would have sufficed. Wins and losses wouldn't define the 2002 club, anyway; the reconstruction of the organizational roster would.

After Selby's near-walk-off veered foul, reality set in. Selby entered the game with a .219 batting average, zero home runs,

Walk-off Grand Slams Since Progressive Field Opened in 1994:

Albert Belle: July 18, 1995 vs. California Angels, off Lee Smith
Albert Belle: July 31, 1996 vs. Toronto Blue Jays, off Bill Risley
Sandy Alomar Jr.: May 3, 1998 vs. Tampa Bay Devil Rays, off Roberto Hernandez
Omar Vizquel: May 23, 1999 vs. Detroit Tigers, off Todd Jones
Bill Selby: July 14, 2002 vs. New York Yankees, off Mariano Rivera
Jim Thome: July 28, 2002 vs. Detroit Tigers, off Juan Acevedo
Carlos Santana: April 29, 2011 vs. Detroit Tigers, off Joaquin Benoit
Travis Hafner: July 7, 2011 vs. Toronto Blue Jays, off Luis Perez
Nick Swisher: June 19, 2014 vs. Anaheim Angels, off Ernesto Frieri
Edwin Encarnacion: July 25, 2017 vs. Anaheim Angels, off Bud Norris
Jason Kipnis: September 19, 2018 vs. Chicago White Sox, off Ian Hamilton (Kipnis' 1,000th hit)

and three RBIs in 18 games for the Indians that season. He would eventually finish a five-year big-league career with a .223 average and 11 home runs in 198 games.

The 5'9" Mississippi kid with the blonde buzz cut didn't stand a chance against Rivera, who five days earlier had thrown a scoreless inning for the American League in the All-Star Game. Rivera retired after the 2013 season, having earned 13 All-Star team nods, tallied a major league record 652 saves and logged a career ERA of 2.21. Rivera served up four grand slams in his 1,115 big league appearances. He hadn't allowed one in nearly seven years.

"You don't remember them all, but I remember that one," Hamilton said. "First off because it's Mariano Rivera, and it's Bill Selby! Nothing against Bill Selby, but usually in that situation, after you hit what looked to be a game-winner, then you strike out and the game is over. Everyone says 'Oh, Bill, you came so close.'

"And then he actually did it."

Selby pulled a 2–2 cutter to right field. Hamilton erupted again. This one wasn't curving foul. It nestled into the right-field seats to the right of the visitor's bullpen at Jacobs Field. The Indians won 10–7. An innocent, unimposing Selby forever entrenched his name into franchise lore.

It marked the first walk-off home run Rivera had ever surrendered. Rivera never allowed more runs (six) in a relief appearance.

In the middle of a season highlighted by transition, redirection and a harsh dose of reality, the Indians finally had reason to celebrate.

"That was tough," said Mark Shapiro, then in his first year as the club's general manager. "That's probably a great memory for Bill and a cool positive for us. When you're heading into waters like that, you have to know that you have to hold onto those great moments. They're important. You have to enjoy them."

Selby's blast boosted Cleveland's record to 41–49, as he handed Joel Skinner his second victory in four games as manager after taking over for Charlie Manuel, who received a mid-season pink slip. The Yankees entered the affair 16½ games better than the Indians. As improbable as it was to foresee a Tribe triumph when Cleveland trailed 7–0, who could have envisioned such a ninth-inning finish?

It was the fifth walk-off grand slam in the ballpark's history. There have been six since.

"I remember at one point looking out at the mound and there was a shorter pitcher and Selby was playing shortstop," Shapiro said. "We had all short guys and I'm like, 'Holy cow. How far have we come from the big dudes that were playing for us?' We were taking pride in just battling.

"That game, that's the beauty of baseball. In any one moment, anything can happen."

76 Colossal Collision

Here came Pete Rose, having rounded third, barreling down the base line, his sight fixated on home plate. There stood Ray Fosse, clad in his chest protector, shin guards, and backward cap, patiently awaiting the throw from center fielder Amos Otis. Rose was not slowing down, not easing up. Fosse was at the mercy of Otis' throw and Rose's aggression. The baseball carried the catcher a few feet up the line, right into Rose's unwavering path. Bam!

It was the 1970 All-Star Game at Riverfront Stadium in Cincinnati. Jim Hickman lined a single to center off of Clyde Wright in the bottom of the 12th inning. Rose, the potential winning run, had been at second base. Cubs manager Leo Durocher, who was coaching third base, followed Rose down the baseline, sprinting toward the plate. Rose collided head-on with Fosse, as their left shoulders met on impact. Rose scored the winning run. Fosse tumbled over in a world of hurt. As Rose's National League teammates filtered onto the field to celebrate with him, the Reds hit machine immediately checked in on Fosse, who stayed down in pain.

Fosse was the Indians' first-ever selection in the amateur draft. In 1965, the organization made him the seventh overall pick. He blossomed into an All-Star five years later, when he finished his first full season with a .307 batting average, 18 home runs, 61 RBIs, and a Gold Glove award. He made the All-Star team and won another Gold Glove in 1971, but his numbers never matched the statistics he registered in the '70 season.

Following the All-Star Game collision, Fosse underwent an X-ray, but it came back negative. He continued to experience pain, but there was no visual evidence to suggest anything was structurally wrong with his shoulder. Still, his production dropped off considerably in the second half of the '70 campaign, when he hit just two of his 18 home runs. He underwent another examination the following year. That X-ray showed that he had a fracture and a separated shoulder, which healed incorrectly. Decades passed and Fosse still could not lift his left arm above his head.

Fosse never made another All-Star team. He never won another Gold Glove. Before the 1973 season, the Indians traded him to Oakland, where he won a pair of World Series titles. He is best remembered, however, for his involvement in a violent collision at home plate, one that decided the 1970 Midsummer Classic. New rules initiated in 2014 barred catchers from blocking the plate and runners from plowing them over.

Fosse died in October 2021 after a lengthy cancer battle.

77 Start of the Franchise

The Cleveland Spiders amassed a 20–134 record in 1899. Twenty wins. One hundred and thirty-four losses. They were designed to fail, as the team owners, the Robison brothers, shipped the top talent on the roster to the other team they owned, the St. Louis Perfectos. The Spiders suffered a 24-game losing streak. They were outscored by 723 runs. They sat 84 games out of first place at the end of the season. The local newspaper quit referring to them as the Spiders and instead called them the "Cleveland Exiles" or the "Cleveland Forsakens" in articles. *The Plain Dealer* described a late-August Spiders win as "an eighth wonder" arriving in the world. "How it happened," the story read, "is beyond explanation." It was their last win for three and a half weeks. Fans stopped supporting the team, so it played most of its games on the road and, ultimately, disbanded after the season.

When the American League debuted as a part of Major League Baseball in 1901, the Cleveland Bluebirds, commonly referred to as the Blues for their all-blue uniforms, became the city's professional baseball franchise. It's the same organization known as the Cleveland Guardians today.

In the American League's inaugural season, the Blues were joined by the Chicago White Stockings, Detroit Tigers, Boston Americans, Philadelphia Athletics, Baltimore Orioles, Milwaukee Brewers, and Washington Senators.

On April 24, 1901, Cleveland played its first MLB game at Chicago's South Side Park against the White Stockings. Chicago won 8–2. The Blues were not very good; they finished seventh in the American League out of eight teams with a 54–82 record, and were led by household names (OK, maybe not *now*) Ollie Pickering, Bill Bradley, Zaza Harvey, George LaChance, Pete Dowling and Earl Moore.

On May 23, they scored nine runs with two outs in the ninth inning to top the Senators 14–13 at League Park. After a 4–18 period in May that included an 11-game losing streak and a six-game skid, they pieced together a 15–11 stretch. In fact, streaks were part of their nature. After suffering through a 5–12 stretch in July, they righted the ship with nine wins in 11 contests. They lost 15 of their last 18 games.

They flipped the script in 1902 upon the arrival of nationally renowned second baseman Nap Lajoie (plus Elmer Flick and Addie Joss). They finished 69–67, good for fifth in the American League standings. By 1903, the team was named the Naps, after Lajoie, the eventual Hall of Famer. For much of the next two decades, the club finished above or near the .500 mark. Cy Young, in his early 40s, joined the franchise in 1909 for a three-season run in the twilight of his illustrious career.

The team adopted the Indians moniker in 1915. Cleveland's franchise is one of four charter American League clubs—along with Chicago, Boston, and Detroit—to play continuously in one city since the inception of the league in 1901.

78 Nap Time

Nap Lajoie dropped a bunt down the third-base line and raced out of the batter's box. He arrived safely at first base. He repeated the process in his next trip to the plate. And the one after that. And that. Against the St. Louis Browns on the final day of the 1910 season, Lajoie tallied seven bunt base hits, a total reached with a little help from an intentionally lax St. Louis defense.

Lajoie, the heart and soul of the Cleveland franchise, was battling Detroit's Ty Cobb for the American League batting title. The winner was to receive a brand-new Chalmers automobile. Lajoie needed a base hit in just about every at-bat of the double header against the Browns to have a chance at supplanting Cobb atop the leaderboard. The Browns wanted to aid his cause. Lajoie collected the seven bunt singles and a triple to center field. Browns manager Jack O'Connor was fired for instructing his third baseman to play deep enough to permit Lajoie to deposit bunt after bunt in the vacant space.

Lajoie was initially thought to have captured the batting crown, but American League president Ban Johnson eventually declared Cobb the winner by the slimmest of margins. The Chalmers company awarded both players free automobiles.

The second baseman, also known for his defensive prowess, routinely found himself among the American League batting leaders. He logged a .338 average for his career, including a .426 mark in 1901, a .384 mark in 1910, .378 in 1902, and .376 in 1904. He totaled 3,243 hits in his career, 657 of which were doubles. He was one of the most prolific hitters both in his era and in baseball history. For that, he was inducted into the Baseball Hall of Fame in 1937.

Lajoie also served as skipper of the franchise from 1905–09. He was such an integral part of the organization that the team was called the Cleveland Naps from 1903–14. Lajoie batted .339 and tallied 2,047 of his hits in 13 years with Cleveland.

79 Red to Toe

Cleveland has cycled through plenty of uniform designs in their lengthy history. No team jersey catches the eye more, for better or for worse, than the club's all-red, top-to-bottom get-up in the mid-1970s. The uniforms made players look like tomatoes. The red tops carried white trim, with "Indians" sprawled out across the chest in capital letters. The pants, which would make any fashion designer sick to their stomach, made the whole ensemble look like a onesie. The team brought back the outfit for one night on June 11, 2004, against, appropriately, the Cincinnati Reds. CC Sabathia, who started the game, resembled a big red apple.

Not all Cleveland uniforms have been so eye-popping. The original jerseys, when the team was known as the Cleveland Naps, were white and bore a script C and a blue collar. During that era, they also sported striped uniforms with "Cleveland" spelled out on the tops. In 1921, a year after the team captured its first title, the team wore white jerseys with "World Champions" displayed on the fronts.

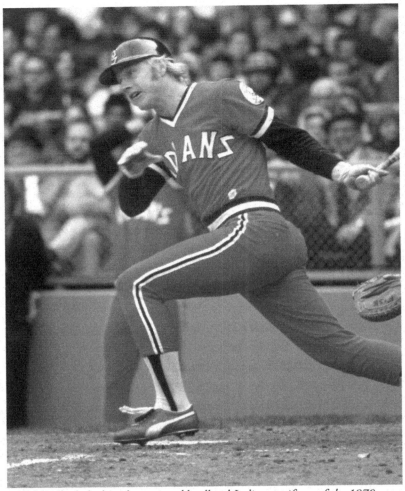

Buddy Bell, clothed in the memorable all-red Indians uniform of the 1970s.

In 1948, the year of the franchise's second championship, the team adopted a look similar to the one it brought back nearly five decades later. The white home uniforms carried a script red "Indians" name on the front with a Chief Wahoo logo on the sleeve. On the gray road uniforms, "Cleveland" was written out in red block letters.

At a couple points in team history, the club has tried out a sleeveless approach. In 1963 and 2005, the Indians instituted white and grey jerseys cut off at the shoulders, with, from the player's perspective, Chief Wahoo on the left side of the chest and his number on the right.

The franchise stuck with the block lettering approach in the '70s and '80s, though the all-red uniforms fizzled out rather quickly. The team added a blue top and reinvented the color scheme on its home uniforms in the late '80s, jerseys that were prevalent in the movie *Major League*. Once the club moved into Jacobs Field in 1994, the Indians donned newer versions of the uniforms the club wore in 1948. The home jerseys were white with red trim and a script "Indians" on the front. The club also had matching gray and blue uniforms.

Fifteen years later, the team returned the gray road uniforms with block lettering and added an alternate cream home jersey with red trim for weekend games at Progressive Field. On August 30, 2014, as part of a throwback night at Kauffman Stadium in Kansas City, the Indians and Royals wore uniforms from the 1974 season. Fortunately for the Indians, that meant the snazzy red tops, but not the abominable red bottoms. Prior to the 2019 season, the club unveiled a new alternate red jersey top, which quickly became a popular choice of attire for home games. They, thankfully, came with white pants.

80 The Best of the Best

Let's take a look at some of the best individual player seasons in franchise history.

The hitters…

1. Shoeless Joe Jackson, 1911
Slash line: .408/.468/.590
His 233 hits are a club record, and he tallied them in only 147 games. He racked up 45 doubles, 19 triples and 41 stolen bases. His .408 average ranked second in the league, behind Ty Cobb's .419. Since hitting statistics have fluctuated throughout history, we can use OPS+ to gain better perspective of how a player fared versus peers in other eras. Jackson's 193 OPS+ indicates his offensive output was almost twice as productive as the average hitter.

2. Tris Speaker, 1916
Slash line: .386/.470/.502
In his first season in Cleveland, Speaker piled up 211 hits, 41 doubles and 35 stolen bases. He led the league in batting average, on-base percentage, slugging percentage, OPS, hits and doubles.

3. Jim Thome, 2002
Slash line: .304/.445/.677
Thome established the franchise record with 52 home runs. He led the league in walks, slugging percentage and OPS+ (197, the second-best mark in team history).

4. Albert Belle, 1995
Slash line: .317/.401/.690
Belle became the only player in major league history with 50–plus homers and 50-plus doubles in a season, and he did so in only 143 games, thanks to the players strike. He led the league in homers, doubles, RBIs and slugging percentage.

5. Nap Lajoie, 1904
Slash line: .376/.413/.546

They ought to name the team after you when you lead the league in batting average, on-base percentage, slugging percentage, doubles and hits. Lajoie posted a 203 OPS+.

Honorable mention: Manny Ramirez, 1999
Slash line: .333/.442/.663

He was the most consistent cog in a well-oiled machine that produced 1,009 runs, the most by a team since the first half of the 20th century. Ramirez hit 44 homers and led the league with a team-record 165 RBIs.

The pitchers…

1. Addie Joss, 1908
The stats: 325 innings, 1.16 ERA, 204 ERA+

It's difficult to judge such an early season, but that ERA+ figure tells us his ERA was 104 percent better than league average, so even by Dead Ball Era standards, this was a dominant performance.

2. Bob Feller, 1946
The stats: 371 innings, 2.18 ERA, 10.0 WAR, 348 strikeouts

Feller led the league with 36 complete games and 10 shutouts, and his strikeout total is 23 more than any other Cleveland pitcher has ever recorded. This was his first full season following a four-year stint in the Navy.

3. Corey Kluber, 2017
The stats: 203 innings, 2.25 ERA, 265 strikeouts

This season earned Kluber his second Cy Young Award, the only Cleveland pitcher to claim more than one during his tenure with the club. He piled up all those strikeouts while leading the league in walks per nine innings, hits per nine innings, WHIP and ERA+ (202).

4. Luis Tiant, 1968

The stats: 258 innings, 1.60 ERA, .495 opponent OPS
This was the Year of the Pitcher, but few were as stifling as Tiant, who led the league in ERA, ERA+ (186), shutouts and hits per nine innings (5.3, a club record).

5. Gaylord Perry, 1972

The stats: 342 innings, 1.92 ERA, 168 ERA+
In his first season in Cleveland, Perry led the league with 29 complete games and merited his first Cy Young Award.
Honorable mention: Cliff Lee, 2008
The stats: 223 innings, 2.54 ERA, 3.8% walk rate
Lee was steady from start to finish and led the league in ERA and ERA+ (167) en route to the Cy Young Award, the second straight Cleveland pitcher to capture the hardware (CC Sabathia in '07).

81 Sunk by the Sun

Kansas City catcher Paul Phillips sent Bob Howry's offering high into the Sunday afternoon sky, one as blue and pristine as the ocean. The baseball hung up in the bright sun. Grady Sizemore camped under where he thought it was headed. He waited for it to return to sight.

By the time it did, it was too late.

When gravity pulled the ball back toward the earth, Sizemore never saw it. It ricocheted off Sizemore's leg and landed on the

Choke Artist

On the last day of the 2005 regular season, as the Chicago White Sox put the finishing touches on the Indians' final-week collapse, Ozzie Guillen rubbed salt in the wound. Chicago's skipper was photographed clutching his own neck with his hands, making a choking sign.

Guillen claimed he was just ribbing a few fans in the stands at Jacobs Field, but even if that were the case, his timing was poor. The Indians dropped six of their final seven games, as they lost their grip on the Wild Card lead and missed out on a postseason berth. Guillen's White Sox, meanwhile, captured the American League Central crown with a 99–63 record, following a three-game sweep of Cleveland to cap the regular-season slate. The White Sox proceeded to top the Houston Astros in four games to win the World Series. They lost only one game during the entire postseason.

ground, Phillips raced into second base with a double and Angel Berroa scored the game-winning run from second. It was a decisive miscue, an unfortunate gaffe that cost the Indians the series finale in Kansas City. Cleveland had entered the matinee with 17 wins in its last 19 games, but they could not afford to drop that one to the last-place Royals.

It was September 25, 2005. Time was running out. The surging Indians had no time to waste, no affordable ground to lose.

The Indians hovered around the .500 mark until the middle of June. They swiftly fell 10 games behind the scorching-hot Chicago White Sox. Ozzie Guillen's club sprinted to a 24–7 start. By late June, they stood at 50–22.

Following their victory on August 1, the White Sox gripped a 15-game lead over the Indians in the American League Central. Despite a seven-game skid in mid-August, they still held a 9½ -game lead on the morning of September 8. Then, the Indians caught fire. Cleveland spun winning streaks of seven, six, and four games before cruising into the series finale at Kauffman Stadium.

That day, the Indians scored three times in the top of the first inning. The Royals roared back, however, and Cleveland needed an RBI groundout by Casey Blake in the top of the ninth to tie the contest 4–4.

Berroa opened the bottom of the ninth with a single to left. Joe McEwing followed with a sacrifice bunt. Then Phillips called upon a shining star. The sun answered the prayer.

After the ball caromed off his lower limb, Sizemore seethed in frustration before picking it up and chucking it back toward the infield. He admitted he took more time than he should have, though his manager, Eric Wedge, surmised that any expediting of the process would not have come quickly enough to nab Berroa at the plate.

The Sunday letdown seemed to send Cleveland into a tailspin. Entering that tilt, the Indians had narrowed their deficit to 1½ games in the division. They sat 1½ games ahead of the Boston Red Sox and New York Yankees in the American League Wild Card chase. The loss to the Royals tacked on a game to their division deficit and shaved a game off of their Wild Card lead. They had a three-game set with bottom-dwelling Tampa Bay and a three-game set with Chicago to close out the regular season. They could not afford any more slip-ups.

The Devil Rays claimed the series opener 5–4. The following day, Tampa Bay trotted out Seth McClung, who entered with a 6–11 record and 7.11 ERA and who had posted an 0–3 record and 16.39 ERA in his previous three starts, which lasted a total of 9⅓ innings. Naturally, McClung blanked the Indians for eight innings in a 1–0 Devil Rays triumph. Cleveland salvaged the series finale, but the Indians were fading fast.

The White Sox swept away Cleveland at Jacobs Field over the final weekend. They won the three contests by a combined four runs. The Indians dropped six of their final seven games, starting with the sun-splashed setback in Kansas City. Despite 93 wins, they finished six games behind the White Sox in the division and two games behind both the Yankees and Red Sox. In the Wild Card era (since 1995), no AL team has won more than 93 games and missed the postseason. Twice, Cleveland has reached that win total and missed the playoffs. The 2019 team also finished 93–69 and also fell apart in the final week against the White Sox and Nationals to fall short in the Wild Card race.

"Wow"

Dennis Eckersley did not look defeated or frustrated or disappointed. He simply appeared astonished. More than anything, he seemed impressed.

The Indians selected Eckersley in the third round of the 1972 amateur draft. He spent his first three big league seasons with Cleveland. After more than a decade as a major league starter, he transitioned to the back end of Oakland's bullpen under Tony La Russa in the late '80s. He rattled off a few years in which he recorded eye-popping stat lines, which garnered him the American League Most Valuable Player and Cy Young Awards in 1992.

By 1995, Eckersley, a 2004 Hall of Fame inductee, had turned 40 and a bit of regression had set in, though he was still effective and still owned the closer's role in Oakland. He entered the game at Jacobs Field on July 16, 1995, in the bottom of the 12th. The Athletics held a 4–3 lead. Kenny Lofton stood on second base with two outs when 23-year-old right fielder Manny Ramirez approached the batter's box. On the seventh pitch of the at-bat, after Ramirez had fouled off several offerings from Eckersley, the slugger drove a 2-2 pitch halfway up the bleachers in left field. The walk-off home run handed the first-place Indians a 5–4 victory and a four-game sweep of the A's.

"There's no other way to put it," said longtime Cleveland executive Dan O'Dowd. "Manny was as gifted a hitter as anybody who has ever worn an Indians uniform."

After Eckersley followed through with his high leg kick and delivered the fastball on the inner half of the plate, the right-hander watched the ball sail into the seats. He walked off the mound and toward Oakland's dugout, unable to hold back a sheepish grin, as though he could not believe what had happened. He then mouthed the word "Wow," a fitting bit of diction to describe both Ramirez's blast and the dominance the '95 Indians displayed.

"When he hit it, he knew it," Indians radio announcer Herb Score said on the broadcast. "He just stood at home plate and watched it."

It marked Ramirez's third consecutive game with a home run. Earlier in the week, he made his first career All-Star Game appearance. The Indians moved to an unthinkable 50–21 with the win, as they increased their lead over the Kansas City Royals and Milwaukee Brewers in the American League Central to a remarkable 14½ games.

"This place was rocking all the time," said Jason Giambi, a rookie on that Athletics team. "It was so hard to take the crowd out of it here. No matter how many runs you put up, as soon as they got one runner on, the crowd started getting back into it. It was such a home-field advantage. That's what I remember as a player coming here. It was unbelievable."

Ramirez wasn't done inflicting damage against Eckersley, though. Three years later, during Game 3 of the AL Division Series against the Red Sox, he tagged Eckersley for a critical home run to pad Cleveland's lead in the ninth inning. Ramirez golfed a 94-mph sinker over the Green Monster, two innings after he clubbed a homer against Bret Saberhagen. The ninth-inning blast off

Eckersley pushed the Indians' advantage to 4–1. They held on for a 4–3 victory. And that marked the final appearance of Eckersley's 24-year career. Wow, indeed.

"That was one of the best hitters I've ever played with," Carlos Baerga said, "and I played with Eddie Murray, Dave Winfield, Albert Belle, Jim Thome, Tony Gwynn. I played with great hitters. Manny is in the top three."

83 Attend Both Parts of the Battle of Ohio

Progressive Field and Great American Ball Park are separated by about a 250-mile stretch of I-71. It's a four-hour trip from Carnegie Avenue to Joe Nuxhall Way, with Columbus situated directly in the middle and little else to distract travelers along the way. There are miles and miles of farmland. There are often miles and miles of construction, too. At one point, there's a famous cheese barn. At another, a large outlet mall.

Since 1997, the Guardians and Reds have tussled during interleague play in what is dubbed the Battle of Ohio or the Ohio Cup. The two franchises boast as much history and tradition as any two organizations in the league. Cincinnati joined the National League in 1890 after becoming a charter member of the American Association in 1882. Cleveland joined the American League in 1901 as the Blues. The teams have never dueled in the postseason and had never played during the regular season until 1997.

From 1989–96, the teams competed for the Ohio Cup in an annual preseason exhibition played at Cooper Stadium in the capital of the Buckeye State. Cleveland claimed six of the eight contests before Major League Baseball instituted interleague play into the regular-season format. On June 16, 1997, the Indians and Reds squared off at Jacobs Field for the first time in front of a sold-out crowd of 42,961. Orel Hershiser struck out Deion Sanders to commence the regular-season edition of the Buckeye Series. Cleveland designated hitter Kevin Seitzer logged the series' first hit with a first-inning double to right. Manny Ramirez notched the series' first home run with a deep fly to right in the ninth inning off Jeff Shaw. The Reds captured the first ever victory 4–1. Wade Miley tossed the first no-hitter in the history of the in-state rivalry in 2021.

The teams played three times in 1997, 1998, and 2003. They did not meet in 2002. They played six times—a three-game series in each city—in the other years until 2013, when they began an annual four-game set, with two contests played in each location, except for years in which the AL Central and NL Central teams all played each other. In that case, it was a pair of three-game sets. Through the 2024 campaign, the Guardians lead the overall series 76–59.

And, yes, there's an actual cup, an Ohio Cup trophy that is stored in the facility of the team that wins each year's season series. If there's a tie, the team that previously held possession of the hardware keeps it another year. The Reds haven't claimed the cup since 2014. They'll try to change that in 2025 under new manager Terry Francona, who racked up a 31–19 record against the Reds as Cleveland's manager.

84 Sibling Rivalry

During the twilight of his career, Sandy Alomar Sr. was often flanked by his two sons in the Texas Rangers clubhouse, the dugout or anywhere else he roamed. Not long after he retired, his sons, Sandy Jr. and Roberto, began their careers in professional baseball.

Little Sandy—OK, so he actually grew to be a 6-foot-5 catcher—signed with the San Diego Padres as a 17-year-old in 1983. His brother followed suit. Robbie signed with the organization 11 days after his 17th birthday in 1985. They briefly played together in San Diego. Robbie spent his first three big league seasons with the club before being traded to Toronto. Sandy made two short cameos with the Padres before being dealt to Cleveland.

A passion for baseball has long been rooted in the Alomar lineage. The brothers' uncles, cousins and their father all dabbled in baseball at one level or another. Sandy Sr. wreaked havoc on the big-league base paths for 15 years.

The brotherly rivalry reached the limelight in 1996, when Roberto's Baltimore Orioles squared off against Sandy's Indians in the American League Division Series.

"My mom would always go nuts when I played against Robbie in the postseason," Sandy said.

In Game 4, Roberto launched a Jose Mesa pitch over the Jacobs Field fence for a game-winning home run. With the victory, Baltimore advanced to the American League Championship Series and Cleveland went home, having fallen short of a second straight World Series appearance. Sandy's game-tying home run in Game 4 of the 1997 American League Division Series salvaged the Indians' season and advanced the club to the American League

Championship Series against Roberto's Orioles. This time, Sandy was the last Alomar standing, as Cleveland proceeded to the World Series following a six-game series win.

"There's only going to be one winner and one loser," Roberto said. "It was great, but it was tough. As a brother, that's the test that you have."

The brothers joined forces in 1999 after Roberto signed a four-year pact with the Indians. Luring him to Cleveland was the club's No. 1 offseason priority. At last, the entire Alomar clan again had one unified allegiance. Roberto was named an All-Star and won a Gold Glove Award in each of his three seasons in Cleveland before he was traded to the New York Mets.

In 2011, Roberto was inducted into the Baseball Hall of Fame. He was joined in the 2011 Cooperstown class by Bert Blyleven, who played with Sandy Sr. and got to know the young Alomar boys in Texas.

"It was always a good competition and a lot of fun to play against him," Sandy said. "But it was a lot more fun when we played together. That way you get to root for him, not against him. He was such a good player that you would want on your team—he could steal, he had all these abilities. But it was always fun competing against your brother and with your brother."

So which brother pays for dinner?

"He does," Sandy said, "because he made more money than I did. He's the Hall of Famer. He has to take care of it."

"I like to take care of my big brother," Roberto said. "He took care of me when I was young."

The franchise has been no stranger to brotherly tandems over the years. Gaylord and Jim Perry anchored Cleveland's rotation in 1974. Joe and Luke Sewell occupied shortstop and catcher, respectively, for the team in the 1920s. Vean Gregg excelled on the mound for the Naps from 1911–14, and his brother, Dave, pitched in one game for the club in 1913, his only major league outing.

Bill Hinchman was an outfielder for Cleveland from 1907–09, and his brother, Harry, briefly joined him on the roster that first year. The Naylor brothers, Josh and Bo, united in Cleveland late in the 2022 season. On July 14, 2023, they became the first brothers in franchise history to each hit a home run for the same team in the same game. They also became the first brothers in a decade—and only the third set of brothers in 60 years—to hit a home run for the same team in the same inning.

85 Catch-22

Nick Swisher only had so much effort left to offer. Grady Sizemore's long ball was not going to be retrieved on the field of play, anyway. By the time the Indians scored their 14th run of the second inning on an unseasonably balmy Saturday afternoon at a brand-new Yankee Stadium on April 18, 2009, Swisher was beat. So, too, were the Yankees, but the Indians were not done piling on.

The unforgettable inning started with the most meager, unimposing hit. It ended with back-to-back booming blasts. Travis Hafner started the procession with a weak dribbler to third base for a single. Jhonny Peralta lined a single to left. Shin-Soo Choo golfed a three-run home run into the visitor's bullpen in left-center to erase the Yankees' 2–0 lead. 3–2.

After Ryan Garko popped out in foul territory behind the plate and Ben Francisco doubled to left, Asdrubal Cabrera brought home a run with a single up the middle that nearly removed pitcher Chien-Ming Wang's shoelaces. 4–2.

Sizemore and Mark DeRosa followed with consecutive doubles to right field. 6–2.

DeRosa had to lunge at Wang's offering outside of the zone to make contact and yet he still poked the pitch off the wall. The ball bounced off a bright yellow advertisement and then trickled back onto the outfield grass as Swisher banged his back against the padding and two runs scored. Victor Martinez laced a one-hop liner to right to plate DeRosa and Wang hit the showers. 7–2.

Hafner and Peralta then greeted rookie Anthony Claggett with consecutive doubles to center. Peralta's base knock, over the head of center fielder Brett Gardner, scored a pair. 9–2.

Choo walked, Garko singled to load the bases and Francisco struck out. Cabrera did not. The shortstop lifted a fastball into the first row of seats in right field, as Swisher made a futile leap at the wall. 13–2.

Sizemore followed the grand slam with a solo shot, one Swisher had no chance at catching. The Yankees right fielder took a few steps and watched the ball sail out of play. 14–2.

When Claggett fanned DeRosa for the third out, it ended a 14-run frame, one that included 13 hits, a walk, a wild pitch, five doubles, and three home runs. The 14 runs were the most ever scored in the second inning of a major league game. The 13 hits were the most ever surrendered by Yankees pitching in one inning. The Indians razzed each other when someone made an out. They shuddered at the horror of what it must have been like to be playing defense during the onslaught.

And they were not finished.

Garko tacked on an RBI single in the third. DeRosa did the same in the fourth and he and Martinez joined forces on back-to-back home runs in the fifth. Hafner launched a solo shot in the eighth and Trevor Crowe completed the scoring with an RBI single in the ninth. All told, the Indians amassed 22 runs on 25 hits and six walks in a 22–4 shellacking of the Yankees. It matched the most runs the Yankees had ever yielded at home. It marked the most runs for the Indians in a game since they registered a 22–0 triumph on

A Chance at a Seven-Hit Game

As Coco Crisp strolled to the batter's box, Omar Vizquel gathered his essentials and headed out of the dugout toward the on-deck circle at Yankee Stadium. Victor Martinez stopped Vizquel in his tracks and committed a cardinal sin.

"He grabbed me by the chest," Vizquel said, "and he said, 'Hey, do you realize that you have a chance to go 7-for-7?'"

It was the final day of August in 2004. The Indians entered the contest with a .500 record. The Yankees stood atop the American League East. Cleveland blanked the Yankees 22–0, matching the league's most lopsided shutout since 1900.

Vizquel singled to right in his first trip to the plate. In his second at-bat, he plated Ronnie Belliard with another base knock to right. He approached the plate for the third time in the third inning and brought home a pair of runs with a double to right. He tallied his fourth hit with a fifth-inning single to left. In the sixth, he scored Crisp with a double to left. He established a career high with his sixth hit on an eighth-inning single up the middle.

The Indians' shortstop became the 59th big leaguer since 1900 to register six hits in a nine-inning game. Only Rennie Stennett, a second baseman for the Pirates, had notched seven hits in a nine-inning affair. He went 7-for-7 in Pittsburgh's 22–0 shellacking of the Chicago Cubs on September 16, 1975.

So Vizquel stepped in against Esteban Loaiza with Cleveland ahead 19–0 and Crisp on first base. He couldn't shake Martinez's unintentionally flustering encouragement. Vizquel flied out to short right field. He finished 6-for-7.

"It just completely broke my concentration," Vizquel said, laughing.

August 31, 2004. That game, of course, came at the old Yankee Stadium.

Hafner and Martinez were a part of both offensive eruptions. Hafner went 3-for-7 with a home run in the '09 affair. Martinez went 2-for-4 with a home run before being replaced by Kelly Shoppach. Both Hafner and Martinez recorded two hits in the 2004 contest. Hafner clubbed a three-run triple in the first inning to open the scoring. Martinez capped the scoring with a three-run home run in the ninth.

The Indians matched the most lopsided shutout win in modern big-league history and supplied the Yankees with their largest loss in franchise history. Cleveland didn't record any 14-run innings, but they scored three in the first, three in the second, three in the third, six in the fifth, one in the sixth, and six in the ninth. A strange-but-true statistic: Cleveland has scored 19 or more runs in a game on eight occasions since the turn of the century, and the Yankees have been the overmatched opponent in four of those eight instances.

Mr. 3,000

The pitch was on the outer half of the plate, but it did not matter. Eddie Murray, hunched over, waving his bat straight up in the air, his knees bent—his back one more than his front—could pull the most wayward offerings through any briefly appearing hole in an infield. So Murray, ever so wise at the ripe old age of 39, twisted his hips and guided Mike Trombley's fastball through the right side of the Astroturf at the Metrodome.

First baseman Scott Stahoviak had no chance at it. He broke toward the base in the event that his cohort on the right side, Chuck Knoblauch, could corral the sharp grounder. The second baseman dove—well, bellyflopped—after the ball, but it was out of his reach. Murray glided around the bag and slapped hands with first-base coach Dave Nelson. He had become the 20th player in major league history to collect 3,000 hits, an unwritten automatic qualifier for Baseball Hall of Fame entry.

The Indians came pouring out of the visitor's dugout. They gathered around the veteran and supplied congratulatory slaps and shakes. Murray lifted his helmet and his cap and acknowledged the applauding Minnesota crowd.

Aside from that milestone achievement by an opposing player on June 30, Twins fans did not have much else to cheer for during the 1995 campaign. Their club fell to 17–42 with a 4–1 loss on that Friday night. Cleveland, meanwhile, surged ahead to 41–17 as they enjoyed a level of success they had planned for years to eventually achieve. That blueprint included a sizable leap forward on December 2, 1993, when the organization introduced Murray and Dennis Martinez—a pair of experienced and accomplished veterans—as its latest additions.

Murray had been selected to eight All-Star teams, had won three Gold Glove awards and had finished in the top five in balloting for Most Valuable Player on six occasions. He was coming off a season in which, at the age of 37, he still batted .285 with 27 home runs and 100 RBIs for the New York Mets.

Manager Mike Hargrove inserted Murray into the middle of his lineup during the slugger's three years in Cleveland. Murray spent the majority of his time at designated hitter, though he did play first base on occasion. The switch-hitter clubbed one home run in each of the Indians' postseason series in 1995 and he delivered a walk-off single in Game 3 of the World Series, the franchise's first Fall Classic victory in 47 years. Murray, the third player in baseball history with 500 home runs and 3,000 hits, was inducted into Cooperstown in 2003. The Indians are one of only two franchises with three players to have notched their 3,000th hit while with the club (Murray on June 30, 1995; Nap Lajoie on September 27, 1914; and Tris Speaker on May 17, 1925). Ty Cobb, Al Kaline and Miguel Cabrera have done so for the Detroit Tigers.

87 Thunderstruck

Andre Thornton's booming bat earned him his nickname. Many pitchers learned, first-hand, that it was a fitting one. When "Thunder" Thornton hit the ball, he hit it hard. And it went far.

The Indians acquired Thornton from the Montreal Expos prior to the 1977 season. He filled a void at first base and general manager Phil Seghi was hoping to cash in on a buy-low investment. Thornton struggled at the plate with the Expos and Chicago Cubs in 1976, but the potential was there. It just needed to be tapped.

Thornton clubbed 28 home runs in his first year with Cleveland. He totaled 33 home runs and 105 RBIs in 1978, 26 home runs and 93 RBIs in 1979, 32 home runs and 116 RBIs in 1982, and 33 home runs and 99 RBIs in 1984. His career seems a bit short-changed, though. His time in Cleveland was marred by on-the-field injury and off-the-field tragedy.

After the 1977 campaign, Thornton, his wife, and their two children were traveling to Pennsylvania for a wedding when they came across an icy road. Their van flipped over. His wife and daughter did not survive the crash.

During spring training in 1980, Thornton suffered a knee injury that required surgery. He missed the entire season. The 1981 season was cut short by a players' strike. Thornton also missed time with a broken thumb.

All told, the powerful slugger tallied 214 of his 253 home runs with the Indians. He earned his way onto two American League All-Star teams. In 1985, manager Pat Corrales named Thornton team captain. In 2007, he was enshrined in the Indians Hall of Fame alongside Jim Bagby Sr., Mike Garcia, and Charles

Nagy—all pitchers, and all guys who were thankful they did not have to face Thornton.

88 No Help Needed

Omar Vizquel's shelf full of Gold Glove awards makes him arguably the greatest defensive player in franchise history. He never turned an unassisted triple play, though. The feat is rarer than a perfect game. Yet three players in Cleveland's history have completed one, more than any other organization in the league.

On July 19, 1909, Neal Ball turned the first one ever recorded. Facing the Boston Red Sox, Ball, playing for the then-Cleveland Naps, caught a line drive at shortstop in the second inning, touched second base, and tagged the oncoming runner.

Bill Wambsganss executed the most recognized unassisted triple play of all-time on October 10, 1920. In the fifth inning of Game 5 of the World Series between the Indians and the Brooklyn Robins at League Park, Wambsganss caught a line drive, stepped on second, and tagged an oncoming runner. Wambsganss was later presented with a medal for achieving the feat. He lost the medal while traveling on a train the following year.

Eleven more unassisted triple plays were registered before Asdrubal Cabrera etched his name into history books on May 12, 2008. Cabrera, like Vizquel, was a native of Venezuela and sported a No. 13 jersey.

"The number kind of got lost a couple years after I left Cleveland," Vizquel said, "but then when Asdrubal came, they gave it to him and it was great to see it back on the field."

Cabrera occasionally wore No. 13 in the minors, but when he arrived in the Indians' clubhouse upon his first promotion to the big leagues, that number uniform was hanging in his locker.

"I never asked for No. 13," Cabrera said. "They held that number for me."

Cabrera began his Indians career at second base, since Jhonny Peralta owned the shortstop position. Quickly, however, the slick-fielding Cabrera inherited the shortstop role.

In the fifth inning of a scoreless tie against the Toronto Blue Jays, Cabrera helped southpaw Cliff Lee dodge harm. Toronto had placed a pair of runners—Kevin Mench and Marco Scutaro—on first and second, respectively, to begin the inning. With Lyle Overbay readying for Lee's 1–0 offering, both runners took off. As his bat splintered across the infield, Overbay lined the pitch toward second base, where Cabrera made a diving grab. He lifted his glove high in the air to show second-base umpire Alfonso Marquez that he caught it. He then jogged over and stepped on second base to retire Mench and tagged Scutaro, who had already rounded the bag. Without pause, he continued his trot toward the dugout. He popped the baseball between his bare right hand and his glove as he grinned.

Cabrera had turned the 14th unassisted triple play in major league history. He was keeping that prized possession. One problem: he didn't. Without thinking, Cabrera tossed the baseball into the stands as he retreated to the dugout.

89 Fifty-Fifty

Albert Belle personified power. His batting stance, which featured him hunched over, his backside sticking out and his bat sitting back, ready to pounce, struck fear into opposing pitchers.

No season better embodied his power potential than the 1995 campaign. That season, Belle became the first player to ever rack up 50 home runs and 50 doubles. He finished the season with a .317 batting average and .401 on-base percentage, and led the league with a .690 slugging percentage, 50 home runs, 52 doubles, 126 RBIs, 377 total bases, and 121 runs scored. He recorded those gaudy numbers in a shortened season, too. Belle played in 143 games, since the start of the season was wiped out by the players' strike.

His 50th and final blast came on the penultimate day of the regular season. His 50th double had come nearly two weeks earlier. With the Saturday afternoon shadows beginning to bear down on Jacobs Field, Belle deposited a fastball from Kansas City hurler Melvin Bunch onto the plaza in left field. The tater tied the game at two. Cleveland would proceed to win 3–2 in 10 innings.

Belle dropped his bat, watched it sail over the fence, and commenced his home run trot, maintaining a focused, emotionless look on his face. His teammates stood and clapped in the dugout. After he retreated to the bench, Belle stepped back out and acknowledged the fans with a curtain call. He raised his right arm and pumped his fist. Slider, the team's pink, furry mascot, bowed down to Belle while standing atop the dugout. The fans, however, wouldn't cease in their appreciation of Belle's feat. So the slugger again stepped out of the dugout and, this time, raised both of his arms above his head and pumped his fists.

Belle finished with 31 home runs over the final two months of the season. In 58 games from August 1 to October 1, he batted .350 with an .885 slugging percentage, 31 home runs, 62 RBIs, 23 doubles, and 60 runs scored.

"Albert was just pure force and power," said former Cleveland executive Dan O'Dowd.

Belle, however, finished second in the balloting for American League Most Valuable Player, largely because of his strained relationship with the media. His numbers across the board exceeded those of Boston first baseman Mo Vaughn, who claimed the hardware. But even Belle could see it coming; he told *USA Today*, on his chances of winning the award: "It's going to be tough. I'm not really considered a media darling."

Belle trumped Vaughn in batting average (.317 to .300), on-base percentage (.401 to .388), slugging percentage (.690 to .575), runs scored (121 to 98), hits (173 to 165), home runs (50 to 39), and WAR (6.9 to 4.3). Vaughn received 12 first-place votes to Belle's 11. In overall balloting, his 308 voting points eclipsed Belle's 300.

Belle never again achieved the 50/50 feat, though he came close. He also stuffed the stat sheet in 1996, when he totaled 48 home runs, 148 RBIs, and 38 doubles in his final season with Cleveland. For the White Sox in 1998, Belle tallied 48 doubles, 49 home runs, and 152 RBIs. He never captured an MVP award,

A Grand Gesture

The California Angels, leaders of the American League West, were the hottest team in baseball. They finished the month of July 1995 with a 20–7 record, having outscored their opponents by nearly 100 runs. Amid that scorching stretch, however, they suffered a crushing defeat at Jacobs Field on July 19.

Lee Smith, then the league's all-time career leader in saves, entered in the ninth, with California clutching a 5–3 lead. He served up singles to Wayne Kirby and Omar Vizquel and walked Carlos Baerga to load the bases with one out. Up to the plate stepped Albert Belle, as the crowd began to chant his first name.

On a 1–2 count, Smith hung a breaking ball over the outside part of the plate. Belle stretched his arms and put his supreme strength on display, as he drove the pitch over the center-field fence. The baseball landed among a cluster of picnic tables in the outfield pavilion. Belle's blast marked the first-ever walk-off grand slam in ballpark history.

despite finishing in the top three in the voting for three consecutive years from 1994–96.

"If he [had] stayed healthy," Carlos Baerga said, "he would be a Hall of Famer."

90 Experience Opening Day

You never know what you're going to get on Opening Day. You spend six grueling months of the offseason thinking you have a semblance of an idea, but then the first game of the year arrives, and, suddenly, anything can happen. Still, there is always that glimmer of hope that the ensuing six months will be special, no matter how the previous season ended. That is what makes Opening Day so cherished and worth attending.

Of course, in Cleveland, anything really can happen. It could rain. It could snow. The sun could shine. The Guardians could win. They could lose. It's a crapshoot.

In 2011, the Chicago White Sox stormed their way to a 14–0 lead in the fourth inning on a brisk afternoon at Progressive Field on the first day of April. What appeared headed toward a historic shellacking turned out to be a relatively close contest. The Indians scored in each of the final four frames to narrow the deficit to 15–10 by the game's ultimate pitch.

In 2007, an unrelenting snowstorm wiped away the Indians' opening series at Jacobs Field against the Seattle Mariners. Paul Byrd had carried a no-hitter into the fifth inning when the flurries started to interfere with the players' eyesight. Cleveland Hall of Famer Bob Feller is the only pitcher to twirl an Opening Day no-hitter, but his gem came at Comiskey Park in Chicago in 1940.

The Indians used to draw upwards of 75,000 fans on Opening Day at Cleveland Municipal Stadium. Granted, Progressive Field does not have that kind of seating capacity, but the club sells out its home opener each year at the ballpark. In 2009, a rain delay of three hours and 49 minutes reduced a sellout crowd of 42,473 to a few hundred by the final pitch, which sealed Cleveland's 13–7 loss to the Toronto Blue Jays. The last out was recorded seven hours and 12 minutes after the game's first pitch. The two teams played another marathon three years later.

On April 5, 2012, the clubs played for 16 innings before the Blue Jays left Progressive Field with a 7–4 win. It was the longest opening game in major league history. The Indians and Detroit Tigers held the previous record with a 15-inning affair on April 19, 1960, which was tied with the 15 innings the Washington Senators and Philadelphia Athletics played on Opening Day April 13, 1926.

Closer Chris Perez, who was responsible for the game going so long after he surrendered three runs in the ninth inning to blow the Indians' 4–1 lead, joked that, "If you're going to break records, you might as well do it on Opening Day."

91 Cookie

There were days when Carlos Carrasco was fearful, daunted by unfamiliar medical jargon and afraid of what measures or treatments might lie ahead. There were days when Carrasco wanted to throw a baseball just to remember what a normal afternoon felt like, but the routine proved too taxing on his body. A casual bullpen session with pitching coach Carl Willis instead collapsed into a tear-filled reality check. The pitcher nicknamed "Cookie," the guy who is always smiling, shed plenty of tears during the summer of 2019—when he couldn't muster the energy for mundane activities, as his weight decreased and his strength vanished and the idea of working his way back to the mound seemed far-fetched; when he was recognized during the Stand Up 2 Cancer segment during the All-Star Game at a packed Progressive Field; when he made frequent visits to the pediatric cancer wing of the Cleveland Clinic, where he forged bonds with children fighting battles similar to the one he waged against chronic myeloid leukemia.

Carrasco was diagnosed during the 2019 season after being unable to shake fatigue early in the year. When he embarked on a leave of absence to confront his condition head-on, he requested the team keep the details of his diagnosis and recovery vague. But he was adamant the press release include his vow to pitch again that season. He needed the distraction and the target, no matter how unfeasible it may have seemed.

"You see just an awful disease taking over someone's body," said his teammate, Jason Kipnis. "He was getting skinny. His energy was down. You can attest when you see Cookie's energy is down, there's something wrong. This guy is a high-energy guy and a clown to go with it. You just watch him struggle some days and you knew it was eating at him. But he still fought through it. He was still putting a smile on his face."

When Carrasco first learned of his diagnosis, he called Kipnis. The two were the longest tenured members of Cleveland's roster, and the second baseman helped walk his longtime friend through some of the medical terminology. The two had studied together a few years earlier when Carrasco was preparing for his U.S. citizenship test. Throughout the summer, Carrasco leaned on teammates for encouragement. He initially stopped caring about baseball, but then realized that would send the wrong message to others facing their own battles. He checked in with teammates when they were on the road, sending texts of support and goofy videos (and, as was often the case, messages intended to instigate) to the players' group thread. And in the background, he kept working, kept wishing. There were days and weeks of sluggishness. He lost weight. He lost strength. But he never lost faith.

On September 1, exactly 10 years to the day of his major league debut, Carrasco completed his short walk to the mound at Tropicana Field. His heart pounded. His eyes welled up. His body trembled with big league debut-like jitters. His wife, Karry, watched from the stands with tears flowing down her face. Players and coaches emerged from both dugouts to supply Carrasco with a standing ovation. And then he threw his first fastball since May, when his life was thrown a 12-to-6 curveball. He finished his inning of work and disappeared into the visitor's dugout in Tampa, where teammates greeted him, hugged him, cried with him, celebrated him and smiled with him. That year, Carrasco was named the American League Comeback Player of the Year. He earned the prestigious Roberto Clemente Award for his plentiful efforts in the community, especially his dedication to continuing his visits to ailing children.

"I wanted to show them that if I could do it," he said, "they could do it too."

92 Spitting Image

The Indians and their six-time All-Star hurler, Sam McDowell, were growing apart. McDowell had only ever pitched for Cleveland. But contract squabbles and unrest paved the way for a parting after the 1971 campaign. On November 29, the Indians dealt "Sudden

Sam" to the San Francisco Giants for veteran pitcher Gaylord Perry and shortstop Frank Duffy.

The trade paid off. McDowell fizzled out once he left Cleveland. Perry won the American League Cy Young Award in his first season with the Indians. Perry posted a 24–16 record and 1.92 ERA. His 24 wins and 29 complete games led the league. He totaled 342⅔ innings and pitched into extra frames on eight occasions. Perry finished sixth in the balloting for American League Most Valuable Player.

Of course, any credit given to the right-hander was often slighted by some spitball-based assumption. The spitball was outlawed after the 1920 season. While with the Giants, Perry was one of the prime suspects incessantly accused of doctoring baseballs. Opposing players and managers griped. Umpires checked him up and down, searching for any sign of a lubricant that, when applied to a baseball, could supply it with some extra spin and dive. For years, Perry pleaded innocence and ignorance and he was never penalized for the act until the twilight of his career. Then in 1974, he released *Me and the Spitter: An Autobiographical Confession*, in which he detailed how he had doctored baseballs with saliva, grease, Vaseline or fishing line oil. He wrote he "tried everything on the old apple except salt and pepper and chocolate sauce topping."

More than anything, Perry was pursuing a mental edge over hitters. He would rub his hands with grease and then shake his opponents' hands the day before his start. He constantly fidgeted with his cap, belt, glove and face. Perry learned his tricks from Giants teammate Bob Shaw, who taught him how to properly apply an agent, how to grip and release the ball and how to conceal his wrongdoing from umpires, opponents and, as he described, from "spying executives up in the box seats." Perry compared it to speaking with Thomas Edison about inventing the lightbulb.

Perry followed up his Cy Young-winning campaign in 1972 with a 19–19 showing in 1973. He returned to All-Star form in

1974, when he compiled a 21–13 record and 2.51 ERA. He won 15 straight decisions over a 17-start span and fell one victory shy of the league record for consecutive wins. Perry finished fourth in voting for the Cy Young Award that season. In 1975, as he approached his 37th birthday, he clashed with new player/manager Frank Robinson and, after recording a 6–9 mark and 3.55 ERA, Perry was dealt to the Texas Rangers that June. Perry and his older brother, Jim, pitched together in Cleveland's rotation in 1974 and for a month in 1975. Their 529 combined wins rank second in league history among brother tandems, 10 wins behind Joe and Phil Niekro. In 1974, the Perry brothers accounted for 38 of Cleveland's 77 wins.

Perry completed his career with 314 wins, a 3.11 ERA, and 3,534 strikeouts. He was elected to the Baseball Hall of Fame in 1991. In his induction speech, he pointed out his daughter, Allison. "When she was a little girl, she would find the writers and would slip to them and say, 'I know where my dad hides his stuff.' And they were all excited and they say, 'Where?' 'He hides it in his garage.'"

93 Bizarre Bartering

Littered throughout baseball history are trades involving peculiar forms of compensation: bats and balls, a team bus, or the cost of a fence repair. Such exchanges were more common in the early days of professional baseball or in the minor leagues. As time wore on, a manager-for-player swap or a goodwill trade, in which a player is sent to another team for next to nothing, became the only abnormal forms of deals completed. Of course, a player cannot just be given away via trade. At least $1 must change hands.

"The rule is you cannot trade a player for nothing," said former team president Mark Shapiro. "Even if it has to be a minor league player who's inconsequential or an amount of cash, like $500, there has to be something."

Over time, Cleveland has been involved in its share of bizarre forms of bartering. In 1890, as the tale goes, Cy Young, who proceeded to win a major league–record 511 games, was purchased by the Cleveland Spiders for a few hundred bucks and a suit.

Harry Chiti was traded for himself. On April 26, 1962, the Indians dealt the catcher—whom they had acquired just five months earlier—to the New York Mets for a player to be named later. On June 15, that player turned out to be none other than Chiti. The backstop never played in a major league game with the Indians.

In the middle of the 1960 season, the Indians and trigger-happy general manager Frank Lane swapped manager Joe Gordon with Detroit Tigers manager Jimmy Dykes. Gordon moved on to the Kansas City Athletics the following year. Dykes managed the Indians for one more season.

During the 1994 season, the Indians and Minnesota Twins completed an exchange in which eventual Hall of Fame outfielder Dave Winfield relocated to Cleveland. Originally, the agreement dictated that the Indians send the Twins a player to be named later. However, that component fizzled when the players' strike commenced. So the clubs settled on the Indians brass picking up the tab at a dinner between front-office executives of the two organizations. Winfield never got a chance to play with the Indians in 1994, but he appeared in 46 games for them in 1995, when the team reached the World Series.

94 A Wild, Unexpected Ride

On June 26, 2024, from the living room in his suburban Washington home, Matthew Boyd flipped on a Guardians–Orioles game unfolding three time zones away. A few weeks earlier, Boyd flaunted his healthy left elbow at a showcase for 18 teams in California. Now, he needed to narrow down his field of suitors and settle on a team for the stretch run of the season.

The Guardians were interested. They desperately needed starting pitching help—anyone with a pulse, let alone a functioning arm. They had developed a reputation for guiding pitchers to new heights and they were in first place about halfway into the season. They had, Boyd thought, plenty of criteria that made them a compelling fit. So he tuned in to their game on an innocuous, early summer Wednesday.

And one of the first things Boyd witnessed? Jhonkensy Noel launching a home run to center field in his first career trip to the plate. His teammates converted the visitors' dugout at Camden Yards into a party scene. Boyd knew he had to be a part of that.

The Guardians were a tight-knit group from the start in 2024. Hope springs eternal for every team when camp begins in February. Every player and coach on every team says they want to win the World Series. A fraction of those individuals actually believe they can. The Guardians insisted they could. Over time, more and more people started to understand their thinking. But who could blame the skeptics? They returned essentially the same roster that compiled a 76–86 record a year earlier. They had a new manager who had never managed, nor even coached from the dugout.

But Stephen Vogt, the organization's choice to replace the most prolific steward in franchise history in Terry Francona, had plotted for this opportunity since he was a third-string catcher toiling away in A-ball. Long before he climbed to the majors, before he made a pair of All-Star teams, before he started his career with 32 consecutive hitless at-bats, before he was cut in spring training, designated for assignment, traded, injured, and lost, Vogt knew he was destined to manage. All those experiences, he contended, would allow him to connect with his players and build deep relationships with any player or coach who sat on the leather sofa in his office. So, despite being only a year removed from his days as a player, Vogt was ready to take the reins in Cleveland.

He faced stiff tests early. The Guardians lost their ace, Shane Bieber, to elbow surgery a week into the regular season. Their rotation spent much of the season in shambles, which prompted the pursuit of Boyd and, later, veteran Alex Cobb. They had to rely on a bullpen full of unknown commodities, with three unproven newcomers—Cade Smith, Tim Herrin, and Hunter Gaddis— delivering sub-2.00 ERAs while pitching nearly every other day and bridging the gap to closer Emmanuel Clase.

Under Vogt's guidance—and he leaned on his lieutenants in pitching coach Carl Willis, bench coach Craig Albernaz, and field coordinator Kai Correa—an overlooked, underestimated roster pieced together one of the franchise's most memorable seasons in recent memory. All season, they boasted one of the top records in baseball. They had five All-Stars: Clase, José Ramírez, Steven Kwan, Josh Naylor, and, implausibly, David Fry, a player to be named later in a trade who blossomed into a valuable hitter and versatile defender. Their bullpen routinely bailed out their ailing rotation. They rose to the occasion against their most daunting competition.

In August, the Guardians watched their nine-game AL Central lead evaporate, but they quickly rebounded. They clutched onto first place in the division for all but six days of the regular season. They added Boyd, Cobb, and Lane Thomas at the trade deadline to fortify their roster, moves that would pay dividends when it mattered most. And then they provided some October theatrics along a wild ride to the ALCS, a journey no one anticipated when it began eight months earlier.

The Guardians eked past the Detroit Tigers in five games in a dramatic ALDS before falling short against the Yankees in five games in the ALCS. In a span of 10 postseason games, they supplied four unforgettable home runs.

1. Fry Silences Comerica Park

The Tigers were hosting their first playoff games in a decade, and they were seven outs away from popping champagne in their home clubhouse. Cleveland hadn't won a playoff game when facing elimination in 27 years, since forcing a Game 7 in the 1997 World Series, a mere 9,848 days earlier. Enter Fry, who two and a half years earlier was catching a bullpen session in minor league camp for the Milwaukee Brewers when a team official told him he had been traded to Cleveland. It was an under-the-radar swap of pitcher J.C. Mejia for Fry, who had to be classified as a player to be named later because he was eligible to be selected by any team in the Rule 5 Draft. Only, that draft never took place because the league entered a lockout. So, Fry became a Guardian. He became an All-Star. And he became a postseason hero who rescued the Guardians from elimination and silenced the Detroit crowd with what proved to be a game-winning homer in Game 4 of the ALDS.

"You dream about it as a kid and think about it all the time," Fry said. "And then it happens, and it goes by really quick."

2. Thomas sends Cleveland to the ALCS

Game 5 of the ALDS at Progressive Field featured a pitching matchup of teacher versus pupil. Or it could be categorized as midseason pickup versus soon-to-be unanimous Cy Young Award winner. That's not to shortchange what Boyd had contributed;

he quickly emerged as one of the most reliable entities in the Guardians' rotation. But Skubal—Boyd's close friend and his understudy in Detroit a few years earlier—was the best pitcher in baseball in 2024, so Cleveland faced a daunting task in a winner-take-all game.

One swing changed everything. The Guardians traded for Thomas at the end of July, and he slumped his way through August, to the point that he had to convince Vogt he deserved regular playing time once the calendar flipped to September. He solidified his everyday role during the stretch run, and he spearheaded the Guardians' Game 1 win against Detroit with a three-run homer. In Game 5, after Skubal loaded the bases, Thomas handed Cleveland the lead—and, ultimately, the series win—with a first-pitch grand slam to the left-field bleachers.

"Pure ecstasy," Kwan said.

3 & 4. Noel and Fry script an instant classic

Clase recorded a 0.61 ERA during the regular season, which earned him a third-place finish in the Cy Young Award voting, the best showing for a reliever in 16 years. He had a postseason to forget, however. With the Guardians ahead by two runs in the eighth inning of Game 3 of the ALCS, Clase jogged in from the bullpen and promptly served up home runs to Aaron Judge and Giancarlo Stanton. The Yankees led by two with two outs in the bottom of the ninth. Boyd had given the Guardians another sterling start, but Clase surrendered the lead, and the club's fate rested in the massive paws of Noel. Talk about a full-circle moment, the reason Boyd signed with the team in the first place. With a runner aboard, Noel, the fearless rookie built like an NFL edge rusher, swatted a Luke Weaver fastball into the October night. Noel has never hit a home run that sneaks past the outfield fence. Everything is a no-doubter. The man nicknamed "Big Christmas" delivered fans the ultimate gift, and he instantly flung his bat to the dirt and strutted toward first, with every person in the home dugout and the stands in a frenzy.

An inning later, Fry authored another heroic chapter, with his own blast to the bleachers, a walk-off homer to cap one of the more unforgettable nights in Progressive Field history. For a moment, the Guardians were back in the series, in improbable fashion.

"I blacked out," Fry said. "I remember being, like, halfway down the first-base line, looking back at the dugout and saying, 'All right, I just have to make sure I touch all four bases.'"

95 Turning the Paige

Numbers were always important to Satchel Paige. It was the accuracy of the numbers that was not so critical. And that would surprise anyone who ever saw Paige pitch, because his blazing fastball had pinpoint accuracy almost every time it left his right hand.

Paige made his major league debut at the age of 42. After Paige spent decades pitching all across the country in the Negro Leagues; in semipro ball; in barnstorming exhibitions; and in the Dominican Republic, Puerto Rico, Cuba, and Mexico, Indians owner Bill Veeck signed him to bolster the pitching staff during the stretch run of the 1948 campaign. Even Paige's birth date was shrouded in mystery for a long time, so he downplayed his age when he broke into the majors as the oldest rookie in league history.

He was quoted once as saying, "Age is a question of mind over matter. If you don't mind, it doesn't matter."

Paige was a pioneer of sorts. He attracted large crowds at every venue he pitched. He blew hitters away with his overpowering fastball and, as he grew older, implemented numerous variations of pitches into his repertoire. He faced major league hitters in exhibition games all over the country, often squaring off against Bob Feller and his team of All-Stars. He was known to exaggerate the numbers he racked up while logging all of the innings over all of the years all over the country. Who could dispute him, though, especially after he proved his worth as a wily old veteran in the big leagues?

On a wall in the lower-level tunnel at Progressive Field rests a portrait of Paige, in his windup, with his quote: "Don't look back. Something might be gaining on you." Paige never looked back. He kept moving forward, kept pitching, kept jet-setting.

When Paige joined the Indians in 1948, manager Lou Boudreau used him both as a starter and a reliever. He amassed a 6–1 record and 2.48 ERA over the final three months of the regular season. He made one scoreless appearance in Game 5 of the World Series against the Boston Braves. The Indians captured the championship—their first since 1920—in six games.

Paige pitched for the St. Louis Browns from 1951–53. On September 25, 1965, Paige tossed three innings for the Kansas City Athletics, as he became the oldest player to appear in a major league game. He was 59 years old and had not pitched in the majors in 12 years. His catcher, Billy Bryan, was 33 years younger than he was at the time. His manager, Haywood Sullivan, was 25 years younger than he was. Paige held the Boston Red Sox scoreless, allowing only one hit: a double to eventual Hall of Famer Carl Yastrzemski. Paige also earned entry to Cooperstown, in 1971.

96 Friends Turned Enemies

Omar Vizquel had become so accustomed to absorbing a fastball in his back that when he stepped up to the plate with first base open in 2006, he was amazed he received a pitch to hit from Jose Mesa.

After Vizquel was critical of Mesa's mindset during his appearance in the ninth inning of Game 7 of the 1997 World Series—an outing in which Mesa blew a one-run lead and forced his team to extra innings—the reliever vowed to plunk the shortstop every time he faced him. For years, he kept true to his word.

In his 2002 autobiography, *Omar! My Life On and Off the Field*, Vizquel wrote, "The eyes of the world were focused on every move we made. Unfortunately, Jose's own eyes were vacant. Completely empty. Nobody home. You could almost see right through him. Jose's first pitch bounced five feet in front of the plate, and as every Cleveland Indians fan knows, things got worse from there. Not long after I looked into his vacant eyes, he blew the save and the Marlins tied the game."

When he learned of Mesa's disgust for the passage—Mesa referred to it as "stupid" and "BS" and said, "If I face him 10 more times, I'll hit him 10 times"—Vizquel lauded the closer's effort in helping guide the Indians to the Fall Classic.

When the Indians played Mesa's Phillies on June 12, 2002, Mesa drilled Vizquel. When they met again in 2006, with Vizquel a member of the Giants and Mesa pitching for the Rockies, the right-hander again struck his former teammate. Mesa merited a four-game suspension for his actions.

"He said he was going to hit me every time he faced me and he did that," Vizquel said.

Vizquel approached the batter's box four months later with Mesa manning the mound. In a 1–1 game, the Giants had a runner on second with one out. A hit-by-pitch would place Vizquel on first and give the Rockies a chance at an inning-ending double play. It made too much sense for it not to happen, especially given Mesa's plunking promise.

Mesa attacked the strike zone instead of his adversary and Vizquel grounded out to second base. The two dueled again a month later, but Vizquel came to the plate with the bases loaded, so Mesa couldn't afford to hit him with a pitch. Vizquel delivered an RBI groundout.

In their final encounter on September 19, 2006, Vizquel stroked an RBI single to right field off Mesa. Vizquel said that's the last time he saw his former locker mate.

"It's so funny, because he was one of my best friends when I was [in Cleveland]," Vizquel said. "We had lockers right next to each other. We lived five minutes away from each other. We fooled around a lot. We cooked together. It was kind of sad that I never got to tell him that I didn't really mean anything bad about what I said in the book or whatever people said about it. It was just a bad incident that turned a detour, and he took it in a different way. It's bad that I haven't really talked to him about it."

Of course, that wasn't the only time Vizquel provoked the fiery hurler. Vizquel and Carlos Baerga once went to Sea World, where the shortstop purchased a mini T. rex figure. He placed it in Mesa's locker one day, and when the reliever first saw it, his teammates made a high-pitched shriek, a surprising noise that didn't sit well with him.

"That was the worst thing we could have done," Baerga said. "That guy wanted to kill everybody, especially Omar."

Mesa joined the Mariners in 1999. When Seattle ventured to Cleveland and he entered the game, Vizquel stood atop the dugout steps and made the shrieking sound.

"I said, 'Omar, I don't think he's very happy about that,'" said former catcher Sandy Alomar Jr. "Then when he came up, the next pitch was behind him. He wasn't joking."

97 Dive Into 100-Plus Years of Memorabilia

The Western Union telegram is postmarked January 25, 1962, and includes a brief, but powerful message in block print, from one icon to another.

> *BOB FELLER*
> *GATES MILLS CLEVE*
> *MY MOST SINCERE CONGRATULATIONS*
> *I AM HONORED TO GO INTO THE HALL OF FAME*
> *WITH YOU*
> *JACKIE ROBINSON*

Both Feller and Robinson were inducted into the Baseball Hall of Fame in 1962, and that correspondence is one gem in a treasure trove of artifacts from the franchise's history, which dates back to 1901. Much of the memorabilia sits inside a dimly lit storage closet in the bowels of the ballpark. Taped to the inside of the door to that room is a black-and-white photo of Babe Ruth, leaning on Feller's bat as he addressed the Yankee Stadium crowd in 1948 for the final time. Ruth succumbed to cancer two months later. The Guardians donated the actual bat to the Baseball Hall in November 2023.

Feller relics are scattered throughout the collection. There's a certificate from the Board of Baseball that named Feller a member of the All America Baseball Team after the Cleveland ace totaled 320 innings, 27 wins and 31 complete games, plus an Opening Day no-hitter (the only one in league history) that season. The document is signed by 12 baseball dignitaries, including Ruth.

There's a 1941 edition of Street & Smith's Baseball Pictorial Yearbook, a 25-cent issue that showcased Feller on the cover. There's an April 19, 1937, issue of *TIME*, with an 18-year-old Feller posing in his white uniform for an issue that came out the day before Feller's first, full big-league season. There's an issue of *Baseball Digest* featuring "Super" Joe Charboneau on the cover during his Rookie of the Year season in 1980. There's a Good Feller candy bar wrapper, a Hi-Feller ginger ale label, a Feller Motorola ad and invitations to Feller's annual postseason homecoming celebration in his native Van Meter, Iowa. There's a stack of congratulatory notes regarding Feller's Hall of Fame election, from Lou Boudreau, Bill Veeck and Hal Naragon, to name a few. General manager Gabe Paul mailed him a letter in January 1962 to seek his approval on a Bob Feller Night in Cleveland. There's also an assortment of materials honoring Feller's time in the Navy: newspaper article cutouts, photos, his maritime jacket, hat and goggles, plus a green duffel bag, a yellow life preserver and a telescope that he used during his time aboard the U.S.S. Alabama.

"Plaques are great. Same with statues," said Jeremy Feador, the team's historian. "But that's what's cool about some of the Feller stuff. We have one of his Navy jackets. He wore that. It's not just this fable or fantastical story."

Elsewhere in the archives are caricatures of Shoeless Joe Jackson, Hal Trosky, Stan Coveleski and other legends from the early days of the franchise. There's a June 1976 issue of Baseball Digest featuring center fielder Rick Manning on the cover, and old game programs, including a 1993 edition with first baseman Paul Sorrento and one from 1989 featuring pitcher Greg Swindell. There's a framed photo of the 1907 Cleveland Naps, who finished 85–67–6. (Yep, that's six ties.) There's an array of old tickets to spectacles at Municipal Stadium, from a green stub good for a $7 lower box seat to watch Len Barker's perfect game on May 15, 1981, to a $6 upper reserve ticket for the 1963 All-Star Game, to a $2 lower box ticket for the Indians' 1948 opener. There's a canvas-sized depiction of a $6.25 upper reserve ticket to Game 3 of the '48 World Series.

There's a box of lineup cards that include Sharpie-scribbled evidence of every in-game substitution. The stack of cards includes those from wins 20, 21 and 22 during the team's record-setting streak in 2017. Jay Bruce delivered the decisive hit that secured that 22nd win, and his navy No. 32 jersey made its way to the archives. Feador saved Tyler Naquin's jersey from his inside-the-park walk-off home run in 2016, a feat that hadn't been replicated in 100 years. He saved Rajai Davis' jersey from the day he hit for the cycle in Toronto that year, the baseball Francisco Lindor launched off the right-field foul pole for a city-rattling grand slam in Game 2 of the 2017 American League Division Series. The ball has a yellow smear, a scar of foul-pole paint.

"People recognize the importance of objects," Feador said. "It's why every family has an attic full of stuff, items they don't want to toss because they're of some significance or memory. Clearly the Christmas tree is of use, but the box full of old kids drawings or grandpa's photographs are important because they connect you to a sense of place. I'm just the dude that makes sure the attic doesn't get cluttered and disorganized and when it comes time to dust off the memories for the holidays, we can bring out the jersey or ball or bat so people can take time to reconnect with the history."

98 The Kid from Puerto Rico

He broke into the majors with a single, a slip and a smile, the first of a slew of signature moments during his six seasons with Cleveland. After lining a pitch to right field, Francisco Lindor tripped while rounding first base and then tried to pin the blame on Detroit's Miguel Cabrera. That smile became a symbol. No one had more fun on a baseball field.

As his dad hit him grounders down a hill, with a herd of cows waiting for any ball that trickled past him, Lindor told his dad he would play on TV one day. Otherwise, he would pursue a career as a dentist.

Sure enough, baseball worked out, and Lindor always seemed to find the spotlight. There was his grand slam against the Yankees in Game 2 of the 2017 ALDS, when the baseball clanged off the right field foul pole and caused Cleveland to shake. There was his game-tying double, with Cleveland down to its final strike in the bottom of the ninth against the Royals, that helped push the club's record-setting winning streak to 22 games.

And the moment he'd mention above all else—his home run in Puerto Rico in 2018.

Lindor was yanked in a million directions during Cleveland's trip to San Juan for a two-game series against Minnesota. He toured his old elementary school, through the courtyard he used to run through each morning, past the concrete walls he used to bounce a ball against, and sprinted into his old science classroom to greet Miss Haddock, his fourth-grade teacher. Students lined the entrance and walkways at the school as he arrived. He later hosted a series of baseball activities with them.

Shortstop Francisco Lindor was a four-time All-Star during his six seasons in Cleveland.

"I want [people] to understand," he said that afternoon, "that this is a real little island, but there are a lot of people with big dreams."

He connected with family members, friends, friends of friends and fulfilled countless interview requests, signed autographs, posed for pictures, held press conferences and attended a Habitat for Humanity event. He quipped that he'd be exhausted by the time he stepped into the batter's box. He had enough energy, though, to will his fly ball over the right field fence, and his fans—many of whom had endured the wrath of Hurricane Maria just seven months earlier, who were without power and who were forced to cover their damaged roofs with blue tarps—didn't want to stop celebrating with their horns and whistles and tambourines.

Lindor was everywhere that week, but when the spotlight called, he was right where you'd expect him to be. And then after the game, as players showered and changed out of their uniforms, there he was again, the man of the minute, hour, day and week. Lindor, sporting a red jersey and red batting helmet, stuck his head out of the window of a red car in a TV commercial for an insurance agency in nearby Guaynabo.

With the eighth pick in the draft, Cleveland had narrowed its draft options to Lindor and Javy Baez in 2011. They were friends and fellow shortstops. The Indians' brass liked Lindor's defensive ability a bit more, so they opted for the switch-hitter who moved to Florida for high school and had the magnetic personality. He developed into a perennial All-Star, a power hitter, a Gold Glove and Silver Slugger winner and the face of the franchise with the unmistakable smile.

Of course, Lindor's story in Cleveland didn't follow a Hollywood script. In January 2021, the team traded him and Carlos Carrasco to the Mets for a package of four players that included Amed Rosario and Andrés Giménez. Lindor proceeded to sign a 10-year contract with New York.

99 Atta Boy, Addie

The days on the regular season calendar were dwindling. The American League pennant came down to a three-team race between the Detroit Tigers, the Chicago White Sox, and the Cleveland Naps. Prior to the action on October 2, 1908, the White Sox trailed the Naps by one game in the standings. The Naps sat one-half game behind the Tigers.

That day, League Park played host to a duel between two of the premier pitchers in the sport. Addie Joss toed the rubber for Cleveland. Big Ed Walsh took the hill for Chicago. Both hurlers were eventually inducted into the Baseball Hall of Fame.

Walsh, who led the league that year with 40 wins, 42 complete games, 11 shutouts, and 464 innings pitched, tossed a four-hitter and tallied 15 strikeouts. He surrendered only one unearned run, on a passed ball, but it proved to be the difference. Joss needed only 74 pitches to register the second perfect game in the modern era, the fewest pitches in a perfect game in league history. The effort was not enough to propel the Naps to the World Series; the Tigers earned the American League berth and lost to the Chicago Cubs in five games. It did, however, serve as a beacon of excellence for Joss' short yet illustrious career.

Joss worked his way from a small hometown in Wisconsin to the Toledo Mud Hens of the Interstate League before his 21st birthday. On April 26, 1902, two weeks after he turned 22, he threw a one-hitter in his major league debut for the Cleveland Bronchos (technically, the Blues, but during the 1902 season, they were widely regarded as the Bronchos). He posted a 17–13 record and 2.77 ERA with 28 complete games and a league-high five shutouts during his rookie campaign. In 1904, he led the league with a 1.59

ERA. He went 27–11 with a 1.83 ERA in 1907 and 24–11 with a 1.16 ERA in 1908.

On April 20, 1910, Joss no-hit the White Sox again, as he became the first pitcher in league history to record a no-no twice against the same team. San Francisco Giants right-hander Tim Lincecum joined him in that regard when he blanked the San Diego Padres for the second time in 2014. Joss' career quickly came to a close, though. An elbow injury derailed his 1910 season. On April 3, 1911, Joss fainted on the field before an exhibition game in Chattanooga, Tenn. Eleven days later, he succumbed to tubercular meningitis. His teammates abandoned their game on April 17 to attend his funeral. That July, a group of American League All-Stars squared off against the Naps in an exhibition created to raise money for Joss' widow and two children. Walter Johnson, Cy Young, Tris Speaker, Ty Cobb and others participated, and the event raised nearly $13,000. The Baseball Hall of Fame possesses a photo of the two teams from that afternoon. Cleveland outfielder Jack Graney is spotted twice in the photo, as he raced from one end of the line of players to the opposite end during the slow-developing panoramic camera process.

Joss was elected by the Veterans Committee to the Hall of Fame in 1978. He was inducted into the Cleveland Indians Hall of Fame in 2006.

100 Pronk's Cycle

Travis Hafner had the home run. He had the double and the single. All he needed on that August afternoon in 2003 was a triple and he had the Indians' first cycle in 25 years. Of course, the man nicknamed "Pronk" by teammate Bill Selby for being part project, part donkey was not the most graceful nor speedy runner. He was the furthest thing from fleet of foot. He had one three-bagger in 80 career games entering that matinee at the Metrodome in Minnesota.

Hafner approached the batter's box in the eighth inning and... black.

The power went out. All over the Northeast.

The entire portion of the country experienced a blackout, triggered by a software bug at a prominent energy company. In some areas, the power outage lasted several days. In other places, power returned later that night. Nonetheless, some missed Hafner's attempt at the cycle. Some missed history in the making.

Hafner socked a pitch from veteran James Baldwin into the gap near center field. He put his head down and moved his feet as rapidly as they would go. Somehow, the guy built like an ox galloped around the bases like a gazelle and reached third safely. Not everyone witnessed it live, but it happened. Hafner became the seventh player in franchise history to hit for the cycle.

His career was really just beginning.

He batted .254 with 14 home runs in 91 games that year, his first with the Indians, who acquired him the previous winter from the Texas Rangers for Einar Diaz and Ryan Drese. Hafner had demonstrated some power and ability to hit for average in the minors, but Texas had no place for him, given that he was not much of a fielder and the Rangers had proven players at his potential positions. Hafner hit .311 with 28 home runs, 109 RBIs, and a .993 OPS in his first full season in 2004. He hit .305 with 33 home runs and 108 RBIs and finished fifth in balloting for the American League Most Valuable Player in 2005. He pieced together his best year in 2006, when he totaled 42 home runs and 117 RBIs to go along with 100 walks and a .308 average. The Indians renamed the right-field mezzanine section at Jacobs Field "Pronkville." There were "Pronk Bars" on offer, chocolate candy bars named after the prolific slugger.

His numbers dipped to .266 with 24 home runs and 100 RBIs in 2007, when the Indians came one victory shy of a trip to the World Series. Hafner then started to battle pain in his shoulder, an ailment that would not subside for the duration of his career. The club had signed him to a four-year, $57 million contract extension in 2007. He stuck around in Cleveland through the 2012 campaign, but was a shell of his former self for his final five years with the club. In those five seasons, he played in only 429 games and logged a .259 average with 59 total home runs. The Indians parted ways with Hafner after he hit .228 in 66 contests in 2012. Hafner finished his career in Cleveland with 200 home runs and an .890 OPS.

Before Hafner's feat, the only players in franchise history to hit for the cycle were Bill Bradley (1903), Earl Averill (1933), Odell Hale (1938), Larry Doby (1952), Tony Horton (1970) and Andre Thornton (1978). Larry Twitchell also did so for the 1889 Cleveland Spiders. Hafner's cycle was the last for a Cleveland player until Rajai Davis did it in Toronto for the 2016 Indians. Jake Bauers then hit for the cycle in Detroit in 2019.

Sources

Many of the quotations found throughout this book were gathered from personal interviews between these players, coaches and executives and the author. Some were provided specifically for this book. Others were selected from interviews for previous articles written while covering the team. Additional quotes and information came from various sources, which include the following:

Websites
baseball-reference.com
TheAthletic.com
MLB.com
asapsports.com
Cleveland.com
SABR.org
Bobfellermuseum.org

Actofvaloraward.org
IMDB.com
SI.com
Indians.com
CBSSports.com
Heritagesportsart.com
Baseballhall.org

Newspapers
Cleveland Plain Dealer
Fort Worth Star-Telegram
New York Times
Chicago Tribune

Books
Veeck, Bill, and Ed Linn. *Veeck—As In Wreck: The Autobiography of Bill Veeck* (Chicago: University of Chicago Press, 2001).